Masculinity in Vietnam War Narratives

Masculinity in Vietnam War Narratives
A Critical Study of Fiction, Films and Nonfiction Writings

BRENDA M. BOYLE

McFarland & Company, Inc., Publishers
Jefferson, North Carolina, and London

Portions of Chapter 3 originally appeared in "Phantom Pains: Disability, Masculinity and the Normal in Vietnam War Representations," *Prose Studies* 27:1 (April–August 2005): 93–107. Reprinted by permission of Taylor & Francis Group, http://www.informaworld.com.

LIBRARY OF CONGRESS CATALOGUING-IN-PUBLICATION DATA

Boyle, Brenda M., 1957–
  Masculinity in Vietnam War narratives : a critical study of fiction, films and nonfiction writings / Brenda M. Boyle.
      p.   cm.
  Includes bibliographical references and index.

  ISBN 978-0-7864-4538-7
  softcover : 50# alkaline paper ∞

  1. American literature — 20th century — History and criticism. 2. Vietnam War, 1961–1975 — Literature and the war. 3. Vietnam War, 1961–1975 — Motion pictures and the war. 4. War stories, American — History and criticism. 5. War films — United States — History and criticism. 6. Masculinity in literature. 7. Masculinity in motion pictures. I. Title.
  PS228.V5B69   2009
  810.9'358 — dc22   2009028835

British Library cataloguing data are available

©2009 Brenda M. Boyle. All rights reserved

No part of this book may be reproduced or transmitted in any form or by any means, electronic or mechanical, including photocopying or recording, or by any information storage and retrieval system, without permission in writing from the publisher.

On the cover: Charlie Sheen in *Platoon* (1986) ©Orion Pictures/Photofest; camoflauge ©2009 Shutterstock

Manufactured in the United States of America

McFarland & Company, Inc., Publishers
  Box 611, Jefferson, North Carolina 28640
    www.mcfarlandpub.com

To the memory of my father,
Dean G. Boyle (1930–1989), U.S. Army, Retired.
In Vietnam, I Corps September 1966 to September 1967
and II Corps January 1970 to December 1970.

And to my nephews and nieces
aiming for careers in the military

Acknowledgments

This book has been decades in the making, so there are many people who over the years have influenced me directly or indirectly. I surely am not able to name you all; I hope you understand that if you've known me since 1975, you've had a part in this.

The people most recently and directly affected by my absorption in all things Vietnam are my family: Kirk Combe and our children, Clayton, Olivia, and Hannah. They've not always understood why films and fiction about "the sorrow of war" were so appealing to me, a wife and mother, and I thank them immensely for allowing me more than a few sacred Friday movie-and-pizza nights to watch war films.

I also want to thank the people at Ohio State who helped me think through formally and theoretically so many of these ideas: Debra Moddelmog, who as my dissertation supervisor always read my writing thoughtfully and with respect; Linda Mizejewski, a model of feminist thinking and living; John Hellmann, who challenged me to support my sometimes conflicted notions; and Phoebe Spinrad, who introduced me to the genre of Vietnam War fictions. I also want to thank Kathleen Wallace for her steadfast friendship and her willingness to read and comment on a very long manuscript. My colleagues at Denison University have provided a stimulatingly intellectual environment to finalize my ideas in this book; for that, I am very thankful.

Thanks are owed, too, to my eight brothers and sisters (in order: Karen Collins, Cheryl Scott, David Boyle, Christine Yuengert, Charles Boyle, Thomas Boyle, Maureen Boyle, and Paula Boyle), most of whom have spent time on active duty in the American Army, but all of whom have significantly impacted how I think about war and the military. And finally, I want to thank my mother, D. Joan Boyle, for raising me and my many brothers and sisters with the belief that we always should do our very best.

Table of Contents

Acknowledgments
vii

Preface
1

Introduction: The New Man Dance Discourse
3

1. "Don't mean nothin'": Race in the Production of Masculinities
23

2. The Nam Syndrome: Improper Sexuality, Improper Gender
59

3. Men Out of Mind: Disabilities in Vietnam War Stories
100

4. A Litmus Test for Masculinity: The Vietnam War at the Turn of the Twenty-First Century
144

Chapter Notes
165

Works Cited
183

Index
197

Preface

I argue in this work that the Vietnam War and the social movements of the 1960s, not just the Feminist Movement, altered the way Americans conceive of masculinity, alterations reflected in visual and textual narratives of the War. I contend that these texts operate as alternative histories because they register continuing anxieties about the War. Though masculinity always is tenuous, war spotlights its precariousness; because the Vietnam War era was a time of crisis for Americans, it heightened anxieties about masculinity. Decades after American involvement in Vietnam, these anxieties still are evident in discourses not always directly concerned with the War in Vietnam, such as the American presidential campaigns at the end of the twentieth century and into the twenty-first and the American wars in Iraq and Afghanistan.

These masculinities discourses appear not only in fictional narratives, but also in films, nonfiction narratives and military recruiting advertisements, suggesting that in several ways masculinity has been rescripted in the national ethos. First, the era since the War has made it imperative for Americans to imagine a plurality of masculinities since a single model of masculinity to which men should aspire might not be desirable and probably never was possible. In pluralizing masculinity, the narratives studied in this work propose that gender is performative, amorphous, and historically contingent, and conclude that masculinities adhere not only to male but also to female bodies. Second, the liberation movements of the era clarified the direct impact of such physical identity issues as race, sexuality, and dis/ability on formations of masculinities. The American truism that war makes a boy into a man is simplistic when it assumes there is one true way to be a male; the War narratives analyzed suggest there are many ways to be a male. Third, that masculinities are pluralized by their extension to people other than white, able-bodied, heterosexual men and that they are mutable intimates that the current binary of sex and gender — sex as chromosomal and gender as environmental — is less definitive than it suggests.

Masculinity, queer, disability, and white race theories afford my readings these conclusions and separate this work from others. I demonstrate the interconnectedness of these identity positions when I use two texts—John Del Vecchio's *The 13th Valley* and Bobbie Ann Mason's *In Country*—to link respectively the chapters about race and sexuality, and sexuality and dis/ability, from within a gendered context. My analysis explores the complexities inherent to gender, especially during wartime, and helps us make sense, too, of those we find now in the wars in Iraq and Afghanistan.

Introduction
The New Man Dance Discourse

American involvement in Vietnam began in the 1940s, intensified during the 1960s and early 1970s, and drew to its infamous close in 1975, but the social transformations evolving from the War era continue to be scrutinized in American culture, appearing in venues as disparate as national policy, homoerotica, and films about other American wars. The War was not the sole revolutionizing event of this period, though. Multiple liberation campaigns, including the Civil Rights, Black Nationalist, Chicano, American Indian, Gay Rights, Women's Rights, and Disability Rights movements, occurred nearly simultaneously to the War and in some cases were instigated by the results of the War. Whether or not a causal relationship exists between the War and the social movements is debatable; what is most important is that Vietnam War narratives manifest these revolutions, with many of the depictions suggesting that what was assaulted most by the era's revolutions was an American sense of a coherent, bounded, or "monolithic" masculinity.

The combined influence of the War and the social movements on American conceptions of masculinity has received little critical attention, however. While previous wars had produced anxieties about masculinity, the Vietnam War was part of an entire *era* that rescripted gender and other social identity roles for many, if not most, Americans. The traditional American ethos contends that boys become men through experience in war, and that conversion makes them real Americans. American boys are convinced that fighting in a war or participating in its violent counterpart is something they should aspire to do, and men who have not participated in a war sometimes are made to think they missed a rite of passage. What it means to be a man, though unspecified in this mythology, is tacitly stated to be white, heterosexual, and able-bodied; what is even less articulated and more assumed is that to be a man is to be masculine and to be masculine is to be a man. This clearly understood combination of identities provides to the myth a coherency and boundedness that mitigates the incoherence of war; it tries to provide certainty in an uncertain environment. One would think, then, that American war narratives of whatever genre would reflect these transformative powers of combat. Surely fiction, film, memoirs and other cultural narratives would support the American mythos by reflecting men who fit the mythical mold. What this study of texts about the Vietnam War and subsequent eras indicates, however, is that a single, monolithic concept of manhood is not evident during that wartime period nor does it consistently appear in the era since the War. Rather than providing conditions to secure masculinity as a singular state, its narratives instead repeatedly and without apology fracture and multiply the ways in which masculinity can be manifest. Instead of transforming boys into masculine men, narratives of the War expose the lie of that American truism through a new discourse of masculinities. The question explored in this study is how that singular definition of masculinity is defied and how the new masculine roles are constructed in narratives of the Vietnam War, narratives that continue to be produced into the beginning of the twenty-first century as part of a new Man Dance masculinity discourse.

By the term Man Dance I mean the self-conscious enactment of gender from among a variety of masculinities. The Vietnam War era provided alternatives to the One True Way of being masculine, to the notion that a male body should behave in prescribed masculine ways. Rather than replacing one correct way with a new correct one, however, the era complicated the relationship between how the body physically is constituted and the behaviors it may manifest. It disrupted the easy equation between male bodies and masculine behavior, the assumption that male bodies would always behave in identifiably masculine ways. In the decades since the War's end, this notion of the mutability of masculinity has become normalized in American life, and the boundaries that previously separated masculinity and femininity have become increasingly blurred. Americans seem conscious that gender is a performance that is socially and culturally contingent.

The current multiplicity of masculinity and its self-aware performance and re-performance is especially apparent in a June 4th, 2004, episode of the radio program *This American Life*, about the role of the American private sector in Iraq. In one segment, a retired Army Ranger lieutenant colonel named "Hank" is interviewed about what he wants to see in his fellow "Personal Security Detail" employees working for the ironically named Custer Battles (Glass).[1] (These are the same kind of employees who

Introduction   5

were captured and burned in Al-Fallujah in March 2004.) Hank says he wants "steely-eyed, flat-bellied professionals," and then describes what it is like to meet another such professional "on a ... [derisive emphasis] mission." Jokingly citing it as a "man dance," Hank says he and the other pro—on any continent in the world—size one another up as they each try to "appear serious, dead serious about this business." As they perform this "man dance," "like dogs sniffin' each other," Hank indicates the two men are keenly aware of it as performance and, consequently, of how they adjust for their audiences. Maintaining "the look" of the personal security under these conditions is imperative, but apparently not when Hank is being interviewed for the program, since he ridicules the performance. In this contemporary episode the relativity of masculinity is revealed, even though it is supposed to look monolithically as "flat-bellied and steely-eyed." This Man Dance masculinity would not have happened had it not been for Vietnam, and is a phenomenon that persists in American cultural narratives.

Considering these texts within historical contexts particular to the Vietnam War era makes it possible to read them as cultural artifacts of the period, a period extending from World War II, from which many Vietnam War combatants derived their models for military masculinity, to the wars in Iraq and Afghanistan in the early years of the twenty-first century. In the conclusion to her landmark book *The Remasculinization of America* (1989), Susan Jeffords denies that a causal relationship exists between 1980s efforts to "remasculinize" American culture and the Vietnam War, and asserts that it is a "misguided effort" to make such claims (186). My longer historical study of Vietnam War narratives, including some that Jeffords includes in her analyses, demonstrates that the War, its representations, and the social movements that were intimately related to it did contribute to narrative reformulations of masculinity. Taking this longer view makes it possible to imagine connections between the War and how masculinities, always a problem during wartime, are pluralized in narratives of the War by the particular conditions existing in American social relationships during the latter half of the twentieth century.

A premise of this study's argument is that in the American tradition war has been offered as a forge for monolithic masculinity, or a single, bounded and coherent form of behavior enacted solely by men. Though this idea has become a truism, it is important to point out its historical contingency. War has been seen as the foremost place and time in modern American culture where and when boys are transformed into men and where their masculinity is then measured; it has been regarded as a haven for developing male masculinity. According to recent socio-political theories, however, Vietnam could not provide that haven. For instance, in *War and Gender: How Gender Shapes the War System and Vice Versa* (2001), Joshua S. Goldstein contests the biological truisms equating the disposition to war and violence with males. He opens his study by addressing the problems of the gender/sex split:

> We *are* a certain sex but we *learn* or *perform* certain gender roles which are not predetermined or tied rigidly to biological sex. Thus, sex [or being male] is fixed and based in nature; gender [or being masculine] is arbitrary, flexible, and based in culture. This usage helps to detach gender inequalities from any putative inherent or natural basis. The problem, however, is that this sex-gender discourse constructs a false dichotomy between biology and culture, which are in fact highly interdependent [2].

Goldstein's findings suggest that biology alone (i.e., maleness: testosterone, cognition, emotion) cannot be held responsible for war. Instead, he concludes, "War is not a product of capitalism, imperialism, gender, or any other single cause, although all of these influence wars' outbreaks and outcomes. Rather, war has in part fueled and sustained these and other injustices" (412). In other words, Goldstein determines that war is not the natural *outcome* of biologically-based or socially-based differences between males and females, but instead, war assists in *producing* the differences. While accepting this paradoxical relationship between gender and sex is important to this study, another mode of Goldstein's paradox needs to be examined: instead of integrating differences among people to produce a uniform/monolithic masculinity, the narratives about the Vietnam War era produce differences among masculinities.

Charles Moskos, a sociologist whose work focuses on the American military, points to the historical variations of the war-as-forge truism:

> A clear conception of the place of military service in American society survived from early in World War II right up to the beginning of the Vietnam War. According to this view, service in the military, and particularly the army, was almost a rite of passage for most American males. Eight out of ten age-eligible men served during World War II, the highest ratio in U.S. history. From the Korean War through the early 1960s, about half of all men coming of age served in the armed forces. But the proportion began to fall — to roughly four out of ten — during the Vietnam War, as the children of privilege found ways to avoid service in an unpopular and ill-defined military quagmire ["From" 56].

One may wonder, then, how the 60 per cent of males who did not participate in the Vietnam War transitioned from boys to men. In *Manhood in America: A Cultural History* (1996), Michael Kimmel agrees that proving "manhood" is a dominant theme in American history (ix), though he contends that during the Vietnam War "one of the most reliable refuges for beleaguered masculinity, the soldier/protector, fell into ... disrepute" (263).

A masculinity with clearly defined boundaries has been important to the American sense of what it means to be American, though. For instance, as discussed more fully in Chapter Four, the "testing" of national leaders for monolithic masculinity is as much about whether their actions during past wars validate *current* conceptions of masculine behavior and attitudes towards *any* war as it is about the candidates' *contemporary* political attitudes towards the Vietnam War. This evolving sense of national ethos is what Lauren Berlant terms the "National Symbolic" in *The Anatomy of National Fantasy* (1991), which she explains is the *formal* space where citizens of the United States are transformed into "Americans." She says that "'America' is an assumed relation, an explication of ongoing collective practices, and also an occasion for exploring what it means that national subjects already share not just a history, or a political allegiance, but a set of *forms* and the affect that makes these forms meaningful" (4; emphasis added). "We are bound together," she continues, "because we inhabit the *political* space of the nation, which is not merely juridical, territorial (*jus soli*), genetic (*jus sanguinis*), linguistic, or experiential, but some tangled cluster of these" (4–5). This notion of the National Symbolic helps to account for the multiple, entangled ways—including gender—by which United States citizens are constructed and imagine themselves Americans. That they are constructed as Americans, instead of inherently living out a "manifest destiny," or living a life deemed correct by the Christian god, is highly relevant to Vietnam War studies. What the War affected, after all, was the American sense of rightness. If Americans were not "right" about the War—strategically, politically, journalistically, in terms of gender, in terms of treatment of the dead and wounded and disabled, in terms of race—then Americans may not be right, either, about preceding and subsequent conceptions of the nation, in addition to the role of the United States in the world's affairs.

In this study, then, the National Symbolic can help to account for the multiple influences on and of the War, which stem from diverse arenas, among which are the collective, the personal, and the popular. The National Symbolic laces together images and language at many levels—

governmental, national, local, personal — to construct how the nation imagines itself. Certainly this imagination of itself would include, for instance, idealized American qualities such as love of freedom and self-reliance. But Vietnam War narratives suggest that an important way by which we have determined "American" has to do with a gender ideal demarcating how men and women should behave.

Thus, the National Symbolic since the final and frantic departure of the United States from Vietnam in the spring of 1975 demonstrates that attitudes toward the Vietnam War have become a measure of gender; war is supposed to be the domain of a clearly defined, monolithic masculinity; masculinity is supposed to be about male bodies. But the Vietnam era made us Americans not quite sure how monolithic masculinity could be identified. What needs exploring, therefore, is how the Vietnam War and masculinity have become intertwined in the American National Symbolic. Through the cultural study of a range of film, literary, advertising, and biographical and autobiographical texts, I explore how the Vietnam War is a venue for the representation of masculinities and, given their historical contingency, how they reflect the present National Symbolic as much as the National Symbolic of the past.

Since the late 1980s and the publication of Jeffords' foundational book linking masculinity to the Vietnam War, masculinity and gender theories have abounded, having begun through the emergence of men's studies immediately after the War's end in the early 1970s, and with feminist studies beginning in the 1960s.[2] Michel Foucault's work, including *The History of Sexuality: Volume 1, An Introduction* (1978), has been instrumental in the later formulations of gender theories: he disrupts notions of history as stable and recordable as behavior, noting that history actually is a record of changeable discourses. In *History*'s chapter "The Deployment of Sexuality," Foucault asserts the Western world's most effective way of governing discourses about sex has been to multiply them instead of repress them (77). Subsequently, the discourse of "sex" is integrated into mainstream society and is thus normalized and, most importantly, controlled. This control indicates the relationship between truth and power, moreover, that truth is not an outcome but a determinant of power:

> [T]ruth isn't outside power, or lacking in power: contrary to a myth whose history and functions would repay further study, truth isn't the reward of free spirits, the child of protracted solitude, nor the privilege of those who have succeeded in liberating themselves. Truth is a thing of this world: it is produced only by virtue of multiple forms of constraint. And it induces regular effects of power.

> Each society has its régime of truth, its "general politics" of truth: that is, the types of discourse which it accepts and makes function as true: the mechanisms and instances which enable one to distinguish true and false statements, the means by which each is sanctioned: the techniques and procedures accorded value in the acquisition of truth: the status of those who are charged with saying what counts as true ["Truth and Power" 1144].

Foucault's ideas about discourse and its control are significant because they indicate two things. First, "truths" are normalized through the production of discourse and not solely through repression of such discourse; by extension one can argue that a discourse linking masculinity with Vietnam can be found in other discourses bordering "masculinity" and "Vietnam." Second, Foucault's new "régimes of truth," or "the types of discourse which [society] accepts and makes function as true," require new narrative forms to tell the stories of Vietnam and masculinity. Together, these two points allow locating the stories of Man Dance masculinities in what might seem the unlikeliest of places, war narratives. Vietnam War texts differ from those of other wars only in so far as they narrate anxieties about masculinity in response to the particular social movements of the era.

Another writer whose ideas have been central to the development of gender theories is Judith Butler, who introduced her theory of gender as performance in *Gender Trouble* (1990). In the Preface to the 1999 edition of *Gender Trouble*, Butler explains that "the view that gender is performative sought to show [in the original edition] that what we take to be an internal essence of gender is manufactured through a sustained set of acts, posited through the gendered stylization of the body" (xv). She clarifies that with "what we take to be 'real,' what we invoke as the naturalized knowledge of gender is, in fact, a changeable and revisable reality" (xxiii). Thus, what people are doing in an American military venue is *performing* a masculinity expected by the American National Symbolic. Butler emphasizes that gender as performance is rarely about consciously *choosing* gender, in the way one chooses a set of clothing to wear for the day; instead, gender is produced on and through subjects so as to naturalize the performance, both externally and psychically. That is, to understand that American military people were performing masculinity in the way Butler describes, we must realize they each had internalized the form of gender suitable to the cultural circumstances of the National Symbolic; they had not chosen their scripts from their "wardrobes" of gender identities. Neither has the American public consciously decided to measure the masculinity of its military participants, nor have the participants elected to wear the cloaks of suitable masculinity. Instead, in accord with the American ethos of monolithic masculinity, the public and the participants both have internalized how suitable masculinity would look in an American war venue.

While Foucault and Butler have focused broadly on gender, Robert Connell has contributed significantly to the particular composition of masculinity theory both in tracing its developments and in attempting to define what is meant by "masculinity." Positioning his ideas against those of popular psychology, which he claims are nostalgic for a period that never actually existed and are biologically essentialist, Connell argues for a plurality of masculinities. In *Masculinities* (1995) he maintains that to examine gender in terms only of race and class is a reification of singularity. That is, to assert a multiplicity of masculinities is progressive; to assert that masculinities are the result of a *multiplication* by the factors of race and class is to simplify what is extremely complicated by effectively privileging gender over the other two "social practices." What Connell devises in *Masculinities*, therefore, is a system to understand practices of masculinities *among* men, thereby avoiding the potentially essentializing hazard of factoring by race and class. These relationships among men he names hegemony, subordination, complicity, and marginalization, terms I use throughout this study. "Hegemonic" masculinity represents the currently accepted model of masculinity which secures the privileges of patriarchy through the domination of women (77). Though hegemonic masculinity's primary aim is to protect these privileges, it manifests itself in particular, local ways. Thus, the hegemonic masculinity valued and displayed at the Pentagon is going to differ from the hegemonic masculinity dominating an American high school setting. Similarly, the hegemonic masculinities dominating high schools in various parts of the world, or even in different geographical locations in the United States, will manifest local concerns. Connell includes the other three categories—subordination, complicity, and marginalization—to examine how men relate to one another within the framework of hegemony. "Subordination" is typified by the relationship between heterosexual and homosexual men (78), though Connell also includes in that category any males who may be perceived as feminine. Though homosexual males may display physically the masculine ideal of hegemonic masculinity, they are nonetheless subordinated to heterosexual men because of their sexuality. "Complicity" is the relationship between men and the advantages granted them by virtue of hegemonic masculinity's existence, whether or not they participate directly in it. "Masculinities constructed in ways that realize the patriarchal dividend, without the tensions or risks of being the frontline troops of patriarchy, are complicit in this way" (79). The fourth of Connell's relationships among men is "marginalization," a category accounting for the ranking of men based on socio-economic class and race, often in situations where gender, race, and class cannot be disentangled. Connell points out that hegemonic masculinity may "authorize" certain marginalized masculinities such as black male athletes to serve as paradigms of hegemonic masculinity, though this authorization is limited and does not grant these men "social authority" (81).

What is problematic in *Masculinities* is the implicit equation Connell makes between men and masculinity. He amends that oversight in his later publication, *The Men and the Boys* (2000), where he continues to argue for plurality, expanding the theory to suggest that gender is an institutionalized social practice whose organization intertwines with other "social structures" like race, class, nationality, "or position in the world order" (29). While this does not appear to indicate a complete retraction of his complaints in *Masculinities* about simplification concerning "intersection" with other "social practices," it does suggest gender is configured in conjunction — "interacting" — with those other practices.

The preceding discussion suggests that an element of masculinity theory crucially influencing how Vietnam War narratives can be approached has to do with the separation of gender from sex and sexuality. In its current popular usage, "gender" is used synonymously with the biology of the body; for instance, "gender" is used on employment applications to indicate whether one is male or female, when the biological term would be "sex." According to Elizabeth Weed and Naomi Schor, the editors of *Feminism Meets Queer Theory*, queer theory has retained the distinction between sex as biology and gender as social behavior, a definition that "is not, in itself, a controversial proposition" (viii). Robert Connell agrees, arguing that to conjoin sex and gender is biologically essentialist, equating males to masculinity and females to femininity, and that "we must acknowledge that sometimes masculine conduct or masculine identity goes together with a female body" (*The Men and the Boys* 16). He further asserts that gender is a social practice that is related to the materiality of human bodies, but is not constituted by those bodies: "Masculinity *refers* to male bodies (sometimes directly, sometimes symbolically and indirectly), but it is not *determined* by male biology. It is, thus, perfectly logical to talk about masculine women or masculinity in women's lives, as well as masculinity in men's lives" (29).

In *Female Masculinity* (1998) Judith Halberstam compellingly argues that masculinity is actually most discernible when it is performed by female bodies, as representations of masculinity in female bodies denaturalize the association between male bodies and masculinity. Moreover, she insists that "dominant masculinity," an element of what this study terms monolithic masculinity, popularly is identified — and unmarked — in the white male body: "Masculinity ... becomes legible as masculinity where and when it leaves the white male middle-class body" (2). Despite most Vietnam War fiction and film featuring how men alone are masculinized in combat situations, the infrequent appearances of female characters in this masculinizing environment end in showcasing masculinity. Part of this study's project, then, is to examine how female masculinities are devised when included in a war scenario, and what the effect is on how male masculinities can then be fashioned.

Though Connell and Halberstam are comfortable separating sex as biology and gender as behavior, Judith Butler argues against this division in "Against Proper Objects," insisting that, especially in terms of academic disciplinarity, to separate the two is a form of violence:

> [T]he very formulation of lesbian and gay studies depends upon the evacuation of a sexual discourse from feminism. And what passes as a benign, even respectful, analogy with feminism is the means to which the fields are separated, where that separation requires the desexualization of the feminist project and the appropriation of sexuality as the "proper" object of lesbian/gay studies [9].

Butler's fear of disciplinary lines being drawn centers on the frequent conflation of sex and gender in feminism and of the conflation of sex and sexuality in lesbian/gay studies; where "sex" implies identity in the feminist sense, "sex" in its lesbian/gay sense incorporates both the feminist sense of identity and also "sexuality" or "sensation, pleasures, acts and practices" (4–5). The hazard, as Butler sees it, is that this split between gender (the "proper" study of feminism) and sex (the "proper" study of lesbian/gay studies) recreates the conditions that have made it possible for males to remain unmarked by sex or gender, and commits females to the unhappy embodiment of both (24).

While Butler specifically is addressing disciplinary concerns for the academy, her caution is warranted. Not only does drawing a line between "sex" and "gender" limit the scope of feminism, she is right to challenge the notion that these things can be split definitively. As she argues in *Bodies That Matter: On the Discursive Limits of "Sex,"* if "gender" is a social construction which incorporates "sex," then "sex" itself originates as a construction, or what Butler terms "a prelinguistic site to which there is no direct access" (5). In other words, if we abandon the notion that "sex" indicates a biology that is given at birth and gender is the social meaning applied to those sexualized bodies, then gender is the preeminent discursive term through which we interpret bodies. She concludes *Bodies* by arguing for a blurring of the lines between queer and feminist, sexuality and gender:

> For surely it is as unacceptable to insist that relations of sexual subordination determine gender position as it is to separate radically forms of sexuality from the workings of gender norms. The relation between sexual practice and gender surely is not a structurally determined one, but the destabilizing of the heterosexual presumption of that very structuralism still requires a way to think the two in a dynamic relation to one another [239].

While skepticism is warranted about the conjoining of gender and sex, particularly because in its popular usage, "gender" has come to mean the biology of one's body and so presents other problems (such as whether one's "sex" can be re-defined), what cannot be ignored in this study's analyses of Vietnam War texts is Butler's contention that gender and sex are intimately aligned. Just as Butler suggests, Vietnam War texts typically reject the easy categorization of gender as behavior and sex as biology as they and other identity categories overlap and are imbricated.

My methodology for investigating how masculinities are constructed in Vietnam War narratives is thus premised on these four approaches: a cognizance of the (Foucauldian) discursive deployment and construction of masculinities; a sensitivity to how masculinities are enacted and thereby are mutable; an awareness of the contradictory hazards of conjoining gender and sex, and of dividing them; and a recognition of the caution that, while masculinity may appear to be "intersecting" with various other identity categories, and thus remains unmarked by these "intersections," masculinity instead is "interacting" with other identity categories, thereby transforming and multiplying in accord with contemporary social needs. Furthermore, the historical contingency of gender is made plain as masculinity's mutations are traced through Vietnam War narratives over the course of several decades, from the beginning of the War until the present time.

Finally, because masculinities are effectively formulated by conditions of the body — race, sexuality, and dis/ability — it is very difficult theoretically to disentangle them. For instance, race and sexuality inflect one another, but certainly the physical and mental abilities of a body cannot be separated from the racial and sexual interactions of masculinities. To demonstrate formally such interactions, the three chapters following this one are chapters primarily dealing with each of these three corporal identities, but they are laced together with overlapping textual readings, or "bridging" texts. That is, in Chapter One masculinity is analyzed through the lens of race in John Del Vecchio's *The 13th Valley*; in Chapter Two, that same novel is read through a lens conjoining masculinity, race and sexuality. The chapter then continues with an analysis of other texts, including Bobbie Ann Mason's *In Country*. Analysis of Mason's novel becomes the focus for Chapter Three having to do with disability, thereby conjoining masculinity, sexuality and able-bodiedness. Therefore, two canonical but very different novels serve as "bridges" to illustrate the interactions among these various masculinities.

At this point, before detailing further the scope of my study, it is important to survey three of the more important critical voices on Vietnam and masculinity: Susan Jeffords, Milton Bates, and Katherine Kinney. Each of these critics offers in her or his book-length study compelling and necessary additions to our understandings of the ways in which masculinity and Vietnam converge.[3] Though Vietnam War narratives abound with multiple and complex formulations of masculinities, critics of Vietnam War representations in general have not scrutinized the monolithic conception of masculinity or recognized the development of Man Dance masculinity.

As Susan Jeffords remarks in the Preface to *The Remasculinization of America: Gender and the Vietnam War* (1989), "an important way to read the war, perhaps the most significant way when we think about the war itself, is a construction of gendered interests" (xi). Jeffords' study focuses on the Reagan era of the 1980s and is intent on exploring how the two gendered positions—masculine and feminine—are opposed to one another, with the masculine position usually dominant or becoming so.

Jeffords' study is remarkable in its critique of the reformulations of the War, specifically those written and produced during the 1980s Reagan years, and so is equally important for how it historicizes gender. What Jeffords means by "remasculinization" is "the large-scale renegotiation and regeneration of the interests, values, and projects of patriarchy now [1980s] taking place in U.S. social relations" (xi). In other words, Jeffords' concerns are with how the War's representation is dependent on the prevailing contemporary cultural needs, and what that contemporary dependence reveals to her is a "backlash" against the presumed "feminization" of American culture during the War and in the 1970s. Her primary focus on gender as behavior, though, to explain the difficulties of this period overlooks to some extent the other bodily identity categories of race, sexuality, and able-bodiedness which closely interact with gender, and the liberation movements associated with some of those categories during the Vietnam War era. While Jeffords' effort to expose the meanings of gender in America during and after the War is laudable, her 1989 focus on gender as *the* mode through which to understand representations of the War is limited. Jeffords is able to conduct this privileging because she employs gender as a monolith; that is, masculinity and femininity both are singular, exclusive and, though unstable historically, nonetheless legibly coherent in the decade she examines. While this is a useful way to explore Vietnam War narratives, and although it is difficult to talk about gender without exploring the two commonly understood gender positions as oppositional, it appears that there is in the current National Symbolic an anxiety about masculinity per se in relation to the Vietnam War for which Jeffords' work does not account. That is, while *Remasculinization* has been essential to deconstructing representations of gender in the Vietnam War, it also seems necessary, in light of the considerable work done in gender and masculinity theories since Jeffords' book was published in 1989, to explore through Vietnam War narratives the specific forms that this continuing preoccupation with masculinity has taken.

Two critical publications more recent than Jeffords' have broached the fracture of monolithic masculinity into "masculinities" in Vietnam War narratives. Milton Bates' *The Wars We Took to Vietnam* (1996) is an extended look at many of the conflicts in American society during the War era. Bates' catalogue of wars includes frontier, race, class, sex, and generational. This historical contextualization of the "wars" is productive and insightful, and moves away from the defensiveness about the War's occurrence found often in critical works. The chapter focusing on gender is titled "The Sex War," a title whose purpose becomes clear when Bates explains the two "sex" wars in the United States during the Vietnam War era: "a significant increase in non-marital (that is, premarital or extramarital) sex; and a redefinition of masculine and feminine identity" (133). That Bates describes them in this way makes two things clear. First, he is referring to heterosexual sex when he refers to the sexual revolution having only to do with marital status, despite the onset of the Gay Rights Movement with the Stonewall Riots in 1969.[4] Second, conflating sex and gender, Bates assumes the coherence of gender identities when he refers to "masculine and feminine identity," even when, as he asserts, coherent gender identity may not be aligned with its traditionally sexed body. In other words, Bates rightfully suggests that changing gender/sex roles was an element of the Vietnam War "battlefield," but his evidence suggests another set of equations, that female equals feminine and male equals masculine. Thus, despite his admirable historical contextualizing, Bates' analysis is limited to accepting gender coherence, an assumption that does not take into account all of the "wars" interacting with masculinity during the War.

Katherine Kinney does not make that same assumption. She says in *Friendly Fire* (2000) that the narratives of the War depict American soldiers as their own enemies, "as the victims of their own ideals, practices, and beliefs, while the ostensible enemy, the regular forces of the NVA and the Viet Cong guerrillas, remain shadowy figures glimpsed only occasionally" (4). Kinney's project, then, is to survey the American "ideals, practices, and beliefs" that reveal themselves in Vietnam War narratives, a project that necessitates (post–Jeffords) the inclusion of gender. Moreover, Kinney acknowledges the multiplicity of gender, exploring gender as it intertwines with other identity positions. However, while she nods to many of these twining identities, she focuses on race and social class. Therefore, while Kinney does elaborate on Jeffords' argument about the centrality and congruity of masculinity, she nonetheless concentrates on masculinity, race, and social class over other physical identity positions that may problematize the distinction between gender and sex. Furthermore, just as Bates assumes heterosexuality in his interpretation of the sexual revolution, Kinney tacitly aligns masculinity with male bodies.

Thus, though histories of the period and War narratives subsequently indicate that other forms of masculinity, such as white male masculinity, homosexuality, female masculinity, and disabled masculinity, have been evident during and after the War, the projects of the three critics sketched here do not deal with them. My work, then, necessarily expands and deepens the analyses begun by Jeffords, Bates, and Kinney in that this study agrees with all three critics that gender as an ideal is historically contingent. It departs from all three in crucial areas, however. Where it departs from Jeffords is in asserting that gender is not the primary analytic by which to understand Vietnam War narratives, but that gender works through and with other identity categories. Where it departs from Bates is twofold: first, while Bates' race war centers on people of color, my study argues that "race" is a category which must include analyses of white people, not just those of color; second, where Bates reads sex and gender as interchangeable categories, this study interprets them as sometimes distinct. Finally, this study joins with Kinney in scrutinizing masculinities from the perspective of race, but departs from her as it examines configurations of masculinity in white male bodies, in female bodies, and in disabled male bodies. Informed by the gender and masculinity theories discussed previously, the interactions of race, sexuality, and able-bodiedness with masculinities are examined in this work.

Chapter One begins the analysis of how these identities interact with masculinity. "Don't mean nothin': Race in the Production of Masculinities" examines how masculinities interact with race, black and white. Given the substantial influences of the Civil Rights and Black Nationalist Movements of the 1950s and 1960s, and the Chicano and American Indian Movements of the 1960s and 1970s, a previous emphasis on reading color (and not whiteness) during the War was understandable. However, we have learned since that period that race and masculinity work as much through whiteness as they do through color; if masculinities are constructed, mutable, and non-permanent, and the meaning of race is also all of those things, then white masculinities are as subject to impermanence and interpretation as are other racial masculinities. Therefore, though race often becomes a euphemism for discourse solely about people of color, especially African Americans, this study avoids assigning the responsibility for race or the "race war" to people of color. It is especially important to examine how race is constructed by white authors since there are so few texts written by people of color. At the same time, this work does not ignore the particularities of masculinities of different races, and avoids the issue of authorial intentionality. That is, while it is imperative to respect the material and psychological differences of raced masculinities, it cannot be assumed, for instance, that because a black male author has written a book, he has inscribed all of his black characters and all of his white characters from a single "black" viewpoint, nor that a white male author would do the same. Finally, this analysis is mindful of the social practices at work during this historical period. An outcome of the Civil Rights, Black Nationalist, Chicano, and American Indian Movements of the Vietnam War era that still obtains at the turn of the twenty-first century is a sensitivity (sometimes termed derogatorily as "political correctness") to the issues of race, so much so that sometimes these issues in Vietnam War narratives are either spotlighted or underplayed, as though race, once faced and discussed, is reconciled and thereby inconsequential. Moreover, the treatment of white race in Vietnam War narratives, except as it is related to social class, is almost always underplayed. The investigation in Chapter One, then, is aimed at inquiring into the interaction of masculinity with race — spotlighted or underplayed — in two texts: John

Del Vecchio's massive combat novel, *The 13th Valley* (1982), and Patrick Duncan's 1989 combat film, *84 Charlie MoPic*.

Just as race is seen to be a defining characteristic of the depictions of Americans at war in Vietnam, so, too, is sexuality. Discussed previously is how Milton Bates' text assumes heterosexuality in his chapter "The Sex War," and how the homosexual acts and desires appearing in many Vietnam War texts rarely are referred to explicitly in the critical work of Vietnam War fiction studies. Chapter Two, "The *Nam Syndrome*: Improper Sexuality, Improper Gender," argues that the reason for this critical obscurity is a generally heteronormative presumption about male masculinity among Americans and a willingness to leave that norm unmarked. Just as in Chapter One masculine whiteness is denaturalized, masculine heterosexuality is denaturalized in Chapter Two by examining the methods of its construction. The chapter's process is to examine depictions of male homosexual desire and of female masculinity especially as they are framed by the Gay Rights and Feminist Movements of the late 1960s and 1970s, and the attempts from within the military establishment to alter regulations against homosexuals and women serving in the armed forces during and after the War. Examining female masculinity is especially important for, as Judith Halberstam asserts in *Female Masculinity* (1998), "the shapes and forms of modern masculinity are best showcased within female masculinity" (3). Also, the definitions and recognition of male masculine heterosexuality hinge on female heterofemininity; to denaturalize male heterosexuality, then, necessitates looking closely at the props on which it relies, and the modes through which females are gendered in Vietnam War narratives. The "bridging" text for this chapter is *The 13th Valley*, which will bring to the chapter the complications and interactions of race in terms of sexuality, while the other texts to be investigated include Norman Mailer's *Why Are We in Vietnam?* (1967), Joe Haldeman's science fiction novel, *The Forever War* (1974), Bobbie Ann Mason's *In Country* (1985) and its Norman Jewison 1989 film adaptation, and Tim O'Brien's short story "The Sweetheart of the Song Tra Bong" (1990).

The third chapter, "Men Out of Mind: Disabilities in Vietnam War Stories," focuses on how masculinities are constructed, conferred and denied depending on able-bodiedness. As Rosemarie Garland Thomson comments in *Extraordinary Bodies* (1997), "Disabled literary characters usually remain on the margins of fiction as uncomplicated figures or exotic aliens whose bodily configurations operate as spectacles, eliciting responses from other characters or producing rhetorical effects that depend on disability's cultural resonance" (9). This simultaneous decentering *and* centering that Thomson describes is antithetical to the project of monolithic masculinity, which depends on (the illusion of) immanence. This chapter discusses how hierarchies of disability are figured in narratives of the War and mirror some of the changes to American law and culture wrought by the Disability Rights Movement of the last several decades. The frequent depictions of bodies that were physically and/or mentally disabled as a consequence of the War not only intensify the urge of the able-bodied to "enforce normalcy," as Lennard Davis so aptly puts it (*Enforcing Normalcy* 1995), but simultaneously interrupt, rather than confirm, the monologue to which monolithic masculinity aspires. The bridging text for this chapter, overlapping sexuality with disability, is *In Country*, followed by analyses of several autobiographical or biographical texts: Corinne Browne's *Body Shop* (1973), Max Cleland's *Strong at the Broken Places* (1980), and Lewis B. Puller, Jr.'s *Fortunate Son* (1991). The chapter concludes with a reading of Larry Heinemann's novel, *Paco's Story* (1986).

Chapter Four, "A Litmus Test for Masculinity: The Vietnam War at the Turn of the Twenty-First Century," contends that the impact of the War has been so far-reaching that the effects of the Vietnam War are rhetorically embedded in American cultural practices more than three decades after its conclusion. It is in these narratives that the normalization of Man Dance masculinity can be seen most vividly. The chapter argues that the American presidential campaigns of 1992, 1996, 2000 and 2004 ironically manifest the influence of the War — ironically, since at the time of the War it was often a badge of honor not to have participated in it — by dwelling on a candidate's attitude toward or participation in the War. This discussion concludes that this late-twentieth and early-twenty-first-century concern about military service in a contentious war is actually a coded concern for the masculinity of a presidential candidate, a masculinity that has been rescripted as a consequence of the War era. This chapter examines the masculinity rhetoric embedded in military recruiting strategies, John McCain's 1999 memoir, *Faith of My Fathers: A Family Memoir*, and the memoir by Harold G. Moore and Joe Galloway, *We Were Soldiers Once ... and Young* (1992) and its 2002 film version. The chapter concludes by investigating the new Man Dance discourse in two memoirs from the current wars in Iraq and Afghanistan, Nathaniel Fick's *One Bullet Away* (2005) and Evan Wright's *Generation Kill* (2004).

A final element influencing this work is my experience of the War. The combat veteran's voice has been privileged as *the* authority on the Vietnam War, combat experience being regarded as the epitome of verifiable evidence. Memoirists of the War are rarely challenged in their assertions, while the filmmakers and novelists who are veterans cite their efforts as motivated by the desire to be truthful and authentic. Repeatedly others of us are told that if we were not in Vietnam, we have no authority to speak about the War, much less analyze it.[5] At the risk of repeating the error of privileging firsthand experience, I contend that there are many of us who did not live directly in combat but nonetheless have valuable insights about the War. For instance, I have experiences that now include not only having been raised as an Army "brat" and being on active duty in the U.S. Army during the Cold War, but also scholarship in international relations, cultural studies, and critical theory. If the Man Dance discourse has taught us anything, it is that though we may not have been aviators or combat Infantry or Marines, our varying perspectives can enrich and complicate Americans' understanding of the Vietnam War and of other wars.

My own experience, enhanced by scholarship, has shown me how devastating the Vietnam War era was to this nation's sense of who it has been and who it can be. The Vietnam War in which the United States was mired for nearly a decade ended several decades ago, but it is still culturally present today, a fact I think largely is attributable to the damage it inflicted on Americans' sense of nation, of right behavior, and ultimately of a coherent and uncomplicated, or what I term "monolithic," masculinity. This is not to claim that there ever was a period in American history when masculinity was not in crisis. It is to say, however, that late-twentieth- and twenty-first-century American culture has managed to maintain the illusion of a monolithic masculinity in male bodies only by ensuring that the rough edges of that illusion — the places where masculinity purportedly ends and femininity begins — are seen as definitive. What the Vietnam War era effected, however, was a change in how we Americans think about masculinity and its confluences with other identity points. That change is recorded dramatically in the many cultural narratives of the War, narratives revealing that rather than the War bolstering monolithic masculinity, it was hostile to that formation and instead produced Man Dance masculinity. The narratives roughen those illusionary edges, uncovering the precarious states of masculinities which haunt those of us who lived during the War, and which endure in American cultural products nearly forty years later. We all still are living and experiencing the effects of the Vietnam War. Analyzing the issues I raise in this study is not the special privilege of the war veteran, but is the cultural obligation of us all.

This multiplication of possible identities during war might be viewed positively as it suggests that men and women both have been liberated from the pressures to conform to dominant forms of masculinity and femininity. It might also suggest that, with this blurring of boundaries between genders, conflicts between and among men and women based on gender hegemony would be reduced, as no person would of necessity be compelled to defend what have become ill-defined boundaries of her gender. While these conclusions might be reached in some cases, I deduce instead that this expansion of the ways to be masculine has been normalized since the end of the War, but, given the patriarchy we live in, it exists concurrently with the traditional form of masculinity in the American National Symbolic. That is, in American culture young men and women are trained to recognize the dominant and traditional forms of gender — men behaving in masculine ways and women in feminine ways— but they often also are trained to resist those pressures.

The evidence before us Americans now is that Vietnam War narratives continue to multiply, complicate and transform masculinities. The cultural battle seen from an early-twenty-first-century vantage point is not about "remasculinizing," or recovering masculinity from femininity. Instead, Vietnam War narratives teach that the struggle in war narratives is not to establish monolithic masculinity as the one, true form but instead to address the social conception of "masculinity" while including all of the physical and mental particularities of identity positions— such as race, sexuality, and dis/ability — integral to gender's formulation. It is the contingencies of these masculinities that make them Man Dance, as there is no longer a single, recognizable form of masculinity suitable to representing war.

1

"Don't mean nothin'"
Race in the Production of Masculinities

For indeed an impressive number of [Vietnam writers] have now come to establish themselves as major interpreters of contemporary American life and culture.... Their sense of profound experiential authority ... allows them to make their largest meanings through the bold embrace of new strategies of imaginative invention; and thus, precisely in the inscription out of memory into art, they become in the fullest sense the creators of cultural myths for new times and other.... ([T]he work of Vietnam writers continues to bespeak a major fulfillment of the true "alternative" spirit of the youth culture of the era, the belief in acts of imagination, often conceived in some new, unmediated relationship with experience itself, that could do nothing less than change the world) [Beidler 2].

According to Department of Defense statistics, at different times during the Vietnam War people of color, including Latino Americans and Native Americans but especially African Americans, and underclass whites were represented disproportionately in front-line ground troops and consequent casualties, and wealthier whites made up the vast majority of officers.[1] Because racial discrimination has remained a controversial point about the War, part of my task in this chapter is to determine how these disproportions appear in the War's representations and how they impact gender. This effort is especially important because those survivors who were disproportionately deployed in combat units during the War are also those least likely to have written about the experience of combat, problematizing Philip Beidler's comment above that those who experienced the War and are writing about it are the creators of new mythology. There is some evidence to suggest, for instance, that while African American officers and enlisted men made up 11.9 percent of the total participation in the Vietnam War,[2] and at least 12.5 percent of those killed, only seven of the nearly one thousand memoirs written by veterans about the War are black-authored, and only three novels have been written by African American veterans (Loeb 202). What does it mean to how race is configured when white authors are largely responsible for creating the "new mythology" of the Vietnam War? *How* are raced masculinities constructed in white-authored texts, especially under the influences of the racially and economically motivated social movements of the era that rejected the assimilationist models under which their members had been operating: the Civil Rights and Black Nationalist Movements, the Chicano Movement, and the American Indian Movement? I contend that this rejection of assimilationism simultaneously represented a rejection of R. W. Connell's "marginalized" and "subordinated" modes of masculinity. In representations of the War, characters often use the popular refrain "Don't mean nothin'" to refer to an issue which actually is very important. Similarly, Vietnam War texts by white authors too often aim to minimize and isolate the impact of race and masculinity on the depictions of men at war. But the attempt ironically causes "race" to resurface in formulations of gender. In other words, race can mean everything, especially in its conjunction with masculinities.

Because white-authored Vietnam War texts often are intent on delineating a universal experience of "the man at war" to accord with the American truism that it is in war when boys become men, they try to level the racial differences inherent in the make-up of late-twentieth century American combat units. Since "white" is regarded as the default race in American culture, this effort means de-racing — or whitening — to universalize. But the texts also are working against the evidence of the war: there is no way to deny the racial discord in the U.S. Armed Forces during the later part of the War, nor is there any way to counter rhetorically the American defeat by a racially marked nation. Thus, influenced by the social and cultural changes wrought by the Vietnam War era Civil Rights/Black Nationalist Movements,[3] the Chicano Movement,[4] and the American Indian Movement,[5] some white-authored Vietnam War texts attempt, in a compensatory way, to circulate the weight of racialization equally, either by including *more* and a wider variety of persons of color, what I term "multiplication," or by referring to race indirectly, what I call "oblique reference." As narrative strategies, "multiplication" and "oblique referencing" afford ways of masculinizing that appear not to be concerned with gender whatsoever as they often use race and military rank instead of masculinity to explain conflicts between American soldiers. In this chapter I investigate two methods of these narrative strategies that silently create racial hierarchies despite what appear to be efforts to avoid that. While these two methods, naming and lighting, are so ubiquitous in fiction and film as to seem generic, as though they mean nothing, they in fact are vital to creating the fractures in monolithic masculinity. In the first example I examine how John Del Vecchio's *The 13th Valley* (1982) both multiplies characters of color and employs a naming rhetoric to refer obliquely to race; names, as used by Del Vecchio, become shorthand signifiers of race. I explore a second method of multiplication and oblique referencing as attempts to distribute race equally in Patrick Duncan's 1989 film, *84 Charlie MoPic*, where a visual rhetoric of film lighting is used to signify the relative racial positions of men in a small combat group.

All three of the Vietnam War era movements signified a refusal to continue acceding to the hegemony of white masculinity which was perceived to oppress their constituents racially, economically, and culturally. To manage these new and influential voices, and to "rewrite America," as Philip Beidler suggests, requires new narrative strategies. What many white-authored Vietnam War texts disclose in constructing racial representations of masculinities in terms of multiplication or oblique references is a new mode of racializing. In *American Crucible: Race and Nation in the Twentieth Century* (2001), Gary Gerstle suggests that this "crucible" of American nationhood has been formed along two contending axes: "civic nationalism" and "racial nationalism." Gerstle asserts that the basis for American nationalism historically has alternated between an advocacy for the "civic" inclusion of all people because they are American citizens, and for a "racial" inclusion of all those whose race coincides with the inherent qualities of being "American."

It is at this juncture of contending ideas of nation where war paradoxically interferes with, rather than contributes to, the construction of monolithic masculinity. Even though war often is used as a way to build and validate loyalties (whether primarily to nation or gender or other identity positions), it discriminates by not providing the opportunity to acquire masculinity uniformly to all males, let alone females, nor has it provided the opportunity in a recognizably distinct way. To try to rectify this inequity, white authors employ a racializing mode that simultaneously acknowledges the particular experiences of individual combatants ("racial") *and* works to make those particular experiences representative ("civic"). The effect is to produce an exemplary experience that can be recognizable as a racially unmarked (i.e., white) experience. In other words, white makers of Vietnam War texts study very carefully the terrain on which they are about to tread, knowing that an ambush point in writing about the Vietnam War is racial difference. In black-authored texts written by veterans, such as David Parks' *G.I. Diary* (1968), Terry Whitmore's deserter narrative, *Memphis-Nam-Sweden* (1971), Wallace Terry's oral history, *Bloods* (1984), and George Davis's 1971 novel, *Coming Home*, the race of white and black men is the predominant point of conflict between them, marking them as more or less masculine. Alternatively, some white authors and filmmakers try to moderate or address the racial differences of the War, with repercussions that appear not to have been anticipated by the users of these strategies. First, the increase in the numbers of characters of color ends up burdening them alone with the responsibility for "race." Second, oblique references to race largely highlight racial differences instead of obliterating them.

Most importantly, constructions of race in Vietnam War narratives impact the way masculinities can be enacted, as race determines whether, according to Robert Connell, masculinities will be hegemonic or one of the three other groups (marginalized, subordinated, or complicit). Though Connell suggests that, as long as hegemonic masculinity is defined as white, masculinities of color will be marginalized, Vietnam War texts trouble that either/or prescription (*Masculinities* 81). That is, the addition of multiple characters of color in white-authored Vietnam War texts may be seen as a progressive effort at evenhandedness or historical accuracy, especially since African Americans were not fully integrated into the American military until the Vietnam War but Latinos and American Indians had been integrated before then. This addition also can be regarded as an author's underscoring a character's being marked as a "race" representative, since even as adding more characters of color disperses the responsibility for representing "race" among a larger group, that group still is limited by the authors to people of color. Oblique references to race, such as the use of lighting in films, have the same effect except, because their race discourse is a tacit one, it easily can be discounted as insignificant or coincidental, or it can be seen as obscuring an issue that cannot be discussed openly. Additionally, unlike the few texts written by veterans of color, white-authored Vietnam War texts do not typically engage overtly in discussions of white as race. This silence insinuates that the white experience is only affected by race in so far as whites come into contact with people of color. The implication, then, is that the white experience is the model for universal experience, when race should be immaterial to combat performance and experience. As the Marines were fond of saying, "There ain't but one color here and that's green. Marine green" (Whitmore 42). "Green" can be read as "universal" which can be read as "white."

The implications of articulating race (through the multiplication of characters of color) and avoiding articulating race (through oblique references) are problematic in terms of masculinities. Through these methods of grappling with issues of race in masculine characters, white-authored Vietnam War narratives attempt to disrupt Connell's categorization of masculinities as either hegemonic or marginalized/subordinate/complicit in creating a single military masculinity that is achievable by any male under any circumstances, regardless of his race. However, in delineating a universal experience by considering race an issue immaterial to the combat experience, many Vietnam War narratives by white writers do not typically avoid the equation of race and behavior, but instead essentialize racial behavior. In other words, the races of Vietnam War characters determine to a large extent their behavior, but because race is seen as integral to telling Vietnam War stories, those racial equations are regarded as "normal" in the racial constitutions of masculine characters. It is this problem of racial definition that I scrutinize in some of these white-authored texts, as they labor to normalize the discourses of race and masculinity in combat.

Two points need to be made here. First, I want to reiterate that what I mean by "monolithic masculinity" is a single masculinity which is held up both as a model for men's behavior and as a masculinity which overcomes the particularities of race, sexuality, and able-bodiedness. This concept differs from Connell's "hegemonic masculinity" because it insists on singularity and wholeness. While "monolithic masculinity" could be a "hegemonic masculinity" occurring typically in the military, I stress the desire for unity and enclosure in masculinity, not the expansive tendencies of Connell's term. Second, it is important to me to use "white" rather than "whiteness." The latter term qualifies white as a racial category, signifying that white is not authentically about race, but instead is more like ethnicity (which, as a cultural as opposed to racial term, permits an unmarked body.) This idea is connected to Richard Dyer's theory in *White* which says "white" people have access to multiple identities because their race remains unmarked (12). The same privilege of unmarkedness is not accorded to the terms "black" or even "African American." That is to say, the word "blackness" typically is not used to discuss the ethnic backgrounds of people of African descent, nor is "African American" typically used as a signifier of ethnicity, as is, say, "Italian American" or "Polish American." "African American" signifies the body while "Italian American" signifies culture. I deliberately say "white," therefore, because I want to mark white as a racial category that cannot be equated to ethnicity. When white, like black, brown, red or yellow, is regarded as a racial construction, then it is a simpler task to think of monolithic masculinity as also a construct which delimits who may belong to it.

Out of the hundreds of white-authored texts written by veterans, I examine John Del Vecchio's canonical *The 13th Valley* and Patrick Duncan's documentary-style film *84 Charlie MoPic* because race is central to both texts' exploration of the causes of conflict, suggesting, therefore, that any treatments of race will be overt, will use "race" to discuss white race as well, and will contain no pretense at a universal experience. However, it is through discussions of race that these two texts paradoxically insinuate that the paramount identity category during war is masculinity, and that all other identities, especially racial ones, are subordinate to that primary category. In underscoring the importance of gender and minimizing the relevance of race to how masculinities can function, both texts suggest that all males, regardless of race, have and should want to have equal access to monolithic masculinity. These two white-authored texts emphasize the racial differences between characters of color and whites by having these characters discuss race often, as though making racial difference conspicuous also will mitigate that difference, or at least vindicate the author against accusations of racism. For these texts, then, if race is framed both as having to do with people of color *and* as a common element of relations between American men in combat, the strangeness of that framing cannot be questioned. In short, the texts imply that what is the problem in war is men claiming distinct identities and not adhering, through will, to the uniform identity they have as a result of being men.

In both texts, race is implicated in formulations of masculinity through frank discussions among subordinates and superiors, Caucasian, Latino American, and African American men; it also is implicated differently in the two texts' narrative strategies. In Del Vecchio's massive 1982 combat novel, *The 13th Valley*, the central character, African American First Lieutenant (1LT) Rufus Brooks, sustains throughout the narrative what I term a "race discourse," an open conversation about race with his subordinates who represent the interests of the Chicano, Civil Rights, and Black Nationalist Movements, ostensibly lessening racial tensions and thereby the importance of race because of the conversation's frankness. Ironically, this discourse on race affirms gender as the paramount identity category among the men. Parallel to this "race discourse," however, is a "race/masculinity discourse," which occurs quietly through the text's practice of naming characters. That is, while the race discourse overtly advocates lessening the consequences of racial markedness, the discourse displaying the interaction of race and masculinity employs a rhetoric of naming that covertly underscores racial markedness and creates a masculinity hierarchy. While Del Vecchio's written text engages in this linguistic rhetoric, Patrick Duncan's 1989 film, *84 Charlie MoPic*, uses a visual rhetoric to discuss race. The white-black racial conflict visually is intensified while the film's plot and dialogue claim the conflict between its two main characters is not about race but about rank. Thus, both Del Vecchio's and Duncan's texts "discuss" race, but through distinctive narrative strategies.[6] In the majority of this chapter, then, I explore the idea that race impacts formulations of masculinities in both of these white-authored texts, despite their claims to the contrary; before I attend to those close readings I provide some theoretical and historical context by which the readings can be understood. This contextualizing includes a brief discussion of the work of two recent critics of Vietnam War narratives, Milton Bates and Katherine Kinney, both of whom address the issue of race in these texts; an overview of the roles blacks especially have played in the American military, focusing on the twentieth century and the Vietnam War; and, finally, a deliberation on the inclusion of "white" as a racial category.

Milton Bates (*The Wars We Took to Vietnam* 1996) and Katherine Kinney (*Friendly Fire* 2000) include race in their analyses of Vietnam War representations, but neither interprets race in conjunction with masculinity; both critics also treat sex and gender synonymously, so that considering masculinity means considering men. Moreover, Bates and, to a lesser extent, Kinney, use the designation "race" to encode what actually are issues about the depictions of African Americans. Bates' objective in his "The Race War" chapter is to "describe those features of African American culture that help to make sense of black people's responses to the Vietnam War" (51), and Kinney claims that the "encounter of black and white men in Vietnam is a crucial structuring trope of the war's representations" (106). Both critics examine only texts written by black authors featuring black experience, suggesting that to these two critics, just as "gender" usually signifies males and females, so "race" is used to signify people of color only and not whites.

Racial difference played a predominant role in the makeup of American military forces prior to the Vietnam conflict. For instance, though there are uncounted references to blacks in the American military for as long as American history has been recorded, those troops almost always have been segregated into their own units or into service-oriented jobs.[7] This separation — and concomitant subordination — led to the configuration of an ideal military masculinity based largely on "regular forces" and so produced a form of masculinity valued and exhibited by white (heterosexual) males, which was, in turn, limited only to some white males. It was not until after World War II and lobbying by groups representing blacks that, in 1948, blacks were integrated into mainstream military units.[8] James Westheider points out in *Fighting on Two Fronts: African Americans and the Vietnam War* (1997) that Vietnam was the first totally integrated war in America's national history (8). This "right to serve" was seen as a victory by blacks, and the military represented to many the vanguard of social institutions paving the way for the racial integration of American society generally. Consequently, the enlisted career military — especially the Army — by the late 1950s was disproportionately composed of African Americans.[9] This disproportion of blacks in the military to the percentage of African Americans in the U.S. population at the time is sometimes used to moderate the complaint that blacks suffered more deaths in Vietnam than was commensurate. An analysis of the Department of Defense database "Southeast Asia, Combat Area Casualties File" reveals that blacks did suffer a disproportionate amount of the casualties and mortalities until 1969, when President Johnson's administration ordered changes to alter such conditions.[10]

My task is not to enter the debate over whether African Americans, Latino Americans, Asian Americans, or Native Americans suffered a disproportionate number of casualties relative to their percentage of the U.S. population. Instead I explore how white-authored texts, the preponderance of those written about the War, construct and attempt to reify monolithic masculinity through particular understandings of what it means to be white. Exploring white as a racial identity is not millennialist thinking. What happened in the last several decades of the twentieth century, however, was a change in the conception of "race" as an outcome of the discursivity of language and power. Under the influence of scientific racism, nineteenth-century Western attitudes developed a biological basis for understanding race, that the external body could reasonably serve as a marker of the internal mind (Appiah 276). This idea of the physical body as representative of mental and spiritual attitudes and aptitudes enabled the eugenics movement at the end of the nineteenth and beginning of the twentieth centuries, and was propagated even further during the World War II era. The white "race" then was not those people who bore white skin, but those people who demonstrated the aptitudes and cultural effects that were then believed to be the outcome of white skin.[11] In that instance, "race" could account for both people of color and whites, and "passing." Following World War II, however, the concept of "ethnicity" was revitalized, and "race" commonly came to signify people whose bodies were marked by color, as opposed to the seeming racial "neutrality" of (white) ethnicized bodies.[12]

White, a work in the burgeoning field of white studies, was published by Richard Dyer in 1997, building on previous work and laying the foundation for subsequent work that explores the way white — as a trope and as a skin color — is situated in the Western world. Dyer's objective is to theorize the meanings of white in a visual culture, and to examine how these theories are put into practice through visual media. As Dyer puts it, "[t]here is a specificity to white representation, but it does not reside in a set of stereotypes so much as in narrative structural positions, rhetorical tropes and habits of perception" (12). White race, then, is not so recognizable as the stereotypes of African Americans and other people of color with which we Americans are familiar, but is done furtively and not always in opposition to coloredness so whites can pass as not-raced, or "the human race." This is what I see happening in many white-authored Vietnam War texts: they take on the issues of race in order to make race immaterial, so that the texts can then create a universal experience of men at war. Given that the constructions of masculinities in some Vietnam War texts often are overt attempts to shift away from racial (i.e., people of color) stereotyping, and towards the simultaneous universalizing and particularizing efforts, and that white is regarded as the default race, analyzing indirect techniques of narrating race — the methods that ostensibly mean nothin' — detects how they disrupt monolithic masculinity. While I do not disregard Kinney's claim about blacks being represented stereotypically in Vietnam War narratives (84), or Dyer's equally convincing claim that whites are not represented stereotypically in western culture generally, I assert that race can be recognized both in the explicit stereotypes (i.e., the many characters of color) and in Dyer's tacit "narrative structural positions, rhetorical tropes, and habits of perception" (i.e., what I have termed "oblique" references to race) embodied in Vietnam War narratives.

I first explore in John Del Vecchio's 1982 *The 13th Valley* how names are used to produce race's interactions with masculinities. This voluminous and best-selling combat novel, complete with authentic-looking maps, Tables of Organization, and "Significant Activities" after-action reports, has been lauded as the definitive Vietnam War novel; its claims to realism and authenticity are one of the reasons compelling me to use it in this study.[13] Also, because there actually were so few black officers in the U.S. military during the War,[14] it is notable that Del Vecchio's central protagonist is a black junior officer who engages his subordinates in scholarly discussions of race, violence, and sexual behavior. My second text is Patrick Duncan's 1989 film titled *84 Charlie MoPic,* a visual narration of race. I examine how *84 Charlie MoPic* defies traditional Hollywood filming techniques, resulting in new ways to perceive the interactions of race and masculinity while depending simultaneously on old "habits of perception." The text is a film-within-a-film: 84C MOPIC is the Military Occupational Specialty (MOS) designator of the enlisted person carrying the camera. Except for a couple of accidental moments, audience members never see this eponymous character, though as the camera's "eye," his viewpoint is essential to understanding the film. Close readings of these two texts demonstrate that race is fundamental to formulations of masculinities, and that even when Vietnam War texts attempt to expunge, minimize or make manifest issues of race as color, race always surfaces as more than color.

The 13th Valley illustrates how names, a seemingly innocuous necessity in fiction, are used to designate where race should be read as occurring, how race impacts the outcome of the characters' lives, and how race is a determinant of the masculinity a character may actualize.[15] Names contribute to our sense of self, though sometimes that can be a fragmented self: for instance, African slaves were given the names of their owners, thereby depriving Africans of their connection to kin and personal history. But even more mundane situations of naming are significant. American wives are expected to assume the surnames of their husbands; that the woman typically takes his name and abandons her original suggests a loss of connection to kin and pre-marital history. It is also presumed that children will inherit their father's surname, validating his paternity and thereby his ownership. Names take on greater import when the expectations and presumptions just enumerated are violated or disrupted, such as a married woman keeping her original name, an only son taking his mother's name, or a person assuming a pseudonym. These are instances of social/patriarchal expectations being disrupted, and thereby often are assumed to have sinister intents.

In war novels, however, soldiers assuming or being endowed with new names is not unusual, as the names are shorthand designators for the character development that occurs in novels not about war, suggesting that naming and re-naming are a central part of the experience of war.[16] Often war names signify the American authenticity of the character or unit. The ideology of the American melting pot and the idea that war is the forge for loyalty both to nation and to gender mandate that war narratives reflect Gary Gerstle's "crucible." Thus, twentieth-century American war narratives often focus on representing the ethnic, geographical, social class and racial makeup of American society in general, and not the makeup of actual units.[17] If war fictions are to represent the totality of American people, then their names should say only that they are from the United States: names should designate them as American citizens, not as hyphenated Americans (such as African-American, German-American, Asian-American). Instead, names in American war fiction texts typically are accompanied by ethnic and racial meaning signifying the characters' places on a continuum of masculinities. This is especially so in Vietnam War texts, which depart from how names are employed in other war's depictions as names may imply many racial, sexual, and gender identities as a consequence of the social movements of the War era.

Vietnam War texts often depart from the racial depictions of previous wars as a result of the unambiguous role race played in the War. Though Del Vecchio's *The 13th Valley* models itself after the "melting pot" World War II novel like Norman Mailer's *The Naked and the Dead*, it attempts to efface racial tensions by making the text's protagonist an African American and an officer, by multiplying the numbers of characters of color, and by having characters of color responsible for issues of race in the War. This equation of color with race backfires, though, making race the central question of its rhetorical strategy of naming:

> The restless infantrymen in the trenches and their clustered sergeants and lieutenants and captains on the landing strip represented a collective consciousness of America. These men, Chelini, Egan, Doc, Silvers, Brooks, all of them, were products of the Great American Experiment, black brown yellow white and red, children of the Melting Pot. Their actions were the blossoming of the past, blooming continuously from the humus of decayed antiquity, flowering from the stems of living yesterdays. What they had in common was the denominator of American society in the 50's and 60's, a television culture, the army experience—basic, AIT, RVN training, SERTS, the oh-deuce and now the sitting, waiting in the trench at LZ Sally, I Corps, in the Republic of Vietnam [145].

Del Vecchio sets his agenda in this passage: to attribute to this group maleness and masculinity in general, but also to ascribe to the particularized and named characters roles in the "melting pot." The five characters named here are central to the plot development, and to the development of a "universal man," a man characterized by his common experience with other men of American culture and war. The Italian American, the Scotch-

Irish American, the African American, the Jewish American, and another African American represent, in Del Vecchio's story, the ability of America to cope with its racial and ethnic diversity. Paradoxically, in attempting to produce representativeness, the text problematizes the full articulation of universality — read "monolithic masculinity" — in its deployment of names. Though these five characters are designated as representative, their names also mark them for distinct treatment. Despite the overt discussion of race among the characters throughout the novel, their names usually racialize them in ways the discussions cannot address because the discussions are on a national/universal, and not a personal, level. This depersonalization both makes it possible for the white character, Egan, willfully to ignore his own complicity in the War, and also forces the characters of color to identify personally with the oppression the Vietnamese are enduring.

Del Vecchio has been lauded for the realism in his novel, a point made repeatedly on the book's cover. *The New York Times* says it is "as close as we will ever get to the 'Vietnam experience'"; *The San Francisco Chronicle* declares that the novel "stands as a vital document to our understanding of the American experience in Vietnam"; *Publishers Weekly* claims that it "conveys to an extraordinary degree the very *feel* of ground combat in I Corps"; *The Atlanta Journal-Constitution* reports that "accurately researched and written in a simple muscular style, the book contains the raw power of combat and introduces a talented writer who was faithful to his impulse to let people know what the Vietnam War was really like"; *Toronto Globe and Mail* suggests that the novel "describes actual combat with an authority only seldom encountered"; *The Dallas Morning News* declares that Del Vecchio "portrays the American presence in Vietnam so intensely, so graphically, so brilliantly that his explosive novel must be read by anyone who wishes to understand that watershed event"; and *The Miami Herald* announces that "Whoever that soldier was who exhorted Del Vecchio to write 'what it was really like' should be pleased to know that is what he has done." These are only seven of the twenty-four examples of what the cover calls "Coast-to-coast Raves for *The 13th Valley*."

Admittedly, enthusiastic testimonies are intended to increase book sales, so these seem useful as marketing tools. What is remarkable, though, is that the dominant theme of praise is for the book's authentic representation of the War, so that a reader may not only learn about the War from the novel but also may have a visceral experience of it. Given the novel's appearance of military and historical authenticity — the maps, Significant Activities Reports, Table of Organization and Equipment, Final Tabulation of "Enemy Losses Inflicted" and "Division Casualties," glossary of military vocabulary and acronyms, and chronology of historical dates reaching back to 2879 B.C.—one might concede that the main characters in the lengthy novel also are represented realistically. However, realism is not ideologically pure simply because it is based on personal experience or historical research; instead it produces war stories reflecting the values and ideologies of the dominant culture (Lorrie Smith 89). That is, application of the terms "realistic" and "authentic" should not prevent readers, even those who were not combatants, from challenging these representations of reality, despite claims that Del Vecchio's "novel must be read by anyone who wishes to understand that watershed event." As Lorrie Smith contends, "[R]ealistic techniques have no inherent value unless the work also investigates the cultural assumptions which animate and give meaning to its images" (90). The late-twentieth-century American "cultural assumption" that I investigate in my analysis of the realistic *The 13th Valley* is twofold: that names can be applied neutrally; and that racial difference can be obviated by discussing it.

The novel has several parallel stories: the battalion has been tasked to locate and assault a North Vietnamese stronghold in the "thirteenth valley," and Alpha Company's mission is to locate and destroy the NVA headquarters. The novel dwells on the relationships among the Alpha Company commander, Lieutenant (LT) Rufus Brooks, a platoon sergeant, Sergeant Daniel Egan, and a soldier, Specialist 4 James Chelini, characters I discuss in some detail. Other characters whose names are central to racializing but whom I will not discuss here include El Paso, who voices Chicano concerns, Doc, who represents the assimilationism of the Civil Rights Movement, Minh, a Vietnamese scout who feels racially oppressed by white Americans, and Jax, who is a militant Black Nationalist. To maintain monolithic masculinity requires immutability; to be "masculine" means to be constant, predictable, and stalwart. The name(s) of each of the three central characters becomes the indicator of where he falls on a continuum of masculinities. In *The 13th Valley*, the more names for a character, the more mutable he is; the more mutable he is, the less "masculine" he appears. Most importantly, the less masculine a character is, the more he is marginalized or subordinated, which is how, according to Robert Connell, racialized people are categorized. Therefore, while the overt story-telling of *The 13th Valley* suggests that race is immaterial, the tacit discourse of race and masculinity in the novel, constructed narratively through the use of names, contends that race is constitutive of masculinity. In my close reading I dwell on LT Rufus Brooks because the other stories pivot on his, and because the varieties of his naming indicate the changeability that excludes him from embodying monolithic masculinity. While Brooks as a thoughtful person of color in a position of power may be read as Del Vecchio's successful creation of a complex black character and a realistic portrayal of what it meant to be a black junior officer in Vietnam in August of 1970, I read Del Vecchio's practice of using a variety of names for Brooks as a strategy to both racialize and marginalize Brooks in terms of masculinity. What occurs in *The 13th Valley* is a covert de-masculinizing of Brooks through the variable identities forced on him as a black man.

Brooks is the only first lieutenant in the battalion who commands a company,[18] and the only African American officer in the battalion. That Rufus Brooks as a first lieutenant is commanding a company was not that unusual in Vietnam, given the high rate of death among tactical commanders and the frequency with which units changed command so that as many officers as possible could have combat command experience. What is unusual is that all of his subordinate platoon leaders are also first lieutenants, potentially confounding the rank hierarchy. Furthermore, since African Americans made up only two percent of the entire military officer corps during the Vietnam War, Brooks' racial identity and military position are significant (Westheider 77). Also, 1970, the year in which *The 13th Valley* is set, was a momentous year in American history. Clyde Taylor calls our attention to the racial disparity prevalent in the United States in 1970 when the killing of four white students by the National Guard at Kent State was nationally publicized and mourned, but the killing of two black students at Jackson State in Mississippi and, a few months earlier, the death of four black students at the hands of South Carolina police received little, if any, coverage (16). In Vietnam, 1970 was also when the new chief of naval operations, Admiral Elmo R. Zumwalt, Jr., attempted to institute reforms in the Navy, which resulted instead in increased racial tensions due to white backlash (Westheider 105). Fraggings of white officers (presumably by black soldiers) had increased by 100 percent from 1969, so that by 1970 racial violence appeared to be the most critical problem facing the military (109).

How Lieutenant Rufus Brooks' names are given do more than replicate a stereotypical African American male of 1982, when the book was published, or of August 1970, when the story is set. Instead, the changeability of Brooks' name suggests that his masculinity is contingent on the degree to which he is raced. It is significant that Brooks is introduced as all mind and no body: "Under the cap the lanky black man sat motionless, sat as if his entire self were his eyes and brain and thoughts and his body did not exist" (33). Though his race as a black man is emphasized in this passage, it is more important that the as-yet-unnamed Brooks, who (we discover later) at this time is dwelling on the divorce papers he has just received from his wife, is a thoughtful man. That is, before he is named, his race and his ideas are not necessarily related. Ironically, this may be the only moment in the text where Brooks' race is not connected to his status as a masculine man. A three-page section following this introduction foreshadows how Brooks has names assigned to him by the author, thus marking him as malleable and pliant (35–38). (In my discussion of *The 13th Valley*, I will use Brooks, without quotation marks, to refer to the character generally. Any names for this or any other character appearing in quotation marks refers to how the text names the character.) In this brief section, Brooks is named "Brooks," "Tango November," "Rufus," "Uncle Tom," "Ruf," "L-T Bro," and "First Lieutenant Rufus Brooks," though most often as "Brooks." Departures from "Brooks" are underscored, tracing the relevance of race to each of Brooks' names, and preparing the reader to understand him and how he can be seen as masculine according to his alternating racial positioning. Ultimately, the anomalous names appear both when Brooks' race is being emphasized and also when his masculinity is most vulnerable, suggesting the inseparability of his masculinity and his race.

According to this early section, Brooks is an intellectual, pursuing a master's degree in philosophy at UC-Berkeley before leaving graduate school to fulfill his ROTC commitment from the University of San Francisco. The San Francisco area was a hotbed of anti-war activism during the late 1960s, and one of the reasons for Brooks' leaving graduate school was the "political tension on campus" (36).[19] His first assignment in Vietnam was as an aide to a high-ranking (white) officer in the 101st Airborne Division Headquarters, where Brooks rankled at how he was named by the other (white) officers "Tango November, their token nigger" (36). He was given the name as the sole African American officer at Division Headquarters, where he was vocal about the mistreatment of enlisted black soldiers in the unit. For a black officer to hazard his own military career by defending black enlisted soldiers was unusual, especially since most black officers were considered "Uncle Toms" (Westheider 55). But the sole alternative to Brooks being named "Tango November" by white officers was to be given another name, "Uncle Tom," by the only other black in the headquarters, a senior NCO; evidently, there was no solidarity in skin color between enlisted and officers. To Brooks' relief, he left Division

Headquarters to become the Alpha Company commander, resuming his "previous quiet manner" and being named privately by his men as "L-T Buddha" (36). It is in the tactical milieu of Alpha Company that *The 13th Valley* is told and where Brooks formulates and writes his master's thesis on the causes of conflict.

This three-page passage (35–38) is instructive in how to interpret Brooks' various names. To the white staff officers, he is the aide to the Division Chief of Staff only because of affirmative action, and so is referred to as "Tango November" (*t*oken *n*igger); that negative impression is compounded by his advocacy for black enlisted soldiers. "Tango November" is a disempowering name, since Brooks has no language to counter it, nor, as a staff officer, any way to vindicate his accusations that black soldiers were mistreated or to demonstrate he was not merely a whiner. Brooks becomes "Rufus" at the same time the black NCO gives him a racially ambivalent name, "Uncle Tom"; unlike the overtly racializing name, "Tango November," Brooks is comfortable with "Uncle Tom." What he does not realize is that the name "Rufus" is racially equated to "Uncle Tom." Once assigned as commander of Alpha Company, where he is at home in the jungle, Brooks is referred to as "Brooks," unmarked by race, and he infrequently is named by his soldiers in sometimes racial but at least complimentary ways (i.e., "L-T Bro" in public, "L-T Buddha" in private). But the signification of "Brooks" as outside of race is temporary and contingent on the combat environment, so that when Brooks is returned to a staff job for only a few weeks, he again becomes "Rufus," and "*again* he fell to chastising his senior associates [about their treatment of black soldiers]" (36; emphasis added). The use of "Rufus," then, signals Brooks' position as "race" character, instances when his paramount quality has to do with his race, not with his authority or ability. It also looks ahead to the discussion in this same passage of why Brooks, a first lieutenant, was appointed as a company commander ahead of the more senior captains; they were exceptionally competitive, and "their combat records were very important to them." On the other hand, "*Rufus* Brooks said he didn't care" (37; emphasis added). Brooks' non-careerist attitude contributes to the admiration of the men in his company, and the belief that "he [Brooks] had attained enlightenment" (38), but it also contributes to the notion that "Rufus" was made company commander ahead of the captains — all white — because of his race.

"Rufus," in other words, identifies the character by race; "Brooks" signals race as inconsequential to the character's identity.[20] I am not arguing that Rufus Brooks exemplifies the stereotype of the complacent black, nor am I arguing that Rufus Brooks exemplifies the stereotype of the noble savage. Instead, I am tracing the way in which Del Vecchio tutors us to read Lieutenant Rufus Brooks, and early lessons indicate that there are numerously raced and gendered Brookses in the text. Though it is possible to imagine that names indicate realistically the cultural assumptions of the time period held by the people Brooks encounters and to which he must respond, race does not appear to play a large role in how Brooks thinks. He is only the sounding board for the complaints of characters of color for whom race explains all differences. Even though Brooks does not articulate opinions about racial difference, the names applied to him ensure that his multiple identities signify "race," which in turn signifies his masculinity.

Raced "Rufus" is also used to signal his sexuality, especially with his African American wife, Lila. Disgruntled by his extending his Vietnam tour, Lila files for divorce. Thus, as Brooks theorizes for his master's thesis the causes of conflict on national and international levels, he also contemplates his personal conflict with his wife. Throughout the novel, Brooks revisits moments in their relationship that may explain its current disintegration, beginning with the first time he and Lila spent the night together (263–265). To Lila, he had made the unforgivable mistake of arranging their rendezvous in a cheap hotel frequented by, to her, "bums and fags." After she storms away, "Rufus" "allowed a [white] man to pick him up," for no other reason than "allowing some white fag to rub his buns" (264). When Lila learns of that encounter, she names him a "lousy ... honky's fag" (265).

What is important about this passage is that here Del Vecchio refers to Brooks as "Rufus" when he is engaged in activities with another man that might easily be marked largely as sexual, not racial. That he is referred to as "Rufus" in this episode indicates that Brooks' encounter with the white man is as much about race as it is about sex. If the encounter is equal parts race and sex, then "Rufus" as a signifier places Brooks outside of the dominant masculine group, which is white (as exemplified by the Division Headquarters) and strictly heterosexual. Lila confirms this with her conflation of race and sexuality as she charges him with being a "lousy ... honky's fag."

Lila's name is important, too, as its mythological significance authorizes her condemnation of Rufus' race and sexuality. Usually called by her first name alone, "Lila" bears the entire weight of her character's meaning. Were *The 13th Valley* a black-authored text, according to Debra Walker King's theory of "literary onomastics," "Lila" could signify resistance to racial and gender oppression.[21] As written by a white author, Lila's resistance is represented as emasculating Brooks and as stereotypical of a black woman, echoing the notorious 1965 indictments by Senator Daniel Patrick Moynihan that single black mothers produced emasculated boys. Lila is characterized as a selfish, preoccupied, domineering woman, and her singular name ensures that readers are unable to imagine her otherwise. Unlike the multiple names by which Brooks is known, Lila's lone name signifies an entanglement of racial, sexual, and gender identities because of its mythological overtones. According to *The Woman's Encyclopedia of Myths and Secrets*, the name "Lila" is affiliated with Lilith, who, in the Hebraic tradition, is the first wife of Adam. He married her "because he grew tired of coupling with the beasts," but when he insisted she lie beneath him while coupling, "[s]he sneered at Adam's sexual crudity, cursed him, and flew away to make her home by the Red Sea" (Walker 541). Lila's mythological name is the template by which we are tutored to read her behavior as "Lilith's." Because her name signals a strong woman who leaves a domineering man, that Lila does leave Brooks, even without the complication of his apparent domination, confirms what we've "known" all along: Lila's character is constructed to signify "Rufus" not just as racially marked (and thereby marginalized), but also as sexually marked (and thereby marginalized). The simultaneity of these racial and sexual identities in "Rufus" complicates our understanding of the Brooks character, even as race and sex are not patently foregrounded by Del Vecchio.

"Rufus" as the "race" man is also used to signal his sexuality with white men in Vietnam. Lila and "Rufus" meet in Hawaii for a week of R&R, but the meeting goes disastrously wrong. While "Rufus" imagines they will spend most of their time in bed together, Lila wants to be a tourist. She is offended by the combat-roughened ideas and language that "Rufus" expresses during the Hawaii trip, and is angry that "Rufus" expects her to behave in traditionally submissive ways. What is important about the scene in Hawaii is that the now racially and sexually marked "Rufus" finds himself impotent during their lovemaking as a result of their arguing and of his flashbacks to combat in Vietnam. Once "Rufus" returns to Alpha Company and the subsequent relief of being named as the racially unmarked "Brooks," he attempts to repair the sexual markedness and lack of control that his impotency (and earlier homosexual encounter) had conferred on him by developing a two-scene sexual fantasy. In the first scene, he intrudes on Lila and another man and tosses a grenade at them; in the second, the image switches to Brooks on the bed with Lila. That Brooks is known as "Rufus" in the moments when he is out of sexual control — the ultimate lack of control in Vietnam War texts is for a man to be impotent or wounded "in the groin"— points to the other moments earlier in the text when he also is out of control and named "Rufus." Another fantasy Brooks has of his wife being with another man occurs immediately after a white officer senior to Brooks refers to him as "Boy" (208). Clearly, Brooks' race is directly connected to his, in this case, verbal emasculation, especially by a white man. The "Rufus" moments are when his race becomes paramount. That Brooks is referred to as "Brooks" during his fantasizing denotes power and control, some characteristics of monolithic masculinity. Unlike "Rufus," whose race and sexuality are disempowering, "Brooks" can manipulate the fantasy and its outcome as a result of the power he has as a racially unmarked (and heterosexually functional) masculine man. However, "Brooks" loses control when the second scene of the fantasy with Lila evolves into the "secret thoughtimage" (481) of a ménage à trois which includes Egan, his white platoon sergeant; previously in-control, unraced, heterosexual "Brooks" becomes, according to the text, racially marked and questionably sexed "Rufus." Even Brooks' sexual fantasies, then, are racialized, and are connected to the way in which his name signals the current state of his masculinity. While Brooks has control over events, he is "Brooks," racially unmarked and a member of the masculine elite. When Brooks does not have control over events, his name "Rufus" signifies the condition both of his racial markedness and of his precarious gender state. Not only does this naming practice by Del Vecchio define Brooks by his varying masculinities, but it also denotes some of the qualities inherent to monolithic masculinity: white and masterful.

This method of racing and gendering characters continues with another main character, Sergeant Daniel Egan. He is closely related to Brooks in the narrative, and his story is important to the outcome of Brooks,' as Egan's role in the ménage à trois fantasy demonstrates. Just as Brooks' name changes denote the precariousness of his masculinity, so do the infrequent references to Egan by anything but "Egan" suggest the stability of his race, sexuality, and masculinity. Because those categories are fixed in Egan, they simultaneously become standard and less material, and so Egan is free to be the spokesperson for the "normal" in Vietnam. At the same time, Egan's fixedness may be read as rigidity, and so he is locked into a particular position as a consequence of his white race and heterosexual embodiment of monolithic masculinity. Egan's normativity is crucial in regard to his and Brooks' theories about conflict, because, to accord with Egan's attitude that war is the natural state of humans, Brooks entirely and almost spontaneously reverses the conclusions of his master's thesis, that conflict is semantically constructed. Egan is seen as a natural soldier: the lower enlisted men emulate Egan, and in combat he is seen as "beautiful," and as "the man who would take any risk to protect his men" (24, 93). The compounding effect of Egan's being depicted as an exemplary leader to his soldiers and as having a singular name, unlike Rufus Brooks, establishes him as a person both normal in terms of masculinity and also racially unmarked. According to the text, however, this same unmarkedness endangers Egan's life and he dies with two other characters, Brooks and Doc, who are marked by their racial positions as African Americans. This fatal outcome reflects some ambivalence in the novel: even though "Rufus'" race is made material to his identity and Egan's race is not, they perish under the same conditions. Their deaths, however, do not mitigate the conditions of their lives, especially white Egan's; as Dyer points out, "whites are not of a certain race, they're just the human race" (3).

Even though the symbol of monolithic masculinity, Egan is not portrayed as a machine; though he uses prostitutes, his combat experience has sensitized him to the needs of his stateside girlfriend, and his hygiene in the field is fastidious. Egan's sensitizing adds to his being represented as normal in the novel's publication year, 1982, especially after the Women's Movement of the 1960s and 1970s and the early Men's Movement of the same period, which focused on men getting in touch with their emotions.[22] What is important to my argument is what Egan thinks about conflict, and how the positive reception of Egan's opinion is reliant on his being represented as "normal." When a discussion about war among the leaders of the company occurs, Egan argues that the Vietnam War is a valid one, and that the threat of communism in South Vietnam necessitates resistance. Despite the arguments against the war offered by characters of color — Minh, the Vietnamese scout, and El Paso, a student of law and history — Egan's argument holds sway. These two characters' names are more evidently evocative than are Brooks or Egan. "Minh" echoes both "Ho Chi Minh," one of the many pseudonyms for the leader of North Vietnam, and the "Vietminh," nationalist freedom fighters, first against the Japanese occupation during World War II and then against the French until their departure in the mid–1950s. (See William Duiker, *Ho Chi Minh* [2000] for more about Ho Chi Minh's names and the Vietminh.) As the voice of historicist "chicanismo," and the "arbiter and the negotiator of intra-company squabbles" (240), El Paso's name alludes to the 1967 birth of La Raza Unida in El Paso. "A major event of 1967," comments Juan Gómez Quiñones, "signaling a change in the Mexican American temper, was the development of the Raza Unida concept, which arose in protest of the cabinet committee hearings held at the conference in El Paso on October 28" (109).

"Brooks" (whose race previously has been narratively structured as irrelevant when he is in Alpha Company) never enters the argument about war; strangely for a person developing a theory of conflict, he regards the particulars of the Vietnam conflict as immaterial to his theory, and he only listens to the others' conversation (332–336). Furthermore, because of Brooks' silence, Minh and El Paso, as characters of color and so in this text symbolizing race, are responsible for representing both the anti-war stance and that of colonized people of color (like the Vietnamese and Latino Americans). Within the company, Brooks is limited to his non-raced identity as "Brooks," not "Rufus." But Egan always remains a unified "Egan," one whose ideas, though contested, remain consistent and dominant. It is Brooks' identity variation that hamstrings him in this case, when he chooses not to weigh in on conflict and is effectively silenced on the issue of race when he, as an advanced student of philosophy, might be the most theoretically knowledgeable.

The racializing by names of a third character, Italian American Chelini/Cherry, also occurs in the novel. Though pre–World War II notions of "race" might have included Italians, the irrelevance of Chelini's Italian ethnicity echoes what David Colburn and George Pozzetta term the "ethnic activism" of the 1960s.[23] As soon as he arrives in Alpha Company, Chelini is christened "Cherry," a name given to new men in combat that suggests vulnerability on Cherry's part, especially because "cherry" connotes sexual virginity. This inability to prevent others' naming and thereby controlling him coincides with the haphazard manner in which Chelini "allowed" himself to be drafted (2), the way in which he is assigned to the wrong type of unit but has no power to change the assignment (1), and his general sense through most of the novel of being an outsider. Similar to the variability of Brooks' naming, whether this character is referred to in the text as "Cherry" or as "Chelini" depends on whether he is able to control his body and his situation. That he is known early in the text as "Chelini," when he is least prepared for combat, and becomes "Cherry" and remains "Cherry" even after combat experience is significant. It is the name assigned to him in Vietnam and which he embraces—"Cherry"—which, because it typically is used to indicate (sexual) inexperience and naiveté, paradoxically signals the greatest amount of power and his moments of invulnerability. Moreover, while Brooks and Egan do not survive this battle in the thirteenth valley, Cherry does.

After Chelini is named "Cherry," he is infrequently referred to as "Chelini" only when he is needed to represent ethnicity, when his being Italian American is important to the text's concern for ethnic and racial diversity, as in the "melting pot" quote at the opening of this chapter. For instance, as "Chelini" signs in with the unit on his first day, he encounters only men of color: the Chicano Top Sergeant, African American Doc Johnson, and African American Jax. "Chelini" observes the black soldiers dapping — "the greeting rite of raps and slaps and shakes" — and power saluting, and concludes, "he'd been assigned to a unit of crazy racist psychopaths" (49–50). As a racist Italian American, "Chelini" functions as the overt judge of Black Nationalist cultural practices, a racism David Colburn and George Pozzetta claim would resonate with the ethnic activism of Italian Americans during the 1960s (134–135). Later in the novel, "Cherry" observes another dapping between a white man (Egan) and a black man (Jax), described as "the sensual caresses of brotherhood" (429). As in the first episode of dapping, "Cherry" cannot bear the sight, but neither is he free in the second episode to name it as "psychopathic" behavior because it involves a white man. Though he does not name "the sensual caresses" as "psychopathy," his body reacts violently to the sight. At the very moment that he sees the dapping in the second instance, "Cherry" develops a severe case of diarrhea, as though that is the only way in which he can purge himself of having seen "psychopathy" without naming it that. So, while "Chelini" functions as an ethnically marked character and is free verbally to pass judgments on behavior he names "racist," "Cherry" is conflicted about the same sort of behavior, which his loss of control over his body illustrates. In-control, ethnically specific "Chelini" more closely approximates monolithic masculinity than out-of-control Everyman "Cherry."

During the final assault on the NVA headquarters, Egan is severely wounded and injected with morphine against his wishes. His drugged state prevents him from getting out from under a helicopter crashing at the site, so first Brooks and then Doc try to shield him from the crash's inferno; all three are incinerated. That Cherry — out of Brooks, Egan, and Chelini — is the only survivor of *The 13th Valley* calls into question the validity of monolithic masculinity, since the man who has only one name, Egan, is intended to model it and he dies, out of control under the influence of drugs. As a white man, Egan is racially unmarked; he is at home in his environment because he both knows the landscape and people of Vietnam and also is a highly skilled warrior; and his personal life and his professional life are prevented by him from overlapping. Even though Brooks is superior in rank and education and is a highly skilled tactician, and therefore should be a model of the type of masculinity valorized by war, he cannot be: though he dies trying to save Egan, both his personal and professional lives are marked by race, which causes them to overlap in conspicuous and limiting ways. Egan dies while under the influence of a drug that had been forced on him by a medic, however, indicating that some things are beyond the control of even the most "masculine" man. Brooks' vulnerability is also visible on his body, as his identities as "Rufus" and as "Brooks" become racialized by the color of his skin. These two men succeed in their mission to take the NVA headquarters, but it would seem, in failing to survive this test of monolithic masculinity, they were unable to fulfill its expectations.

Survival is not traditionally associated with masculinity, since masculinity is often confused with heroism, and deserters, for instance, are not typically deemed "heroes" but do survive. Neither does death translate automatically into heroism or masculinity. Masculinities as they appear in military venues, especially after Vietnam, do not always equate to heroism, and masculinity post–Vietnam has accrued new forms which make it possible to include the vast number of men who "survived" the War. To have survived the Vietnam War, which popularly is understood as senseless and brutal, might be regarded as a laudable, masculine achievement, especially for those who experienced combat. Now, those whose skills made it possible for them to leave Vietnam alive might be considered masculine; those who did not participate in the War and now feel guilt about it might be considered masculine because they admit their shame; those who evaded the War altogether can be judged the right kind of masculine to be the nation's commander-in-chief. In her discussion of how national catastrophes are handled by memory, Marita Sturken claims that the bodies of survivors at the National Vietnam Veterans Memorial, for instance, can signify possibly conflicting ideologies: "Although the body of a wounded veteran at the memorial may testify to the war's cost, his presence may also be intended to reinforce the precise codes of honor and sacrifice in war that resulted in his injury" (12). In short, survival can testify to two diametrically opposed attitudes toward the War, and to have survived the War may then be interpreted as masculine.

Since "normal" and invariable Egan is represented by Del Vecchio's text as a consummate survivor in warfare, he may be read as the model of self-contained, monolithic masculinity as it appears in this novel. But if survival becomes a primary criterion for being regarded as masculine, that Cherry is the only one of the three to survive does not mean he replaces Egan as the model. Though his name, "Cherry," does denote him as a Vietnam War Everyman, and one who somehow has gained the power to bestow names, by the conclusion of the novel he loses that power as he exceeds the boundaries of monolithic masculinity in verging on insanity. Over the course of the novel, coincident with his increasing excessiveness and control, he also gains the power to name: he names himself a "man-god" (470) and when Minh, the Vietnamese scout, is killed by a mortar round to the head, Cherry names the parts of his brains (586); finally, when Brooks, Egan, and Doc are memorialized, Cherry names their deaths with "Fuck it. Don't mean nothin'," thereby assuming Egan's language to name a meaningful event (636). Were Cherry to retain this power to name, he might be read as occupying the space of masculine model vacated by the dead Egan, whose assertion that war is the natural state of man was affirmed by Brooks right before both died (630). However, when Cherry attempts this final naming, he is silenced by a (white) officer. Even the Vietnam Everyman is still ethnicized and so cannot overcome the perquisites of being white and having military rank.

These three characters demonstrate how the Vietnam War has problematized the construction of monolithic masculinity in the National Symbolic. That is, when war is supposed to strengthen and confirm a man's claim to monolithic masculinity, the conditions of the Vietnam War described by white veteran Del Vecchio accentuate, rather than downplay, the tenuous hold each character already had on masculinity outside of the arena of the war. The penalties for being racialized ("Rufus") are too great to bear the equal weight of non-normative sexuality ("Brooks"); it is not enough for a man unmarked by race and sexuality to model monolithic masculinity — he also has to survive (Egan); and it also is not enough to survive, since the model of monolithic masculinity has definitive, implicit boundaries which must not be exceeded (Cherry). The conclusion drawn by *The 13th Valley*, then, is that the conditions in Vietnam could not support monolithic masculinity. But the novel produces this conclusion only as the result of multiplying characters of color, and then using a tacit rhetoric of names that racializes characters in order to place them either in or outside of the bounds of monolithic masculinity. This practice extends to many other Vietnam War texts, where names become shorthand for personal qualities.

Patrick Duncan's film, *84 Charlie MoPic* (1989), uses the oblique method of addressing race as it demonstrates how images of masculinities in the Vietnam War are mediated by ideology. Just as attempts to moderate the racism of the Vietnam War era in *The 13th Valley* are undone by Del Vecchio's use of names, so too does *84 Charlie MoPic*'s visual rhetoric have a dual and sometimes contradictory racial effect. Even as the film addresses the ideological mediation of images, it attempts to temper that mediation by creating a documentary-looking film with characters directly addressing the camera. Duncan claims the film's aim was an ideological one, to explain the war's loss as a result of treating war as business: "We had people who considered it a business. They saw the cost in lives in the same way a guy in Detroit figures workers are going to lose a few fingers; that's written into the insurance program, and they can swallow it as a part of overhead" (Jaehne 12). But the film medium inherently cannot avoid the mediations Duncan wants to circumvent, since the film genre's reliance on images undoes this aim as it demonstrates visually, against the spoken language used by the characters, how masculine relationships in the film framed by racial difference should be deciphered.

"84 Charlie MoPic" is the shorthand military designation for a military cameraman, "Combat, Moving Pictures." The birth name of the man serving this function is never revealed, nor does the film appear deliberately to include an image of MoPic. He and the white second lieutenant, LT (2nd Lieutenant Drewry), join a long-range reconnaissance patrol of five men to make a training film: OD (Staff Sergeant O'Donnigan) is the African American, hard-nosed, steely-faced leader of the patrol who "plays by Charlie's rules"; Cracker (Specialist 5 Frye) is the self-named "poor white trash" weapons specialist who is second in command after OD; Pretty Boy (Specialist 4 Baldwin) is the handsome, white, soft-spoken medic from California; Hammer (Specialist 4 Thorpe), the white "lifer," is heavy weapons specialist/machine-gunner for the group; and Easy (Private Easland) is the white, "short," joke-cracking, 4-Purple-Heart-winning radioman. Combat-seasoned OD resents the filmmakers' intrusion not only because he has a tightly-knit group whose job is contingent on their isolation and interdependency (Cracker, Hammer and Pretty Boy all refer to the others as "brothers," and all five wear identical bracelets to signal their brotherhood), but also because in the hierarchy of rank, LT nominally is in charge. What is worse to OD is that LT is not only a "fucking new guy," untried and untested in the rigors of war, a "cherry," but also an opportunist. To LT, war is a business, a big corporation where "the advancement potential is enormous." While rank and attitude appear to explain the conflicts between OD and LT, the visual rhetoric of the film connotes racial animosity.

These characters might be Vietnam War film stereotypes, confirming what Richard Dyer refers to as "habits of perception," or the results of how we are tutored to view images. Since the end of the War, Americans have been habituated to interpreting it in certain ways: "good" South Vietnam was a democracy being invaded by a "bad" communist government of North Vietnam; the United States was prevented from winning by a micromanaging, business-like government; most soldiers were wounded, either physically or psychically; those who returned in one piece routinely were spat upon by vindictive Americans; and Vietnam was the only war America ever had lost.[24] What *is* uncommon about *84 Charlie MoPic* is how it is filmed; shot entirely from the shoulder of the cameraman, spectators are denied the explanatory shot/reverse shot to which Hollywood has accustomed us and on which we rely to explain our relationships to the images we see.[25] In addition, the film uses the conventions of neo-realism: frequent and noticeable use of a hand-held camera in location shooting, lighting which approximates the location's given illumination, ordinary characters in ordinary settings, speech marked by dialect, unprofessional actors, unpleasant topics, and working-class as opposed to middle-class life (Kleinhans 159). *84 Charlie MoPic* is self-conscious about its use of the handheld camera, especially when all of the characters at one time or another look directly into the camera: "Look at the camera, not me," says MoPic. Background sound is minimal and there is no soundtrack music; the film uses contemporary music (Donovan) that the soldiers hear on Armed Forces Radio. Finally, because the film is shot outdoors and relies on natural lighting, there appears to be less manipulation of the images by the filmmaker.

The film has been judged as highly realistic. "One of the best," exudes Michael Lee Lanning, a combat veteran of the Vietnam War. Except for the "detracting weakness" (*Vietnam,* 209) of the soldiers' variety of hats and headgear, *84 Charlie MoPic* is "without a doubt the most accurate portrayal of a Vietnam patrol filmed to date" (208). Richard Bernstein furthers the argument for Patrick Duncan's film being read as realistic when he says, "it is, at least most of the time, effective and believable, a new sort of cinema verité, producing the illusion of being within the platoon, sharing its danger, its battle-hardened jokes, its young man's obscenity, even its awareness of the camera" (30). It is so realistic that Stanley Kauffmann complains *84 Charlie MoPic* is redundant: "Why did we need a fictional re-creation of a Vietnam documentary? The genuine articles exist" (24). In her review/interview entitled "Company Man," Karen Jaehne explores how Duncan used his own experience as a soldier from the lower class to create the film: "Duncan can understand directing a film as 'work,' just as he went to Vietnam initially as 'work or as an alternative to jail,' as he says. Yet Duncan believes that if your job is to make a Vietnam film, the film will betray your lack of experience if you have not done time" (12). Milton Bates points out, however, that "Patrick Duncan successfully disguised his California locale by cropping close. This tactic worked until the final frames, which are unfortunately intersected by a power line" (223).

In pretending to be an unmediated reproduction of images, the film purports to reproduce the "true" Vietnam experience. It deals with race in a similarly self-reflexive way, by explicitly making race an issue. Like *The 13th Valley*, white-authored *84 Charlie MoPic* tries to erase or moderate the racial divides of the era by addressing them directly. Though the spoken language scripted between the characters does ameliorate racial divisions, the image-dependent film medium discloses race as significant to the way these men interact. The film does this through what Richard Dyer calls "habits of perception," or the scopophilic ways in which spectators "so believe in the presence and reality of images that we may take them at face value" (Kolker 2). These habits include the desire to recognize "truth" about the Vietnam War, one of the most prominent "truths" being that racial difference is overcome in the brotherhood of combat. Though it attempts to minimize racial difference by emphasizing this "brotherhood," *84 Charlie MoPic* suggests that masculinity still is inflected by a racial hierarchy.

Any realistic effect of *84 Charlie MoPic* is achieved through the use of a 16mm shoulder-held camera. While the audience is aware of the cameraman because we see the effects of his presence and hear his voice when he instructs the soldiers, we only see him, accidentally, three times. His image is notable, for those moments when we are shown MoPic emphasize pivotal points in the diegesis. In the first instance, the visual text reveals its ideological intent. MoPic has put down his camera to urinate and Hammer retrieves it to interview MoPic. Hammer, Easy, and Pretty Boy are boyish-looking, but MoPic is even younger and more innocent-looking. When asked by Hammer why he volunteered for this mission, MoPic explains that, while working in the processing lab where the films of all MoPics were sent to be developed, he had developed many films of combat which ended abruptly and were anonymous, intimating the death of the cameraman; those mysteries compelled MoPic to find out for himself what had occurred *behind* the camera. This desire is prescient, since his film also ends abruptly and virtually anonymously. The film also suggests that MoPic already is anonymous — we never do learn his "civilian" name — and that the lessons an audience receives while viewing all films do not tutor it to question the ideology of the camera's eye, the person manipulating the camera. The text, then, quietly asks us to challenge the notion of its objectivity. By making explicit the ideological perspective of the camera person, as in MoPic's first appearance, the text impels the audience to consider carefully the depictions rendered.

The second image of MoPic comes when the group is fleeing from the enemy and urgently trying to get to the pick-up point; we have almost forgotten the cameraman in the commotion. As they hasten through the brush — the audience is there, bumping along with the camera — MoPic stumbles and falls, causing him and the camera to lie side by side on the ground, when he looks directly into the camera, and then quickly recovers his feet. What the audience cannot miss, though, is the look of utter fear on MoPic's face, summarizing the attitudes of all the men: fascinated by the enigma of war, and terrified at its proximity.

The third time MoPic appears on film is at its conclusion. Four men have survived — LT, a badly wounded OD, Easy, and MoPic — and they are waiting for a helicopter to retrieve them from a "hot" landing zone. LT mistakenly throws the yellow grenade, indicating the landing zone is safe, when he should have thrown a red one. So when the helicopter lands amid hostile fire, the four have to dodge the bullets to board the helicopter. LT and MoPic escort the hysterical Easy to the helicopter, where MoPic leaves the camera on the deck as he and LT return to help OD. From the helicopter deck the camera captures the image of the three approaching the helicopter when MoPic is shot once, attempts to get up and is shot again, stirs, and is shot a third time. The camera reveals, seemingly non-ideologically since no person now is controlling it, the helicopter lifting off without MoPic and then only a frame of the sky and a booted foot.

The image of the three returning to the helicopter is captured by the unmanned camera, inferring objective truth value in this image-making that could not have occurred with a person subjectively controlling the camera. That is, the way ideology was made explicit by the first instance of MoPic's being on film, as Hammer controlled the camera and MoPic explained why he wanted to be in the bush, alerts the audience to the way in which "seeing is not believing,"[26] and how the images presented by the text are, in fact, mediated ones. In the second two instances, however, when MoPic is out of control of the camera, the text purports to reveal unmediated (and, therefore, "truthful") images of terror and death. That the text includes both types of images blurs the lines between mediated and unmediated images; it is difficult to discern upon which the text is insisting. As Dyer suggests, however, film is by its constitution a mediation. That is, even if a filmmaker sets as her goal the objective representation of an image, it still is an image that is a re-presentation; film images are always already mediated. Thus, *84 Charlie MoPic*'s attempt to represent without mediation is doomed from the beginning, just as is the man whose story it tells.

"Racial imagery," says Dyer, "is central to the organisation of the modern world" (1). While any number of filmic elements could be examined for discerning how raced masculinity is depicted and imagined in *84 Charlie MoPic* or other Vietnam War films, I look at the element ostensibly the least mediated: lighting. Because the film is shot entirely outdoors and during daylight hours, one could argue that little to no special lighting is afforded to any of the characters or scenes. The film "says" otherwise, however. While the film is an attempt to render the fraternity of warrior brothers, the lighting rhetoric used in the film establishes a racial hierarchy not unlike the one occurring linguistically in *The 13th Valley*. As Dyer points out, "the very process of [racial] hierarchisation is an exercise of power":

> Movie lighting in effect discriminates on the basis of race.... [S]uch discrimination has much to do with the conceptualisation of whiteness. There is also a rather different level at which movie lighting's discrimination may be said to operate. What is at issue here is not how white is shown and seen, so much as the assumptions at work in the way movie lighting disposes people in space. Movie lighting relates people to each other and to setting according to notions of the human that have historically excluded non-white people [102].

In emphasizing the geographical home of each of the men, *84 Charlie MoPic says* race does not matter, so that as "Americans" the men in combat all are masculine "brothers." But the lighting of the film *shows* that race does impute gender differences among male characters. *84 Charlie MoPic* does not depict the representative ethnic and racial distribution appearing in narratives like *The 13th Valley*. The most common information we receive about the characters is their geographical homes: Pretty Boy is from California, Hammer is from a small, mid-western town, Cracker is from South Carolina, and Easy is from New Jersey. Their nicknames reinforce their geographical identities, as opposed to racial or ethnic ones. However, these particular geographical locations are representatively American, and, except for South Carolina (Cracker is the only character asked about race relations), are "written" by the text as white, and therefore race non-specific, since "race" is not about "white." When LT asks Cracker about being commanded by a black man, he snaps, "That's a real world question. Ask me that when I'm back in South Carolina." Cracker's claim empties the War of racial meaning; this is important, since Cracker, hailing from the Deep South, is meant to be the representative of bigotry and racial prejudice (especially after events motivated by racism in the South were nationally publicized during the Civil Rights Movement of the 1950s and 1960s). Spectator habits of perception assume that if the character representing a racial attitude says race does not matter in Vietnam, it must not; we believe Cracker because as an underclass white Southerner, he has the most to gain from the oppression of blacks. Audience understandings of racial attitudes in certain regions of the United States, even if they are based on stereotypes and misinformation, guide how we read characters.

The homes of the other three characters — MoPic, OD, and LT — are never disclosed. If the characters are representative, that state is not geographically-based. When MoPic remains behind the camera, he is a generic American: ostensibly unlocated by geography, unmarked by race, unmarked by class, and unmarked by gender. When visible, he is humanized by race and sex, but no other identities adhere to him from outside the scope of the military. OD is similarly humanized, but only within the same limited scope. When LT asks OD for an interview, OD refuses, saying, "The Army has no business in my private life," implying that his anonymity is by choice, unlike the physically imposed anonymity of MoPic-behind-the-camera. Subsequently, the audience knows nothing of OD outside his behavior during this mission; that he is black also activates certain racial habits of perception that are not suggested by the white skin of the other characters, such as his nickname ("OD"="overdosed") preposterously echoing the widespread heroin use by "minority" soldiers near the end of the War (Starr 118). When Easy interviews LT, LT tells the camera that it was "politics" that kept him from an appointment to West Point, but that he still intended to make the Army his career because "the advancement potential is enormous." LT will not permit anonymity, as does MoPic, nor does he choose it, as does OD. Because these three characters are geographically unidentified, and because the conflict between OD and LT is captured by MoPic, they are central to the discourse of race that *84 Charlie MoPic* invokes. The other characters *articulate* ideas about race that appeal to the audience's habits of perception; these three characters *enact* the images that tell another story about race and masculinity. The question, then, is how those images are enacted through the film's image-making. This is where lighting becomes relevant.

Paradoxically, the darker places in the landscape represent safety to the group, and the places that are well-lit are the most threatening. The challenge for MoPic is to capture details in faces with a minimal amount of lighting, since the reconnaissance unit does not linger in the well-lit, dangerous spaces. When they take breaks or establish a camp site, it is always in the cover of the woods, and this is where LT's interviews of the men take place. As a result, the lighting is important, since light impacts how each man's story can be perceived.

Dyer argues that lighting of white characters is hierarchized:

> There are appropriately hard-edged, relatively opaque subjects (the lunatic, the felon, the native) and appropriately soft-edged, more translucent ones (angels, fairies, saints and people like them). At the extremes there are the opaque non-white subject and the pellucid white subject, but in between the technology permits the reproduction of whiteness as a differentiated and hierarchised structure. Class as well as such criteria of proper whiteness as sanity and non-criminality are expressed in degrees of translucence, with murkiness associated with the poor, working-class and immigrant white subjects [113].

All four of the characters who are geographically specified — Easy, Hammer, Pretty Boy, and Cracker — are presented by the film as white men, and yet all four also are filmed under lighting conditions that hint at degrees of whiteness and subsequent masculinities. Easy, the first to be interviewed, is always filmed in fully shaded or night lighting, alluding both to the safety in darker spaces, but also to the not-quite-white look of the actor. This dark lighting contributes to the physical characterization of Easy: he is fearful, dope-smoking, lazy, demoted several times, and wounded an equal number of times. Hammer also is filmed in shade, but not in the deep shade of Easy. This lighting suggests that, though Hammer is white, he is low in the white hierarchy, since he is in the military only because he was given the option of jail or enlisting. Pretty Boy, on the other hand, is filmed almost always in full or dappled light, contributing both to his positive characterization as a Californian, as a medic, as a man who defied death multiple times and also, in a sense, as a martyr when he is the first man of the unit to die. Cracker also is interviewed in full light, ambivalently framed by LT (the opportunist and potential racist) on one side and OD (the racist who denies race is relevant) on the other.

This framing reveals Cracker both as a man from a racist background, but also as one whose racism is qualified by his claims that "the Army's the only real equal opportunity employer I ever saw" and his "love" for OD. Of the four men, then, those filmed largely in shade (Easy and Hammer), even though they are white, are defined by their corporeality, and those white men filmed largely in full light (Pretty Boy and Cracker) are defined by their minds. Dyer interprets the historical distinction between body and mind as a racial qualifier: "Black people can be reduced (in white culture) to their bodies and thus to race, but white people are something else that is realised in and yet is not reducible to the corporeal, or racial" (14). The lighting in this film accomplishes those racial distinctions in terms of gender, so that those seen most for their corporeality are marginalized or subordinated, while those seen more for their minds are closer to the monolithic ideal.

The lighting used for MoPic is unambiguous as it underscores his importance to the diegesis. The first time MoPic is filmed, for instance, he is sun-dappled, a mixture of lighting that, to Dyer, is characteristic of white men: "White subjects may have the soft and the sharp, the light and the dark, the translucent and the palpable warring *within* them. However, this is more often true of white men [as opposed to white women], portrayed with greater contrasts of light and dark, hard contours but areas of translucence, the spirit in the flesh" (113). MoPic is filmed in a space of the deep forest where some light filters through, the majority of which shines on his face, especially his eyes. The light singles him out as white and as a character whose vision is integral to the story. That MoPic's two later appearances feature him in full light adds to his fulfillment of Dyer's white ideal — more mind than body — and to his importance in the story as the "eye."

LT, on the other hand, is lit as a racial enigma. In the opening shot of the film at base camp, he stands in front of the camera to introduce the film. The sun is behind MoPic, casting his shadow on the sand and forcing LT to squint as he looks towards the camera and the sun. This "spotlight" on LT emphasizes his importance to the narrative, but he forgets his lines for introducing "Lessons Learned," so MoPic prompts LT, reinforcing the camera's/MoPic's primacy in the creation of these images. In the background of this introductory scene, the reconnaissance unit marches into the frame from behind LT, led by OD. This is a semiotic spectacle: in full sunlight it makes clear visually the oppositions between LT and OD. While the light is harsh on LT, his helmet casting shadows on his face which exaggerate his facial features, the same light virtually obliterates the facial features of OD's beret-clad, and hence shadow-free, head. While the "spotlight" of the sun emphasizes the centrality of LT to the narrative, what it primarily emphasizes about OD is the shininess of his skin, thereby rendering ambiguous what diegetically should be his centrality to the narrative. This scene sets up, then, the roles of the three prominent characters: MoPic, with his shadow cast by the "spotlight," is obliquely imperative to the story being told; LT, facing the "spotlight," is central and translucently raced as white; and OD, also facing the spotlight, is problematized as the lighting focuses on the blackness he embodies. That is, while the lighting verifies the normalcy of the relatively disembodied MoPic and the embodied LT, it frames OD's blackness as a deviation from the normal.

This visual signification counters what is considered normal to this unit: playing by "Charlie's" (the enemy's) rules, something OD does exceptionally well and about which LT is ignorant. During the same encounter that ends in Pretty Boy's death, the unit captures a severely wounded NVA soldier. Hammer tries to kill the prisoner, but is stopped by LT as he argues the prisoner could provide intelligence to analysts back at base camp. But the reconnaissance unit is being pursued and must move fast to the pick-up point, so they cannot carry both Pretty Boy's body and the prisoner. LT then argues the prisoner should be left behind but alive; it is LT's ignorance of "Charlie's" rules that forces OD to point out that the prisoner already knows too much about the unit for them to leave him alive. After they agree the prisoner should be killed, OD insists LT use a knife rather than a pistol. But when LT stabs the man he does it ineptly and OD must complete the killing. The complete shade of this scene is important: in the case of LT, a white man, it indicates his "murkiness," his being out of his element of full light, and so, of his indiscretion and ineptitude. For OD, on the other hand, the darker lighting reveals the features of his face, marking his physical and mental competencies. As a result, OD surfaces here as more masculine, more masterful than LT.

Nonetheless, the final scene's lighting illustrates the primacy of white LT. The four survivors arrive at the pick-up point, a village that is littered with dead Vietnamese. Easy, OD, LT and MoPic stumble into the village, which, as in the opening scene, is lit fully. Unlike the earlier parts of the film, where LT nominally was in charge but OD was the actual leader, LT has established himself as the actual leader through his map-reading skills and calling in of artillery. Also, while LT's punji-stick wound from the beginning of the mission has been forgotten, OD still suffers from a disabling wound somewhere in his abdomen. OD's is the only wound the camera has not located specifically. LT's hand is shown impaled by the punji stick; the camera zooms in on Pretty Boy's bullet-pierced hand and bloody face; Cracker's sucking chest wound is graphically displayed; and Hammer's wound to the upper thigh is shown as he duct-tapes it. Not only is OD's wound not shown, it never is clear where he has been wounded. All the audience is shown is that, as a result of his wound somewhere in his torso, he hardly is able to walk. Another result of OD's being wounded is that Hammer has to lead the group and immediately is killed by a mine. This pattern of wounds being shown or not shown contradicts the vocal articulations of brotherhood despite racial difference in visually reinforcing OD's bodily difference from the others. In the final scene, the lighting is the greatest signifier of the preeminence of white LT, however. The full light refers to a habit of perception established by the first scene: light "relates people to each other and to setting according to notions of the human that have historically excluded non-white people" (Dyer 102). Not only is LT's body relatively whole and he controls the group, but the light also confers on him what it does not do as it obliterates the facial features of OD: a greater degree of control and thus, masculinity.

Therefore, as a result of the lighting scheme in *84 Charlie MoPic*, even though it is perceived as "natural" and unmediated, the politics of race and masculinity are illuminated. Though the articulated discourse about race, expressed directly by Cracker and indirectly by Hammer and Pretty Boy, insists that race does not matter in combat, the signs of racial difference and its relationship to the ways in which masculinity can be conceived are revealed through a medium whose fundamental element is light. Even in a film like this one, which overtly challenges the idea that it mediates the subject it portrays, signification of race through lighting and the ways that audiences have been tutored to recognize racial signification cannot be avoided. Moreover, race in film can be regarded as constitutive of monolithic masculinity; lighting is highly mediated in film, revealing how masculinity is differently constructed according to racialized perceptions.

The narrative strategies of both *The 13th Valley* and *84 Charlie MoPic* disclose how race can be both a component of monolithic masculinity and also its undoing. Despite the discussions of race articulated by its characters which attempt to mitigate the deleterious effects of racial conflict during the Vietnam War, *The 13th Valley* narrates race through a rhetoric of naming, employing names subtextually to racialize characters' bodies and thus to hierarchize their masculine identities in terms of the degree to which they can control events. Achieving monolithic masculinity does not guarantee survival, though, as Egan's death represents how even the most "normal" of masculine characters can be beyond control of his own circumstances. Similarly, *84 Charlie MoPic* attempts to ameliorate the tensions of racial difference in the Vietnam War through overt discussions of the topic. But spectators' habits of perception engendered by the film medium, in conjunction with the craft of the filmmaker and cameraman who light certain characters in particular ways, serve to mediate that overt message, and race is reconstituted through uses of lighting. What these texts demonstrate is that as long as "whiteness" is represented both as not-race and as normal, monolithic masculinity can maintain its boundaries of white, heterosexual, and in control. However, once the constructions of white as race are explored, and the illusion of what is normal is deconstructed, it becomes apparent that race is constitutive of masculinity. That is, these white-authored texts hold characters of color responsible for the representation of race, just as Dyer explains that, conventionally, lighting becomes a "problem" only when people of color are involved. To be racialized, however, is to be more body than mind; to be more body than mind is to be out of control; to be out of control is to be excluded from the category of monolithic masculinity. When critics like Katherine Kinney and Milton Bates consider "race" only in terms of people of color, and largely in terms of African Americans, they ignore the intertwining of race with masculinity, presuming, when they equate gender and sex, that masculinity is a common factor among men, and that it is only race that distinguishes them. But when "race" includes white characters and "normal" can no longer exist, then neither is there a place for the norm in terms of masculinity; then, masculinities also distinguish men. Discussing race in a singular manner, as a matter of color, maintains the illusion of the achievability of monolithic masculinity.

Finally, this analysis suggests that race and gender are not *produced* by the narrative strategies employed by white authors of Vietnam War texts, but are *inside* these strategies. That is, the tools used to multiply characters of color — naming — or to refer to race obliquely — lighting — appear by definition to be gendering and racializing devices. Characters must be named in fiction and figures must be lit in films, and those names and that lighting will always accrue significance. But the efforts of the new "mythmakers"— the film-making and novel-writing white veterans of the Vietnam War — to achieve race and gender neutrality may falter from the outset, as the available techniques of narration are usually configured to reify the very power structures the authors indict. This narrative limitation has serious consequences for representations of the War, and helps to explain why so few veterans from those groups disproportionately represented among combat casualties have attempted to narrate their own experiences. Nothin' does mean something, after all.

2

The Nam Syndrome
Improper Sexuality, Improper Gender

> *War stories are always looking back and looking ahead. They are telling the story of a war that has already occurred at the same time they are preparing for a war yet to come. Stories are often told by interested parties, parties who have particular points of view about specific wars or wars in general or both. Stories are told to individuals and to nations, and they play a significant role in determining whether individuals and nations are willing to go to war. The stories are important because they tell audiences not simply about wars but about moralities, about men and women, and about one's place in the social order* [Jeffords, "Telling" 232].

The "story" connecting the Vietnam War, masculinity, and sexuality is evidenced by an essay published two decades after the War's end in 1995, opposing homosexuals serving openly in the military.[1] Writers R. D. Adair and Joseph C. Meyers, both mid-level officers in the United States Army, quote Admiral James Stockdale, a navy pilot and POW in North Vietnam for most of the War, to bolster their argument that admission of homosexuals to the military would be further evidence of the "ethical decline" that began during the Vietnam War. Stockdale is quoted as saying:

> Society as a whole has adopted the judicial process as its moral yardstick and forfeited common sense and personal responsibility.... Too many have become relativists without any defined moral orientation. Too many are content to align their value systems with fads and buzzwords, and mindlessly try to obey what amounts to a hodgepodge mixture of inconsistent slogans.... However, if anything has power to sustain an individual in peace or war, regardless of occupation, it is one's conviction and commitment to defined standards of right and wrong.... Each man must bring himself to ethical resolution [181].

Notably, Stockdale does not specify homosexuality as an ethical lapse. Essayists Adair and Myers previously have claimed that "race and gender" inequities were addressed correctly by admitting blacks and women into the regular forces, since "race and gender are not behavior." They follow that claim immediately by saying:

> Sexual conduct is. We all have choices to make in life about who we want to be. By these choices we define and limit ourselves from being other things. A homosexual can no more claim an absolute right to admission to the army than can anyone else who fails to meet the standards that the army and society deem optimum for building the force [176].

That Adair and Myers employ Stockdale to substantiate homosexuality as a moral/ethical degradation in the military is peculiar, especially since Stockdale does not specify homosexuality in his rubric. Further, that Adair and Myers use "race" to signify people of color and "gender" to signify women demonstrates the cognitive difficulty of distinguishing biology from social behaviors. To these authors, "race" and "gender" are ineradicable markers on the body whose meanings are biologically immutable and not the result of social construction. However, before blacks and women were permitted to join the Regular military, they, too, were cast as "failing to meet the standards that the army and society deem optimum for building the force." Therefore, when Adair and Myers contend that "sexual conduct" is a social choice, unlike "race" and "gender," what they really mean is that *homo*sexuality is a choice and that the possibility of this choice changes over time. Because they do not explicitly conclude that *hetero*sexuality is also a choice (one apparently made in order to comply with military regulations rather than personal option), the supposition is that heterosexuality is "normal" and the only "choices" to be made would be deviations from normalcy. Adair and Myers' essay, then, demonstrates the contradictions inherent in the long-running arguments against homosexuals serving in the U.S. armed forces, arguments derived from a moral understanding of the Vietnam War: choosing one's sexuality is a moral choice, but the only sexuality one *may* choose is deviant. To a large extent, then, homosexuality is regarded as deviant because it is both gender and sexually anomalous. Because the Vietnam War era is seen as a significant turning point in American culture, it is convenient for Adair and Myers to deploy Stockdale for their current purpose. Yet their use also underscores how closely linked in the National Symbolic are gender, sexuality, and Vietnam, and how those who lived through Vietnam, such as Stockdale, are the current purveyors of truth applicable to many "moral" contingencies.

During the 1992 American presidential campaign, Democratic candidate Bill Clinton pledged to issue an executive order compelling the armed services to lift the ban on homosexuals in the military. Clinton's commitment was the logical outcome to a history of not just the exclusion but also the persecution of these male and female service members, a history which had alternately intensified and waned depending on the social climate and military needs of the time. As Randy Shilts contends in *Conduct Unbecoming: Lesbians and Gays in the U.S. Military, Vietnam to the Persian Gulf* (1993), women in general and homosexual men particularly were suspects in the "conspiracy" against heterosexual male masculinity in the post–Vietnam War All-Volunteer Army. As products and producers of culture, the literary and film texts about the Vietnam War—Jeffords' "war stories"—trace the actual developments of both these groups during and after the War, even as gay men and women ostensibly were not a part of the military, and women were not a part of the Regular military but still formed their own corps into the late 1970s.

The inscriptions of both male homosexuals and females enacting traditionally masculine roles in these texts have been relatively ignored by critics, however, suggesting a heteronormative presumption about depictions of the war.[2] That is, when critics contemplate how masculinity is incarnated in Vietnam War texts, rarely do what R. Connell terms "marginalized" forms of masculinity enter the critical picture. However, sexuality influences the configurations of masculinities, and to disregard these instances of non-hetero sexuality is to disregard multiple other forms of masculinity. In texts whose subject is war, most of the characters are men; as Michael Kimmel contends, "Homophobia is the central organizing principle of our cultural definition of manhood.... Homophobia is the fear that other men will unmask us, emasculate us, reveal to us and the world that we do not measure up, that we are not real men" ("Masculinity as Homophobia" 131).

I suggest that some critics have been unconsciously heterosexist, complicit in maintaining heteronormativity as the monolithic masculine standard while they ignore the gender implications of sexualities in these recurrent images. In this chapter I examine the images in four Vietnam War texts chronologically to illustrate how ideas about male and female homosexuality and female masculinity have been altered over the course of the last several decades by changing ideas of "normal" sexuality, who is permitted to make choices about sexuality, and how this change has contested formations of masculinities. This exploration challenges both the malleable nature of what Connell refers to as sexual "social practices" and also how they have influenced the figurations of monolithic masculinity. The texts include two that focus on male sexuality before the war was concluded, since women were not admitted to the Regular Army until 1978, and two that were published after women had been integrated into the army. Norman Mailer's 1967 *Why Are We in Vietnam?* and Joe Haldeman's 1974 *The Forever War* are the two texts I use to interrogate images of male homosexuality during the Vietnam War. To investigate the status of female masculinity, I look at Bobbie Ann Mason's 1985 *In Country*, its 1989 Norman Jewison film adaptation, and the 1990 version of Tim O'Brien's "Sweetheart of the Song Tra Bong."

What these four Vietnam War texts disclose is that masculinity is a malleable condition contingent on how sexualities are constructed. Equally importantly, these texts suggest that masculinity and sexuality may morph even from within the same set of circumstances, as the chronological reading of these texts illustrates how the interaction between masculinity and sexualities has altered historically from within the single context of the Vietnam War. In the early years of full-fledged American involvement in the War, with a heteronormative World War II and Cold War attitude still dominant, masculinity and sexuality were seen as synonymous in a work such as Norman Mailer's *Why Are We in Vietnam?* At the close of the Vietnam War, as the feminist and the gay liberation movements began to make their mark on mainstream American society, *The Forever War* evidenced the pressures of those movements to detach masculinity from sexuality. After the conclusion of the War and the integration of women into the regular military, the 1980s ushered in what Susan Faludi calls "backlash" and Susan Jeffords terms "remasculinization," or efforts to return to the synonymous state of relations between gender and sexuality visible during the War. This desire to reinstate previously rejected norms is apparent in the difference between Bobbie Ann Mason's 1985 novel and the 1989 Norman Jewison film adaptation. Mason's novel, however, illustrates the appeal and normalization of feminist notions and introduces a sexual ambiguity through female masculinity emerging as the gay and feminist movements matured. Read through the context of these movements, and the growth of theories of sexualities in the academy, Tim O'Brien's short story "Sweetheart of the Song Tra Bong" refers to the normalization of gender amorphousness, and also materially alters his female protagonist's conditions so that her sexuality, too, becomes amorphous. Positioned in a gendered and sexual liminal space, Mary Anne can be read as the "queer" that, by the early 1990s, was more and more overt in American culture.[3] Before moving to the close readings of those texts, however, I provide some historical background with which to understand both Clinton's presidential campaign pledge and the social context within which the four texts may be understood, and also a reading of *The 13th Valley* that bridges gender, race, and sexuality.

Randy Shilts claims in a 1993 *Newsweek* article, "The Vietnam War provides some of the most striking examples of the military's tacit acceptance of homosexuality in times of war" ("What's Fair"). Though the military services had policies excluding homosexuals from serving as early as the beginning of World War II, when homosexuality was regarded as a mental illness, the exigencies of war demanded the enlistment of all able male bodies, so the option to discharge male homosexuals was left to local commanders (Berubé 14).[4] Homosexuals were not officially and uniformly banned from serving until the 1950 enactment of the Uniform Code of Military Justice (UCMJ), and this code's reinforcement in 1982 by President Ronald Reagan's Department of Defense (Scott and Stanley xi; *Homosexuality,* GAO 3). As a result of the conflicting demands—to prevent homosexuals from joining or to discharge them if they already belonged, and the needs of a country at war—the numbers of servicepeople discharged for homosexuality has varied dramatically in wartime and peacetime, a pattern which continued during and is highlighted by the war in Vietnam. This hypocritical treatment of homosexual service members is one element apparently motivating Clinton's pledge, since various civilian groups already had been lobbying in favor of openly homosexual men and women serving in the military. Decades before Clinton's move in the early 1990s, studies commissioned by various governmental bodies had determined that the armed services' reasons for excluding homosexuals from service—"to maintain discipline, good order, and morale"—were not, in fact, substantive. That is, no evidence could be generated to support service-wide contentions that homosexuals were a danger to national security or to other servicepeople, even as far back as 1957 when the "Crittenden Report," whose publication was suppressed, was conducted on the part of the U.S. Navy (*Homosexuality,* Crittenden 14). Reports contemporary to Clinton's effort that reached conclusions similar to the Crittenden Report include the 1992 U.S. General Accounting Office's report, "DoD's Policy on Homosexuality," the 1991 PERSEREC (U.S. Defense Personnel Security Research and Education Center) report entitled "Homosexuality and Personnel Security," and the 1991 Penn + Schoell poll results titled "A Report to the Human Rights Campaign Fund on Public Attitudes towards Homosexuals and Their Place in the Military."[5] Despite these reports and President Clinton's January 1993 order to Secretary of Defense

Les Aspin that Department of Defense policy be revised, military leaders continue to insist in documents published as recently as 1995 that homosexuality is "incompatible with military service" ("Summary" 167).

Randy Shilts points out in *Conduct Unbecoming*, his massive history of homosexuals in the American military since the late 1950s until the Persian Gulf War, that "the military is far less concerned with having no homosexuals in the service than with having people think there are no homosexuals in the service" (154). I would add that the American military since the conclusion of the War also has wanted the public to think women are fully integrated into the military and thus have enough "masculinity" to function in a military unit, but that full integration stops with combat because women in combat would have to be "too" masculine. That is, the military conflates sex and gender: to be in combat, American women would have to reject what has been socially designated their primary sex role, as feminine bearers of children, to appropriate one of the socially designated sex roles of men, as masculine bearers of arms. To a great extent, then, the desire to eliminate homosexuals and women from the military explains the "hysteria" surrounding Clinton's move to revise DoD policy towards homosexuals. It has been crucial to maintain an image of the United States armed forces, illusory or not, that implicitly is dependent on a monolithic masculinity which is by definition heterosexual and male. The integration into the regular forces first of black men (with Truman's executive order in 1948) and then of women (in the mid-1970s) contributed to the erosion of the belief that "soldier" equals white and male.[6] While Shilts points to attempts at shifting military policy in favor of homosexuals much earlier than the 1990s, anxieties about the total disintegration of an idealized, monolithic masculinity as the model for the American soldier bolstered arguments, then and during Clinton's campaign, against enlisting personnel who openly defied traditional gender and sex roles.

The Vietnam War era raised concerns about traditional "sex roles" (i.e., "gender") with the Feminist Movement especially problematizing the essentialist notion that a woman's body parts determine how she may and may not interact in the social sphere. Major events influencing this altered gender idea include: the 1966 founding of the National Organization of Women; the 1967 "Summer of Love"; the 1968 demonstrations against the Miss America pageant; the 1969 Stonewall Inn riots; the late-1960s widespread use of the pill; the 1970 Gay Pride March and Women's Equality Day demonstrations; the 1972 founding of *Ms.* magazine; and the 1973 *Roe vs. Wade* decision, legalizing abortion (Bloom xi–xiv; Farber, *The*

Age of Great Dreams 167–189). American "new feminist" scholars such as Mary Ellmann in *Thinking about Women* (1968), Kate Millett in *Sexual Politics* (1969), and Shulamith Firestone in *The Dialectic of Sex* (1970) challenged the patriarchal notion that women could and should be categorized socially by their biology. Firestone's text opens with such a challenge to biological determinism:

> Sex class is so deep as to be invisible.... But the reaction of the common man, woman, child—"*That?* Why you can't change *that!* You must be out of your mind!"—is the closest to the truth.... That so profound a change cannot be easily fit into traditional categories of thought, e.g. "political," is not because these categories do not apply but because they are not big enough: radical feminism bursts through them. If there were another word more all-embracing than *revolution* we would use it [1].

Firestone concludes that a challenge to biology would "threaten the *social* unit that is organized around biological reproduction and the subjection of women to their biological destiny, the family" (206). Thus, while biology arguably is stable and coherent, the social behavior that translates biology, or gender, is considered alterable.

These War-era feminist critics argue convincingly that biology and gender are not synonymous, yet "gender" has been appropriated since the War to signify both. For instance, rarely is an applicant for a job, to a school, or for a scholarship, among others, asked what is her "sex"; when she is asked what is her "gender," the question has to do with the biology she was born to or had chosen for her, not her social behavior. Though Judith Butler objects to the separation of gender and sex on disciplinary grounds (see Introduction), I contend that this co-optation of "gender" in lieu of "sex" has occurred in Vietnam War studies to disallow the reading of some non-hetero sexualities. In her 2000 screed against women in the military, *The Kinder, Gentler Military*, journalist Stephanie Gutmann relates an instance in 1995 of this embrace of "gender" by the military when she was looking for information about military women.

> I'd just called Army public relations to check a fact in an article I was writing. When I told the officer (most public relations people in the services are military officers) that I was doing a story on "sexual integration in the military," there was an awkward silence and then a strained laugh. "The term we use now," the Pentagon flack finally said primly, "is *gender integration*" [16].

Gutmann interprets this semantic switch (since "now" indicates there was a time when "sex" was used by the military to refer to male and female bodies) as, derogatorily, "political correctness." It may very well be an abuse of the desire to make language operate more precisely. How "gender" is employed in the case of the public relations officer and, I would argue, society at large, is not to distinguish between the biological and social constructions of bodies, but instead to conjoin the two. In other words, the Vietnam War era raised awareness of the social construction of gender as distinct from "givens" of sex. This awareness aided in de-essentializing the body, both female and male. Since that time, however, "gender" has come to stand in for "sex." This lends the appearance of subtlety, of biology and behavior as distinct, but the meaning of "gender" has returned to the essentialist roots of "sex"—in the case of an applicant, it does not ask whether she is masculine or feminine, which appears to be the result of personal preference, but whether she is male or female, not understood generally to be a choice. Gutmann explains the current preference for "gender" over "sex" thusly: "'gender,'" she proposes, is "an antiseptic word popular because it is more sexless, less dangerous, than the word *sex*" (19). In conjoining "gender" and "sex" so that both signify the physical body, the possibilities of escaping biology are diminished. "Women," then, will always be feminine *by nature*, as will "men" always, therefore, be masculine *by nature*.

Such fears of the power of language and its enactment are disclosed in Vietnam War fictional texts, which can be used to trace the historical developments concerning women in the military and male homosexuals that led to Clinton's decision. Shilts' message, that the appearance of no homosexuals in the military outweighs actuality, is especially relevant since images of male homoeroticism and homosexuality, and female masculinity surface regularly in Vietnam War texts. Yet rarely do critics refer to, much less analyze them. Because images of male homosexual relationships and desires and masculine females disrupt the traditional conception of a legible, heterosexual, masculine male soldier, if one relies on critics, those images appear as negligible anomalies. However, I believe these images appear frequently enough that they offer patterns for analysis and telltale traces of the concerns about Vietnam. Images of masculine women appear often in Vietnam War texts, especially after the War when women were integrated into the Regular forces, further blurring the boundaries between "properly" gendered women and men. Because these images concern themselves as much with sexuality as they do with gender, they suggest that the 1990s furor over homosexuals in the services is simultaneously a concern about acceptable gender roles and sexualities.

Sexuality is not only connected to gender in Vietnam War texts but, as I demonstrated in the previous chapter, is also closely configured with race. The interrelationships of these three identities are exemplified in *The 13th Valley*, which deploys names subtextually to racialize, and thereby gender, each character. But a sequence of events that is integral to constructing the racialized *and* sexualized masculinities of two of the three central characters occurs immediately before the climactic battle of the novel, demonstrating how masculinities are intimately connected to interrelations between race and sexuality.

Near the end of *The 13th Valley*, Staff Sergeant (SSG) Egan and LT Brooks discuss the causes of conflict, when the company is hiding amid the enemy and Egan is about to go out on ambush (534–539). Calling Egan "Danny," a familiarity Egan does not return, Brooks asks him, "what causes conflict?" (534). Egan is uncomfortable with how "meekly" Brooks poses his question, but Egan expounds on his theory that war is the natural state of man. Though the two men are under enormously threatening conditions as the North Vietnamese hunt for them, only Brooks is described as speaking "softly" or "whispering," even though the novel has shown the military professionalism of both men in their total commitment to the safety of the men under their charge and to conducting war operations well. The loudness or quietness of each man is not intended to suggest that they care more or less for the safety of the men; both are revered by the other soldiers in the unit. Their sonority has to do instead with their relative authority on why war occurs. So, even though Brooks challenges Egan's idea that war is the natural state of man, because Egan speaks in a full voice and Brooks does not, "Brooks" appears to Egan and the reader as less masterful because of this "meekness." (Keep in mind that names in quotation marks indicate the identity positions a person may have. Thus, "Rufus" is the predominantly racialized identity of the character Brooks.) When Egan says, "The only justification you need for Nam is we're doin' it. It is, thus it is right. That goes for everything. If it is, so it is" (537), and Brooks calls that "crazy," meek Brooks has no power to refute Egan's conclusion. He suggests "tolerance" of difference to alleviate war, but Egan naysays the suggestion: "You'd have to change it all — every last man, woman, and child — if you wanted ta break the cycle of peace-war-peace-war. You'd have to build a new base. If you can't change the system that produces war there's one thing you best mothafuckin do — you better win them fuckin wars" (538). Brooks can only say "Amen" to Egan's argument before Egan changes the subject back to their war. For the first time in their relationship, "Brooks" is made inarticulate; he literally is silenced, even though Egan's argument is solipsistic. Before this scene, as I outlined in Chapter One, only the racialized "Rufus" part of Brooks' character had suffered ostracization and "Brooks" had maintained a tenuous coherence within the company that was not predicated on race or gender. This scene, however, changes the status of "Brooks" to "meek" as he is isolated by his liberal attitude toward conflict.

The isolation of "Brooks" sexually, which began with his relationship with Lila, also is completed in the final part of this scene, when Brooks looks to Egan for ideas about personal, not national, conflict (538–539). Broaching the subject with his admission that he had suffered from impotence while in Hawaii with his wife, Brooks then asks Egan whether he had ever fantasized about his "lady" being with another man. Egan "answered robustly" that everybody does that. At this point, "Brooks seemed transparent" to Egan, as though Egan, now the master because he understands better than the philosophy graduate student Brooks why humans engage in war, also understands more about Brooks than Brooks understands about himself. More importantly, Egan's prevailing point of view in the text—"Egan was born for the jungle valley, raised for the jungle valley war. He was the essence of the infantry"—facilitates a mastery that simultaneously empowers the assertive Egan and disempowers submissive "Brooks" (600). When Brooks asks Egan whether he had ever fantasized a ménage à trois including another man, and then just being with another man, Egan assures Brooks that this fantasy is a common one among male soldiers, and that it even has been given a name: the "Nam Syndrome" (539). As the master, Egan is the one whose opinion dominates and who can identify what is normal, both in terms of how national conflict occurs and about personal sexual affairs. "Brooks," because he is now in a sexually and racially liminal state like "Rufus," can only listen and learn.

Del Vecchio is elusive in this scene as the two men talk in a code of sexual insinuation. Their topics proceed from impotence, to a second man with the first's female lover, to a ménage à trois of two men and a woman, to the woman serving as the intermediary between two men, to no intermediary between two men, but their conversation is ended and punctuated by the simultaneous sound of a rifle being shot and the explicit naming of anal sodomy. When Brooks first asks Egan about images of his female lover being with another man, Egan consoles Brooks by telling him that those thoughts are "normal" because everybody has them, and yet Brooks, an officer previously and unusually in tune with his subordinates, had been unaware of the widespread nature of this fantasy. If Egan names what is normal and Brooks is ignorant of what is "normal," the implication is either that Egan does not know what he is talking about or that Brooks is not "normal." Del Vecchio suggests here that the non-normalcy of "Brooks" is not because Brooks has experienced the "Nam Syndrome," but because he is ignorant about what is normal among his troops. Similarly, Egan is "normal" because he can name what is normal; the power to name outweighs the power to rationalize. Yet Del Vecchio will not commit on this point, leaving "Brooks" in a gender, sexual and racial liminal space, as all of his named identities — "LT," "Rufus," and now "Brooks" — are compromised.

Brooks drafts a copy of his thesis, rejecting Egan's notion that war is the human condition, and concludes that Western (i.e., white man's) languages are too linear to reflect reality and so create conflict (556–565). That Brooks persists in explaining conflict as a result of social effects might problematize my suggestion that Egan is the master of Brooks. As soon as Brooks articulates this thesis, however, he begins to behave in "uncharacteristic" ways, perhaps because the thesis does not accord with the newly liminal "Brooks" (565). When Egan has been wounded severely, is heavily sedated and thus is quiet, Brooks has the opportunity to reiterate his social constructivist position on conflict, but instead reverses in a matter of seconds the argument he has maintained since the beginning of the novel. "'What causes war? People cause war. People being people. It's that simple.... When there are no more people,' Brooks says woefully, 'then there will be no more war. War is part of being human. It's like love and hate and breathing and eating. And living and dying. Just like you said, Danny'" (630). Certainly Brooks is distraught over Egan's injury, the practical effects of which probably have something to do with the adjustment of his theory. But Brooks' theory already was predicated on the conflict he had experienced with his wife, Lila, so the theory was not devoid of first-hand experience. The question, then, is not so much what has caused Brooks' reversal; the point is that Egan is so drugged with morphine that he cannot speak, and so Brooks in effect becomes Egan's mouthpiece, even though they have not discussed this issue since Brooks wrote his thesis opposing Egan's viewpoint. Unable any longer to maintain his argument for a "semantic determinant theory of war" (115) as he sees men suffering the consequences of "language," it appears that the "LT Rufus Brooks," all of whose identities are marked by their racialization and sexualization, can only speak what "normal" and unmarked Egan has spoken all along: war is the natural state of man.

This sequence is important to the outcome of the novel, especially since neither Brooks nor Egan survives this battle, making it difficult to judge whose estimate of the causes of conflict are sanctified by Del Vecchio. John Hellmann suggests that, because these two expire in a wholly unheroic way, leaving behind Cherry/Chelini, the novel ends nihilistically. "*The 13th Valley* thus ends with a traumatized American [Cherry] forced to regard the aspects of his ideal self-concept, the characteristics of his mythic heroes, as lost in the furious meaninglessness of Vietnam. Gazing at this spectre, the American consciousness can only blaspheme or deny" (*American Myth* 134). Yet no other critic has commented on the entire sequence of events, nor, since Jeffords' 1989 work, has the conversation between Brooks and Egan elicited any critique.[7] In her chapter "That Men without Women Trip," Jeffords interprets the sexual fantasy episode as another instance in Vietnam War narratives of the exigency of the "masculine collective" to develop in opposition to women. "While sexual images must be foregrounded in order to act as constant reminders of the structuration of gender that reinforces the ideology of collectivity, they pose a constant risk of displaying the dependence of that collectivity on the very relation it denies—the association with women." The Nam Syndrome is, then, one of many frequent retellings and reworkings of masculine collectivity against the feminine: "They can never completely achieve their separation from the feminine and so must constantly retell their relations to it" (*Remasculinization* 72). While Jeffords' disquisition of *The 13th Valley* is laudable, especially as she examines the "Nam Syndrome" scene, I disagree with her on several points.

Jeffords' claim in the first quote above, opposing the "masculine collective" to "women," is problematic because she is comparing gender—"masculinity"—to sex—women—and not "femininity," even when she goes on later to problematize the comparison of gender to sexuality. To Jeffords the "Nam Syndrome" exemplifies the proximity of male heterosexuality and homosexuality, demonstrating the problems of a logic that positions gender difference against sexuality. She offers Freud's explanation for male homosexuality (as a pathway to the "normal" state of heterosexuality) to explain Egan's assertion that the Syndrome represents normalcy: "With Freudian theory thus acting as an apologetics for homoeroticism as a heterosexual matrix, the Nam Syndrome becomes a necessary part of male development, an essential phase to be passed through on the way to 'normal'" (72).

While Jeffords finds the "logic" of the Nam Syndrome problematic, it seems to me that her conclusion can be challenged in so far as she uses "gender" to refer to male and female bodies. Jeffords makes claims for the "masculine," not the "male" or "man's" collective, but she compares it not to "femininity" or "the feminine" but to "women," even as she complains about a logic that compares gender to sex. Furthermore, while Jeffords does associate race and sexuality in this scene, she does not connect the episode to how the characters previously have been differently characterized in terms of race, nor does she use this interaction of race and sexuality to complicate her conception of masculinity. Unlike many critics, Jeffords does not assign "race" only to characters of color; however, she does minimize the relevance of racial difference, asserting the preeminence of gender in the bond between the two men. Finally, she does not associate this conversation to Brooks' and Egan's subsequent behaviors in the sequence I have analyzed above, behaviors demonstrating the interrelationship and constructedness of race, sexuality, and gender.

The objective of my discussion in this chapter is to illuminate how these three identities—especially sexuality and gender—interact and accrete as they work to disrupt monolithic masculinity. For the purposes of this project, my starting point is gender, but I contend that Vietnam War texts disclose that these identities do not necessarily originate and conclude with gender; instead, they are intertwined and multi-faceted, so that they often are difficult to untangle. Such is the case with *The 13th Valley*: masculinity is contingent on race, but race cannot be defined without an explication of sexuality, and sexuality hinges on, among other identities, masculinity. That is, how the men behave is not solely or even primarily incidental; that they are men, in other words, does not mean that what they have most in common is masculinity. It is the sexuality portion of this tangle that I focus on in this chapter.

When gender, sex, and sexuality are considered separately, males in Vietnam War texts often have little in common in terms of gender; moreover, often it is females who are more "masculine" than those males who are, by popular definition and by the gender/sex system, supposed to be masculine. Brooks' wife, Lila, for instance, is depicted as not-feminine, aggressive and hateful because she wants "time for her own thing" (478). On the other hand, Egan's erstwhile girlfriend Stephanie is represented as feminine because she is mated to the "normal" monolithically masculine Egan. What that femininity translates to, however, is an unhealthy submission to the verbal and physical abuse of Egan and other men. Following the conclusion of the War, in Vietnam War texts females more often are depicted as "masculine," especially after women had been admitted to the Regular forces (1978) and to the service academies (1976) (Skaine 61–62). But fictional representations of the War often characterize these women, like Lila, as exceeding the bounds of monolithic masculinity; a woman at war, in other words, cannot be "normal." Randy Shilts argues in *Conduct Unbecoming* that women in the military have been viewed by white, male heterosexuals as anomalous creatures for serving in what traditionally has been a male arena, and so have been treated either as whores (who cannot get enough sex from men, and so join a largely male institution) or lesbians (who cannot bear the thought of sex with men, and so join an institution where there are like-minded women).[8] Shilts cites the early 1980s as a particularly tenuous moment for women in the military and, thus, for heterosexual men dependent on traditional gender roles to define their heterosexuality:

> The most profound resistance to the encroachment of women on traditionally male terrain happened under ordinary circumstances and away from much public notice. In thousands of small ways, men tried to reassert the old roles while women were trying to adapt to the new. Insidious sexual harassment resulted, especially in the workplace as women's numbers grew. Women also found that job success created a disconcerting double bind. An aggressive male employee was complimented as assertive; an aggressive woman was a bitch. One source of the resistance to strong women was a barely articulated fear of lesbians. It had become a cliché among women trying to succeed in traditionally male domains to assure [male and female] colleagues, "I'm not a feminist, but...." But of course the great majority of women did indeed subscribe to the feminist ideology; what they really meant was, "I'm not a lesbian..." [416].[9]

Shilts' assertion elucidates the problem of conjoining gender and sex; if masculinity is aligned only with males and femininity only with females, *and* sexualities are viewed as closely connected to, if not synonymous with, gender, then the logical outcome will be that men who are feminine and women who are masculine are not only "gender traitors" but also are assumed therefore to be sexually "traitorous." The Vietnam War texts I examine published *before* the War's end make that jump in logic, from gender to sexuality, so that male characters who do not follow the masculine gender dictates of their sex are assumed also to be violating heteronormative sexuality dictates. Texts produced *after* the War, and once women had been "regularized" in the services, confound this deduction, as characters of both sexes may cross gender boundaries and not be assumed to have crossed boundaries of "normal" sexuality. In clouding the "natural" associations between gender (masculine/feminine), sex (male/female/trans/inter-sexed), and sexuality (hetero/homo/bi/trans), these later texts make it more likely for "gender treachery" to occur and for these identities to proliferate, once again confounding the possibility of monolithic masculinity. Whether they also depict sexual treachery is always the subtext in these fictions.

It is Judith Halberstam's project in *Female Masculinity* to create such a possibility of proliferation. Halberstam approaches this gender/sex conundrum in her introduction by insisting that naming itself confers gender or demonstrates gender expectations, resonating with my argument about names and race in Chapter One. She uses public rest rooms to demonstrate the problem of a binary gender system for persons whose gender is not "readable at a glance" (23), suggesting that the naming of rest rooms as "men's" and "women's" enforces this binary by conferring, rather than reflecting, meaning (25). That is, for women (especially) who do not initially appear to be women, but are not "men" either, the men's/women's split presents a dilemma. The women's rest room, insists Halberstam, is policed by other women using "gender codes" which are reliant on the appearance of being a woman, or femininity; men's rest rooms, on the other hand, are governed by "sexual codes" which encourage and promote sexual relations, but are not reliant on the appearance of being a man, or masculine (24). The meanings of both codes can be extended beyond the rest rooms, however, to a panoptically gendered world. To neutralize these codes, Halberstam contends that "nonce taxonomies" should be developed from the female masculinities that exist currently, categories that function as interventions "in the hegemonic processes of naming and defining" and thereby "challenge hegemonic models of gender conformity" (8–9). As Halberstam says, "The widespread indifference to female masculinity ... has clearly ideological motivations and has sustained the complex social structures that wed masculinity to maleness and to power and domination" (2). In other words, the uninspected pairing of gender and sex maintains the male-equals-masculinity-equals-power equation. One may assume that the "ideological motivations" are integral to telling war stories, and that war story tellers are invested in maintaining traditional gender, sex, and sexuality norms, since war now and during the Vietnam War era was conceived as not just a masculine, but a male heterosexual endeavor. The texts I examine testify to Halberstam's assertions about gender codes and sexual codes. Those produced before the War's end dwell largely on "sexual codes" through a focus on sexuality, while the texts produced later disclose an interest in "gender codes" through their interest in female masculinity; both ultimately are concerned with the construction of male masculinity as they demonstrate its malleability.[10]

Sexuality (and Gender) during the War

> Though the call for such avowal [of manliness] was strong throughout American culture and, therefore, throughout the U.S. military, there was one group of soldiers for whom this desire was most pronounced, particularly in those early years of the Vietnam War. The people who most need to prove something, after all, are the people who are most in doubt. Where proof of manliness is concerned, this meant young men who thought they might be queer [Shilts, Conduct 32].

Norman Mailer's *Why Are We in Vietnam?* (1967) is one of the earliest examples of both Vietnam War literature and those Vietnam War texts concerning themselves with sexuality. The novel demonstrates how gender and sexuality were synonymous in the War's early years, so that crossing masculine gender boundaries equaled crossing boundaries of heterosexuality. This equation changed as the War continued and after its conclusion, when stories about the War were re-formulated. *Why Are We in Vietnam?* is the story of a hunting party in the Alaskan wilderness which uses specialist weapons and transportation to kill a grizzly bear. The eight male members of the party can be divided into three groups: the teenager DJ and his friend Tex; DJ's father and his two subordinates from work; and the professional leaders of the hunting party, Luke, Ollie, and the helicopter pilot. DJ narrates the story from a two-year vantage point, on the eve of his and Tex's departure for Vietnam. Told in a frenetic, hipster voice, the story explicitly is concerned with generational, social class, and racial conflicts, as fathers and sons, hunters and leaders, and DJ and his alternate black self, "some genius brain up in Harlem" (27), combat one another for mastery of masculinity. Implicitly, however, *Why Are We in Vietnam?* narrates the problems of "proper" gendering in mid–1960s American society.

Critics of Vietnam War literature generally have overlooked the text, though John Hellmann's *American Myth and the Legacy of Vietnam* (1986) set the stage for other critics to read it as a novel about the impact of the mythology of the American frontier.[11] Hellmann says the novel addresses "what a contemporary frontier means for a society that has given itself over to corporation and machine" (79), especially emphasizing generational and social class conflict. Philip K. Jason's reading departs from Hellmann's, as Jason refers to the novel as "a study in American character" (*Acts and Shadows* 10). Katherine Kinney reads *Why Are We in Vietnam?* through the lens of race, suggesting that the text's last-minute return to the uncertain race of the narrator insinuates an answer to the novel's question that is largely about race: "'Who is the voice of America?' black or white, is the novel's last question, the ironized battle point from which to approach Vietnam" (110). While Hellmann does suggest that one element of the frontier myth is reliant on a series of "sexual and social sublimations" (80), few other critics of Vietnam War narratives analyze how the trope of sexuality operates in the novel. However, Kate Millett, a contemporary feminist critic writing in 1969, critiques the novel as one more in Mailer's collection of books linking sex and violence, concluding, "Yet because Mailer has insisted so often that the violence which masculinity presupposes, even requires, cannot be denied, we must conclude that the reason 'why we are in Vietnam' is only because 'we' must be. Such is the nature of things" (322). Making Mailer sound eerily like SSG Egan of *The 13th Valley*, Millett sees traditional monolithic masculinity as dependent on heterosexuality, a state that characterizes Vietnam War texts published during or immediately after the War.

The novel is broken into alternating "Intro Beeps" and chapters, so there are ten Intro Beeps, a "Terminal Intro Beep and Out," and eleven chapters. The Intro Beep sections represent the narrator of the present, DJ, who interjects his reading of the hunting story just told, while the chapters tell the story of the hunt two years previously. Until Chapters Ten and Eleven, an Intro Beep section separates all of the chapters. Though there is a concluding Intro Beep, there is no Intro Beep between the final two chapters. That DJ does not attempt to interpret this section of the hunting party story emphasizes especially the actions of these two chapters. From the opening "Intro Beep 1," sexualities repeatedly are invoked in *Why Are We in Vietnam?*, and the Alaska hunt is concluded with an image of DJ and Tex on the verge of consummating their lust for one another. As DJ-narrator has his mother complaining to her psychiatrist early in the novel, the two boys are inseparable (20). But I contend that the sexual moment concluding the action of the hunt also marks the relationship between the two teenaged boys, readying them in terms of masculinity for their future in Vietnam.

The hunting party is led by Luke Fellinka, a man whose job is to locate prey for his wealthy clients to kill. Rusty, DJ's exceptionally competitive father, suspects that the absence of a corporate honcho will lead to Luke's cheating him of the experience for which celebrities pay large amounts of money. Concerned about Luke's indifference to his need to kill a grizzly bear and thus retain his status as a corporate "Ranger Commando" (84), Rusty strikes out with DJ on their own, and the two of them kill a grizzly. But the experience leaves DJ hating his father, as Rusty claims to have killed the bear when DJ thought he had.

With Rusty having acquired his trophy bear, the hunting party could be over, but as DJ-narrator continues in Intro Beep 9, "The climax within Alaska is yet to come — you will get rocks off you thought were buried forever" (149). So angry with his father that DJ is afraid he will kill him, in a near mirror image of the Rusty-DJ escape, DJ and Tex leave the campsite to strike out on their own. Their objective is to purify themselves of the "mixed glut and sludge" (180) of the hunt thus far, which they do by leaving their weapons behind as they hike further into the mountains. Their conversation is fraught with homosexual overtones, but the narrator is quick to point out they are "real Texas men" (179), as though the "glut and sludge" inherited from the corporate male and from which they want to separate themselves is anxiety about his ability to perform sexually. After a day of seeing all the markers of unexplored wildness — a white wolf, an eagle, a grizzly, a herd of caribou, and a bull moose — the exhausted boys sleep, but are wakened prematurely by the cold. Unable to return to sleep, and electrified by the northern lights, each boy is stimulated by the other's closeness, imagining himself "pronging" the other. But each boy also fears the other would kill him as a result; before killing one another becomes an issue, the "radiance of the North went into them" and their sexual lust is transformed by "some communion of telepathies and new powers" into blood lust, turning them from "near as lovers" to "killer brothers" (204).

While it is plausible this scene is an illustration of the sexual sublimation occurring in homosocial groups, it also suggests that masculinity is as much about the ability to sublimate as it is never to have thoughts needing to be sublimated; monolithic masculinity is marked by anxiety about straying outside of heterosexual boundaries. Significantly, this scene more or less concludes the hunting trip and the novel. Only the Terminal Intro Beep follows it, a summary of the putrid conditions created by the hatred and greed of Europeans transported to North America, conditions that also have made it possible for Tex and DJ to go "off to see the wizard in Vietnam" (208). I suggest, then, that the culminating event of the hunt, a parallel to the "hunt" in Vietnam, is not Rusty's claiming the bear and DJ's subsequent full-blown hatred for his father, but instead, the developing sexual relationship between Tex and DJ. What is clear is that this sexuality cannot be separated from the boys' efforts to become the men their fathers are not, or from their gender as masculine men.

Norman Mailer wrote this novel in the spring of 1966, following a year of escalating American involvement in Vietnam. More troops were required to meet the military mission there, so the local draft boards of the Selective Service became less selective. Consequently, 1966 began a period when fewer service people were being discharged for "nonconforming sexual orientations":

> Between 1963 and 1966, ... the Navy discharged between 1,600 and 1,700 enlisted members a year for homosexuality. From 1966 to 1967, however, the number of gay discharges dropped from 1,708 to 1,094. In 1968, the Navy ejected 798 enlisted men for homosexuality. In 1969, at the peak of the Vietnam buildup, gay discharges dropped to 643. A year later, only 461 sailors were relieved of duty because they were gay. These dramatic reductions occurred during the period of the service's highest membership since World War II [Shilts, *Conduct* 70].

Why Are We in Vietnam? is not a rhetorical question, I suggest. The novel insinuates that there is enough conflict in the United States during 1966 to satisfy any blood lust, and one of those conflicts, perhaps the primary one, has to do with male sexuality. DJ and Tex deny their desire for each other not because they feel it is a moral wrong, a gender violation, or they will be labeled, if only in their own minds, as homosexuals. According to DJ, Tex already had "buggered" many people; their hesitation comes not from fear of the act itself or its morality, but from fear that such an act would redistribute the power each had in their friendship as "killer brothers" (204). While they both desire each other, they cannot find a way to engage mutually in the fulfillment of that sexual desire without disturbing the delicate gender/power balance in their relationship; the desire for each other transforms after the hunt to their preying on older married women and corpses (155–157). The answer to the book title's question, then, could be that this is how the United States disposes of its "miscreants," that Vietnam is where the violent hunting and sexual behavior in which DJ and Tex are engaged or hope to be engaged is appropriate. I suggest, however, that DJ and Tex are not anomalous, but represent the state of masculinity at the beginning of the War: gender and sex are so closely bound that they are indiscernible. In other words, Mailer's text narrates men as embodying a masculinity that includes a whole realm of activities, including the sublimated desire for anal sodomy, all of which have a place in the Vietnam War.[12] An answer to the question *Why Are We in Vietnam?* is that the middle years of the War were a good venue for genders/sexualities to be tried out and on without the threat of being discharged for homosexuality.

However, the literature of the War indicates that as the War continued and fewer discharges for homosexuality occurred, social anxieties about homosexuality peaked. The emergence in 1969 of the Gay Liberation Movement and its alignment with other progressive movements of the time also would have provoked a growing visibility of homosexuals.[13] A science fiction rendition of the Vietnam War, Joe Haldeman's *The Forever War* (1974), records this growing anxiety as the novel lends a fantastical air to the War. It also previews a margin growing between gender and sex that was not apparent in Mailer's *Why Are We in Vietnam?* signifying the War's influence on the differentiation between these two. Among the many critical works addressing Vietnam War literature, only three of the better-known ones deal with *The Forever War*: Thomas Myers' 1988 *Walking Point: American Narratives of Vietnam*, Philip K. Jason's 2000 *Acts and Shadows: The Vietnam War in American Literary Culture*, and H. Bruce Franklin's 2000 *Vietnam and Other American Fantasies*. Myers' reference is only an aside, appearing as an endnote that contends *The Forever War* "speak[s] to history" (230). Jason produces an entire chapter on Haldeman's work, including two pages devoted to *The Forever War*. Only as he is concluding this section does Jason mention the trope of malleable sexuality in the novel, and then, only in terms of homosexuality (59). Jason's overlooking the trope appears to reveal a heteronormative disposition; that he leaves unremarked the fact that women, "butch" or not, are required by law to serve the sexual desires of men suggests this "law" already is assumed to be a part of heterosexuality. In his chapter entitled "The Vietnam War as American Science Fiction and Fantasy," Franklin does not mention the trope of sexuality, focusing largely on the uses of technology depicted in the novel, while he insists "America's war in Indochina cannot be separated from American science fiction, which shaped and was reshaped by the nation's encounter with Vietnam" (151).

The novel begins in 1997 and concludes in 3143; because of time travel, the central characters and lovers, William Mandella and Marygay Potter, live through this period but age "subjectively," as the eponymous interstellar war is waged from 1996 until 3140. Mandella's and Potter's civilian lives are overtaken by the war, as they both are high–IQ conscripts in the service of the United Nations Exploratory Force (UNEF) and fear being separated forever as a result of being stationed in different universes and times. The enemy is Taurans, creatures who initiate the war by jumping through a "collapsar field" near Earth, and whose presence appears threatening to earthlings, known as Terrans. Little is known by the Terrans about the Taurans, as the two species are incapable of communicating with one another, but the Terrans attribute sinister intentions to the Taurans, thus prolonging the war. The novel parallels contemporary notions of many Americans' assumptions about the Vietnamese: unknown and foreign "little people" who act en masse because they have an unlimited source of bodies and care little for the value of life. Moreover, the Terrans (earthlings) are willing to ransom everything they value to win the war, so that over the centuries the Earth grows unrecognizable to those soldiers in space defending it. The story is parable-like as it cautions against those attitudes that, when the novel was being serialized in the early 1970s, reflected the obstinacy of the American government towards Vietnam, even as evidence for failure mounted.[14] In addition to being a cautionary tale against nationalist attitudes, however, *The Forever War* also deliberates on contemporary American attitudes about gender and sexualities, as the war is punctuated over its long course by changing notions of gender and sex norms. This meditation on the amorphousness of gender and sexuality is largely a function of the novel's being about the Vietnam War but also a function of its being science fiction.

One type of science fiction promises to feature ultra-sophisticated technology and hardware; as a genre it focuses more on plot and less on characterization, thus maximizing its relevance as a cultural bellwether. James Gunn suggests in *The Science of Science Fiction Writing* that a premise of science fiction is environment determines how humans behave, and science fiction's role is to examine how humans can liberate themselves from this eco-determinism. "Science fiction," he claims, "exists in a world of change, and the focus is on external events: What is the change and how are humans (or aliens) going to respond to it?" ("Worldview"). In an essay defending the value of science fiction, John Clute opines that the genre is about changing the world, used "to dramatize ideas about the world and the tools we may be able to invent in order to transform it, and to speculate about the implications of those ideas and tools." Moreover, adds Clute, most American science fiction published between the early 1920s and 1975 told the embarrassingly predictable story "of the technology-led triumph of the American Way in the star-lanes of the big tomorrow" ("In Defense"). Even though Haldeman contends that the "Forever War" could be about any war, *The Forever War*, as science fiction written after the demise of the "technology-led triumph" era, is especially revealing about the Vietnam War (ix). The three components that characterized science fiction before Haldeman — focus on plot, the human ability to alter the world, and the same story told repeatedly for half a century — distinguish *The Forever War*, as the novel departs from one-dimensional characters, the predictable story, and the glorification of American technology. Most important for the purposes of this study, however, is how human sexualities and, hence, genders are Haldeman's narrative devices for gauging human responses to environmental alterations. As futuristic environments alter, so does the significance of genders and sexualities, discounting a masculinity that endures environmental change.

The opening chapter plunges the reader into Mandella's world; in two pages, we learn that he is only a few months into basic military training in 1997, but already he knows eighty ways to kill people, has a vocabulary littered with military jargon and euphemism, and is part of a combat unit that includes women. The chapter concludes with a scene of mandated heterosexuality accompanied by a reversal of traditional sex roles, making clear from the outset of the novel that this is a world where sex and gender roles are enforced by law. In this scene, an exhausted Mandella retires to his bunk where he finds lustful "Rogers," a woman who, according to a roster that rotates assignments, has been designated his current sexual partner. Though he indicates he is not interested in her sexual advances, she persists, and he thinks, "Why do you always get the tired ones when you're ready and the randy ones when you're tired?" (5); Mandella resigns himself to the inevitability of Rogers' advances. In a later scene, Rogers is described as "butch" (6), but Mandella opts to "sack" with her even when there is no roster, suggesting that her masculinity does not alter their sexual relations. Traditional heterosexual sex roles are not entirely reversed, however; Mandella sleeps with other women, and these women sleep with other men, but though the heterosexual couplings are not reproductively oriented, there is no hint that women sleep with women, or men with men. Furthermore, when Mandella offers to sack with Potter, he intimates that the sexual moves she has learned from another male partner are good because they will benefit his sexual experience (30).

Though in *The Forever War* women legally are required to be responsive to male sexual advances, men are responsible for birth control; men make deposits in sperm banks and have vasectomies (112). This point is interesting, especially in light of the widespread use of the contraceptive pill when Haldeman was writing. But the reader is not told how birth control happens until sexuality—or the advent of homosexuality as a means of birth control—becomes an issue for Mandella. That females learn heterosexuality in order to benefit the males is especially pronounced when the unit retires to Stargate 1, a base where eighteen men and two women are assigned. As the narrator puts it, "The crew there was very glad to see us, especially the two females, who looked a little worn around the edges." Though previous episodes indicate the men and women were equally willing to sleep with different partners of the opposite sex, it turns out that only the women are "compliant and promiscuous by military custom (and law)" (41). Consequently, the newly-arrived women from Mandella's group are put to work that evening as their male counterparts look on. Peculiarly, the male onlookers assess not the sexual performances of the women they know and have "worked" with (and, presumably, have "trained"), but instead those of the "eighteen sex-starved men," complicating the construction of heterosexuality as it includes a homoerotic judgment.

However, men and women only have sexual relations together, and though there appears to be bending of traditional sex roles in terms of who initiates the relationship and who submits to it, it is clear from the Stargate 1 episode that women, whether traditionally feminine or masculine, are lawfully responsible both for submitting to male advances ("compliance") and for generating sexual relations with a variety of men ("promiscuous"). Throughout this early portion of *The Forever War*, no one objects to or resists the law, and Mandella is the only one depicted as hesitating, suggesting that these legal arrangements are not disagreeable. The novel thus elucidates late–1960s anxieties about changing heterosexual sex roles; if women can be freed from the strictures of virginity as a result of the Sexual Revolution, they also can be exploited by that freedom. Though the early parts of the novel suggest a gender-amorphous world where masculine females exist and are killed in combat, and feminine males are reluctant to dominate sexual relations, the focus is on cementing a heterosexual world despite surprising gender roles. The depiction of heterosexuality in the early part of the novel, then, is less about the malleability of gender than it is about the fixity of heterosexual relations in a sex-blended military unit, reflecting a 1970s presumption that gender and sexuality were synonymous.

The intensity and constructedness of this heterosexual mandate is apparent when Mandella has visions of himself as a machine copulating, but more so when he and Potter return to the Earth to find that homosexuality is advised as a means of birth control. Even in the mutable world of *The Forever War*, sexuality always appears to be a complicated mix of law, choice and social necessity, not an inherent and irresistible biological drive. Though Mandella wants to believe that his hypnosis-induced combat brutality is not his "true" nature (66), he is unwilling to believe that sexuality also is a function of suggestion. Changes in pronouns from the sexualized "him" to the gendered "thim" do not bother Mandella, but the effeminate gestures and makeup of a male Captain, hinting to Mandella that the Captain has chosen to be homosexual, conflicts with Mandella's idea of what men by nature should be. Mandella also struggles with his conception of what women should be when he discovers his mother has a lesbian lover. Interestingly, this section is omitted from the 1974 serialization in *Analog* magazine and in the first edition (1975) of the novel. According to Haldeman's Author's Note, the editor of *Analog* declared the section "too downbeat" for publication in that magazine (ix). One would think that images of a changed world would not upset readers of science fiction. It appears that the images of altered ways of life, particularly the suggestion that sexuality was a choice, are what were considered unacceptable.

Homosexuality is not mandatory but is regarded as normal at this point in the narrative; those claiming to be heterosexual are "eccentric," and suffering from an "emotional dysfunction" (180). Mandella is referred to secretly by his subordinates as "The Ol' Queer" because he continues to identify as heterosexual and, separated from Potter, remains abstinent. Once Mandella learns of this new social order, he is uncertain about how to treat his colleagues, acknowledging that "So much of my 'normal' behavior was based on a complex unspoken code of sexual etiquette. Was I suppose [sic] to treat the men like women, and vice versa? Or treat everybody like brothers and sisters?" (189). What is considered "sexual" is vague, as Mandella's first example, "men like women," uses social relationship, or gendered terms, and the second example, "like brothers and sisters," cites biological relationship, or sex terms. What is clearer is that, as a result of heterosexuality's de-normalization, Mandella is confused by the reoriented tangle of gender and sexuality. As he is relegated to the outsider status of "eccentric," he understands but does not accept the mutability of sexuality and, perhaps, gender; his response to this knowledge is to isolate himself with Potter on a planet for outcasts named "Middle Finger," where together they reproduce. This attitude, regarding gender and sexuality as not synonymous, marks a departure from Mailer's novel, as Haldeman's central character recognizes that sexuality is a choice and that gender does not necessarily coincide with it. That is, like DJ and Tex before they have arrived in Vietnam, Mandella conceptualizes the Forever/Vietnam War as a stage for the enactment of sexuality; unlike DJ and Tex, Mandella is forced by the peculiarities of this War to see sex and gender as distinct from one another and as a matter of performance, signifying the peculiar pressures that the Vietnam War put on masculinity. Gradually, and in spite of an American ethos that depended on the notion of monolithic masculinity to support its claim to transform boys into masculine men during war, the War was revealing gender as a construct, one distinct from the sex of the body and chosen sexual behaviors.

Gender (and Sexuality) after the War

> The issue of women in the military was never about women; it was about men and their need to define their masculinity. That, more than the fighting and winning of wars, appeared to be the central mission of the armed forces [in the period following the Vietnam War], at least for many men. That was why they sought to limit the role not only of women in the military but of gays, as well. These exclusions were, in this sense, all part of the same package, a defense of traditional masculinity in a changing world. The fact that the world was shifting made the defense all the more impassioned [Shilts, Conduct, 492].

In the decade between Haldeman's 1974 *The Forever War* and Bobbie Ann Mason's 1985 *In Country*, cultural representations of the War emerged especially in film while the Feminist Movement developed more fully. Since *In Country* is written by a woman and features a young woman and her concerns about traditional sex roles, Mason's story has been read as focusing more on gender than sexuality. However, the Gay Rights Movement also maturing during this period was influencing and influenced by the Feminist Movement, producing crossover works like Gayle Rubin's renowned 1975 essay, "The Traffic in Women: Notes Toward a Political Economy of Sex," and Eve Kosofsky Sedgwick's 1985 *Between Men: English Literature and Male Homosocial Desire*. In her brief history of the Gay Rights Movement, Annamarie Jagose suggests that the movement was as motivated by gender as by sexual liberation. Quoting Michael Hurley and Craig Johnston, Jagose contends that "[h]omosexual oppression was theorised [in the late 1960s and early 1970s] overwhelmingly in terms of gender, since 'male homosexuals share the oppression of patriarchy in that our sexuality, if not our general behavior, is believed to be non-masculine'" (39). An ironic outcome of this concurrent production was a growing distinction between gender and sexuality. As Shilts points out, the label "feminist" was popularly understood in the 1970s and 1980s to signify not just attitudes about gender, but also attitudes about sexuality: "feminist" signified "lesbian," an equation pervading Bobbie Ann Mason's novel. The central female character, Sam Hughes, explores both her gender and her sexuality as she searches for her own identity through her father who died in Vietnam in 1966, before she was born. While Mason's narrative places Sam in heterosexual relationships, the attribution of "feminist" leanings to her female protagonist produces ambiguity about Sam's sexuality.[15] An American audience's fear of Sam's sexual ambiguity is underscored by the changes to the novel's characters in Norman Jewison's 1989 film adaptation, where the casting and characterization of Sam in the film endeavor to counter the sexual indeterminacy of Sam in the novel, making the story less about her and more about a male character.

Susan Jeffords' 1989 study focuses on the "remasculinization" of American culture during the 1980s, when *In Country* was published. Jeffords suggests that the Vietnam experience appears transformative in literature and film until gender is made the focus of inquiry. "With gender the focus of analysis," she says, "it becomes clear that Vietnam is instead a point of translation, one in which the specific manifestations of gender relations may appear to be altered, but in which the masculine point of view from which gender is presented is maintained" (51). Jeffords further contends that, though *In Country* is written by a woman from a woman's point of view, it confirms the "masculine point of view" which argues masculinity is a collective that crosses other boundaries of identity (i.e., race, social class) (62). In other words, *In Country* disappoints the desire for transformation in Vietnam War texts, despite its being conceptualized and enacted by female voices. While I agree with Jeffords' assessment that the final scene of the book at the Vietnam War Memorial confirms collectivity as an American value evidenced by the War, I also believe that, as a result of conjoining gender with sex, Jeffords overlooks a possible reading of Sam as a female masculine character, an omission that forces Jeffords to read Sam only as another conveyor of male masculine values. Alternatively, Judith Halberstam argues that female masculinity also can be heterosexual, but she analyzes instances of lesbian female masculinity because the heterosexual version "represents [only] an acceptable degree of female masculinity as compared to the excessive masculinity of the dyke" (28).

I contend that just as Mason's *In Country* Sam represents a state between masculine and feminine, she also inhabits a space between hetero and homo, a liminal state that is both about possibility and also about threat. Her outsider status is evident from the outset of the novel: "Sam likes the feeling of strangeness. They are at a crossroads: the interstate with traffic headed east and west, and the state road with north-south traffic. She's in limbo, stationed right in the center of this enormous amount of energy" (17). It is this liminality that Jewison's film dispels, thereby revealing the cultural fear of uncertainty, manifested as a growing boundary between gender and sex.[16] As Barbara Tepa Lupack charges in her essay dealing with the film adaptation, "Jewison alters both the novel's perspective and structure and minimizes the text's subtextual concerns with gender issues and definition" ("History" 160). For the remainder of this section, then, I compare Mason's novel and Jewison's film to underscore how fear of the divide between gender and sex and the consequent liminality of those two states is revised by Jewison to be palatable to a 1980s American film audience.

Fear that masculine females were lesbians was evident in American culture during and in the decade following the War. Though Shilts estimates that lesbians did make up a disproportionate amount of the women in the military (Conduct 140, 561), he also argues that women generally were singled out as a result of the inroads they had made in a traditionally male venue, and that those women often were seen as *either* traditionally feminine *or* lesbian:

> Between 1972 and 1982, the number of enlisted women in the Army had increased by nearly 550 percent, from 12,349 to more than 67,000. The number of female officers had nearly doubled from 4,400 to 8,650. Women now comprised 10 percent of the Army's officer and enlisted strength, and comparable increases were evident throughout the services.... For heterosexual men t]he old moorings were slipping. Once women had simply been wives and mothers. Now they did not need men to define themselves; they had their own jobs.... Some steps further along this feminist path, many men feared, lurked the women who represented the ultimate rejection of men: lesbians, who refused to define even their sexuality by their relationship to men, who did not need men for anything. As such, lesbians were the sum of all fears for the confused heterosexual male of the 1980s. Lesbianism was the phenomenon that could deprive heterosexual men of women who would participate in the construction of their heterosexual identity [415, 417].

In the novel, Sam "betrays" femininity, both in what she thinks of traditional gender roles and in terms of her own physical activities. She is not a member of the military, but she is an inheritor of the Feminist Movement, as her mother had been an early "wild child" in defying gender expectations during the 1960s, and, to some extent, is still subscribing to its tenets, and her uncle, Emmett, still refuses to act the part of an employed-outside-of-the-home masculine man. In attitudinal and physical ways, Sam dissociates herself from her female peers: she runs "because it set her apart from the girls at school who did things in gabby groups, like ducks. When she ran, she felt free, as if she could do anything," even though she is sexually harassed and threatened by men when she runs (75). Sam lives with Emmett, her mother's brother and a Vietnam veteran, who allows her boyfriend, Lonnie, to sleep over at their house. Sam uses the pill, though her friend Dawn cautions Sam about its "side effects," to which Sam retorts, "I don't care. Having a baby would be a pretty big side effect" (43). When Dawn suspects she's pregnant, Sam agrees to buy the pregnancy-testing kit since "'If you get talked about the way Emmett and me do, and the way my mother did, then nothing is embarrassing.' Sam cared less and less what people thought" (82). Dawn dreads being pregnant because she has played housemaid and mother to her father and brother, as her own mother died while giving birth to her (105). Once Dawn confirms she is pregnant, Sam urges her to have an abortion. The first time Sam suggests this, Dawn is offended (141); later, once the man responsible for impregnating her expresses pleasure about her condition, Dawn admits she is too afraid to abort the fetus: "I could do a lot of crazy stuff, but not that. I'm just too chicken to do that." As Sam the nonconformist views it, "Having kids is what everybody does. It doesn't take any special talent" (177). As if to affirm the sexual ambiguity of her androgynous name, Sam endeavors at every instance to defy the gender roles expected of her.

Sam also is marked physically as not-feminine. The novel describes her as bucktoothed, round-faced, and sporting short, auburn hair (39). Her running produces a muscular body, a condition remarked on by Tom, a friend of Emmett's and a Vietnam vet. Despite a relationship with high-school-aged Lonnie, Sam lusts after mid-thirties Tom; once they have an opportunity to have sex, though, Tom is unable to have an erection. Subsequently, Sam enfolds Tom in her arms: "Since he couldn't get inside her, she wanted to enclose him with her arms." Emphasizing the sexual and gender ambiguity of this scene, Tom exclaims, "My God, Sam, I've never felt muscles on a girl like you've got" (129). Rather than interpreting this outcry as an accusation, as though her muscular body could be responsible for Tom's impotence, Sam interprets it as a compliment. Sam sees herself as hard, dark, and on the cultural edge. When Lonnie advises her to get a dress to wear to his brother's wedding, a traditional rite of heteronormativity, Sam insists, "I don't want a dress" and instead sees "herself in black leather pants. And a lot of metal" (187).

Sam's sexual and gender differences in the novel are complemented by the womanly characterization of her uncle, Emmett. In an early scene, Emmett wears an Indian-print wrap-around skirt, which Sam explains to Lonnie is an imitation of Klinger on *M*A*S*H*, a character who dresses as a woman in search of a discharge (for homosexuality) from the Army. Emmett initially is proud of the skirt, striking "an exaggerated fashion-model pose" and "pranc[ing] like Boy George" (27). But when Lonnie challenges Emmett to wear the skirt in public, Emmett becomes defensive: "'It's healthier for a man to wear a skirt,' Emmett said solemnly. 'He's not all cramped up and stuff'" (30). After Emmett reacts hysterically to the thunder of an approaching storm, he is described as "stately in his skirt — tall and broad, like a middle-aged woman who had had several children" (32).

Emmett meets the feminine gender expectations of a middle-aged female mother as well, as he remains unemployed outside of the home, puttering around the house, cultivating plants and the health of the house's foundation. As his mother explains it, Emmett has "always got to be piddling around with something" or "playing paper dolls" (146). Emmett's parents are divided in explaining what they perceive to be his current degradation, but both attribute it to a deficiency in manliness; while his father thought the war would "make a man" of Emmett, as though he were questionably male beforehand, his mother connected his manliness to an inability to reproduce, since she thought he had become sterile as a result of having the mumps when he was eleven.

The novel emphasizes Sam's centrality to the novel in making her point of view the dominant one. Her thoughts are more accessible than any other character's, thereby advancing the reader's sympathetic attitude toward and interest in Sam. The story obviously is about her psychic and physical development and how the people around her contribute to it, and the aftereffects of the Vietnam War are the medium for her discovery. However, the Norman Jewison film adaptation, also titled *In Country*, turns the point of view from Sam to Emmett as it reconstructs the crazed and vengeful Vietnam vet into the victim of a horrible national errand.[17] Though directors of film adaptations may choose to alter any element of a novel for aesthetic or plot reasons, the things they do choose to change are significant. In this case, the effect of the film's refocalization is to belittle the quests for gender and sexual identity that compel Sam (and, to a lesser extent, Emmett) in the novel, but also to underscore the importance of the quests to the novel. The casting of Emmett and Sam and the revision of key scenes from the novel expose this effort by the film to minimize the liminal status of both characters, calling into question the cultural need these alterations would satisfy.

A relatively unknown actress, Emily Lloyd, plays Sam in the 1989 film. Lloyd brings to the role some of the energetic inquisitiveness that characterizes Sam in the novel, but there are several elements of Lloyd's acting and physical characteristics that are problematic to interpreting

Sam's dark outlook in the novel ("Emily Lloyd"). As a British actress Lloyd works hard to sound American, though her use of a syrupy and enthusiastic Kentucky accent sounds more saccharine and less cynical than Sam might have sounded had Jewison intended a different kind of character or one more faithful to the Sam of the novel. While Sam sees frequent long-distance running as emblematic of her independence and so one imagines her stride as easy and practiced, Lloyd's running is infrequent, goofy and awkward, arms akimbo and a stride that threatens to trip her with every step. While this awkwardness may be a function of Lloyd's own lack of athleticism, it casts Sam physically as an out-of-control naif. Lloyd's character's naiveté also transforms Sam from a young woman who enjoys smoking dope with her uncle to a girl who not only would not dream of smoking, but also, to her uncle's annoyance, extinguishes his cigarettes while he is smoking. Not only does Lloyd not embody Sam's attitudes, but her physical appearance also counters the physical appearance of Sam. Where Sam has short, dark hair, Lloyd has long, blond, Farrah Fawcett-type locks. Where Sam has multiple piercings, Lloyd's are unnoticeable. Where Sam imagines herself in black leather, Lloyd is costumed in pastel T-shirts and shorts. Where Sam is muscular and skinny, Lloyd is curvaceous. When in the novel Sam is broody, skeptical, and rebellious, her defiance of gender and sexual mores is conceivable. When in the film Lloyd is naive, whiny, and obedient, it is less plausible she will break any rules. As both the psychological and material antithesis of Sam, Lloyd's femininized, heterosexualized part ensures that Sam, a dominant masculine female in the novel, will not be the focal point of the film. Instead, she serves as a device for telling the re-masculinized Emmett's story, a role that insinuates the threat of Sam's female masculinity portrayed in the novel.

Emmett is central to Sam's story in the novel because Sam lives with him and because he is a Vietnam veteran. Sam believes Emmett is a victim of Agent Orange poisoning, as he has chronic headaches and a persistent case of acne, and her desire to solve his problems sets her on the path of discovering more about her own father and, thus, about herself on the threshold of adulthood. Though Emmett also appears to suffer from Post-traumatic Stress Disorder (PTSD), he attributes his lack of ambition to the futility of finding a job that is not environmentally exploitative (45). In short, for most of the novel Sam initiates their activities and motivates Emmett, who inexplicably is unable to initiate activities outside of their home. Near the conclusion of the novel, however, and once Sam's running away prompts Emmett to confess to Sam his painful "war survivor story," *he* initiates the trip to visit the Vietnam War Memorial with Sam and her father's mother. There the three of them are "reborn," as Emmett finds the names of the buddies he survived, as Mrs. Hughes touches the name of her son and leaves a perennial plant, and as Sam sees her own name replicated on the memorial. In the novel, then, Sam's story leads to the "rebirth" of all three characters. This is not the case in the film, the consequences of which are to minimize the power of Sam's narrative and to maximize Emmett's.

Another relatively unknown actor at the time, Bruce Willis, plays Emmett. Though this was an early film in Willis's career, predating such familiar Willis vehicles as most of the *Die Hard* series, *Pulp Fiction* (1994), *The Bonfire of the Vanities* (1990), and *Look Who's Talking* (1989), Willis by this time had already had parts on various television shows, notably his leading role in *Moonlighting*, and his most significant film had been *Die Hard* (1988), the first of the series ("Bruce Willis"). Thus, though Willis now is known as a major Hollywood actor, at the time he, like Lloyd, was relatively unknown.[18] Consequently, since the film is not primarily intended as a star vehicle, which might have explained its re-focus on Emmett, it seems to be telling a wholly different story, one about the victimization of the Vietnam veteran. Susan Jeffords describes this effort as "remasculinizing," but I also read it as an erasure of what made Sam central to the novel. To accomplish that in the late 1980s required abridging, if not eliminating, the traces of female masculinity in the novel, since the national mood cited by Randy Shilts above required that Sam's gender and sexual ambiguity in the novel not be mistaken for lesbianism by a mainstream audience in the film. In other words, to rescript Emmett/Willis as the symbol of restored masculinity mandated rescripting all of the evidence discussed above of Sam as a gender or sexual transgressor; Emmett's restoration to "masculinity" required a simultaneous restoration of Sam to "femininity." This change in Emmett was effected in several ways in the film. First, in the scene where Willis is wearing the skirt, he immediately is defensive about it. There is no reveling in wearing it, nor is he regarded or imaged as a "stately ... middle-aged mother" (32). The effect of Willis' being immediately defensive is to disallow his open gender violation, and to insist that, despite his domesticity, he is nonetheless a masculine male. Another way that the film rescripts Emmett is to write his parents out, eliminating any hint that Willis may have seemed unmanly before the War. Even if an audience is unfamiliar with the novel, the film can insinuate that Willis was entirely altered by the War, not by any dispositions he took with him to the War, and thus recasts Willis as a victim of the War, not of his past or current environment. This recasting also supports Lloyd's obsession to confirm Willis' victimization from exposure to Agent Orange and his suffering from PTSD.

In the novel, the impetus for the trip to the Vietnam War Memorial and the conclusion of the book comes as the result of Sam's actions forcing Emmett to tell his survivor story. After reading her father's journal, and being disgusted by the abjectness of his life in combat, Sam decides all of the vets she knows must have been engaged in similarly despicable activities. She "runs away" to the nearby swamp, hoping to experience firsthand the "in country" environment. Emmett hunts her down there and tells her his own war experience as the lone survivor of a small patrol unit. He survived only because he feigned being dead under the body of another American soldier, and he was afraid when Sam ran away that she, too, might leave him by dying: "You were gone, and I didn't know what might have happened to you. I thought you'd get hurt. It was like being left by myself and all my buddies dead." Even though Sam and Emmett have lived together for most of the time since his return from the War, Emmett only reveals now that, as a result of the trauma of the War, he is "damaged," "like something in the center of my heart is gone and I can't get it back," and expends all of his energy on "staying together, one day at a time" (225). As a result of this episode, Sam expects Emmett to "flip out," but instead, it is she "who went sort of crazy after Emmett came to find her at Cawood's Pond" (229). While Sam feels alienated, lethargic, and disinterested (even in running), Emmett is invigorated by his confession to instigate their trip, with Sam's grandmother, to the Vietnam War Memorial in Washington, D.C. (230). At the Wall, the three characters are equally enlightened: conservatively-minded Grandmother Hughes concedes the power of the unconventional war memorial to evoke an emotional response; Sam sees her own name inscribed and decides that all Americans are part of the memorial; and Emmett finds, to his delight, the names of his dead buddies.[19] Also as a result of his confession to Sam, Emmett resolves to turn his life around by going to work, and Sam agrees to go to college. In the Mason text, gender is a matter of choice that does not have to impinge on constructions of sexuality, so that female masculinity and male femininity may abide together without requiring those two positions to negate one another. The implication of the concluding scene at the Wall, when Sam finds her name on it and Emmett delights in finding (or not) those of his friends, is that Sam will continue to be a masculine female and that Emmett will continue to be a feminine male, but that for either to switch does not require the other to switch as well. The film concludes differently, however, as it rejuvenates male masculinity at the cost of the female masculinity visible in the novel. Though in the Cawood's Pond episode Willis does declare to Lloyd the maddening and daily ordeal of holding himself together, he does not detail how he survived, nor does he initiate the trip to the memorial. In the novel, Emmett's talking about how he survived Vietnam and his subsequent emotional void affirms the (feminine) role he has played; in the film, Willis's not revealing how he survived but revealing the emotional void suggests a sensitive, though not *too* sensitive, masculine man.[20] To this point in the film, it has been Lloyd initiating any activities, so *her* suggesting the visit to the memorial continues the pattern of her trying to solve Willis' problem. When Emmett initiates the trip in the novel — when he asserts a masculine position — Sam's masculinity is not obliterated for that assertion to take effect, and she is able to hear and withstand the details of his trauma without being made "feminine." In the film, however, Lloyd is never permitted to display female masculinity, nor is she privy to Willis' deepest wounds. Her job is simply to get Willis to a place where he can be reborn, phoenix-like. The end result of the film, then, is to insist on gender binary oppositions and on traditional gender and sexual roles: for male masculinity to be, female masculinities may not; for male heterosexuality to be, female homosexuality may not.

This transformation in the film, I contend, is a reaction against what Jeffords conceptualizes as contemporary fears of the collapse of gender as a stable form, and the subsequent failure of heterosexuality, circumstances the novel seems to welcome. The differences between the 1985 novel and the 1989 film reflect the early 1980s changing gender roles of women in American society that Randy Shilts outlines, and what Susan Faludi calls the subsequent "backlash" against those changes during the course of the 1980s. What Faludi calls "outbreaks of fear and loathing of feminism," in *Backlash: The Undeclared War Against American Women* (1991),

> are backlashes because they have always arisen in reaction to women's "progress," caused not simply by a bedrock of misogyny but by the specific efforts of contemporary women to improve their status, efforts that have been interpreted time and again by men — especially men grappling with real threats to their economic and social well-being on other fronts — as spelling their own masculine doom [xix].

Thus, I contend that the film is a conservative reaction to the liberal gender moves of the novel evident in American culture during the 1980s, a reaction trying to reinstate the equation between gender and sex and, hence, monolithic masculinity.

Though Tim O'Brien's short story, "The Sweetheart of the Song Tra Bong," was published in the same time period that Jewison's *In Country* was released, it does not resort to the gender binaries insisted upon in the film.[21] Instead, the story describes a mode of existence for female masculinity that is simultaneously horrific and exhilarating. Critics have read "Sweetheart" through the lens of gender, in so far as the story underscores the disparate experiences of men and women in the Vietnam War. This reading, however, is dependent on a problem I cited at the beginning of this chapter: the conflation of gender and sex, of social behavior as the result of biology, offering through the use of "gender" an "antiseptic," "less dangerous" word for "sex" as a descriptor of the body and its abilities (Gutmann 19). What this curiously unselfconscious sort of reading omits, however, is the possibility of gender being performed outside of a heterosexual norm. I contend that, in ways similar to Mason's *In Country*, "Sweetheart" leaves open such a possibility, thereby suggesting a separation of the gender/sex pairing and a new and viable pressure on the masculinities of the Vietnam War: female masculinity.

The outer story is narrated by "I" or the "Tim O'Brien" narrator. His tale is concerned with the inner story that Rat Kiley, an unreliable narrator, tells about the unit to which he previously belonged. The two units are quite dissimilar, as the current unit frequently "humps the boonies" (hikes around the jungle) and the previous one stayed in one place. This dissimilarity immediately establishes an opposition, especially because the event Rat describes could not possibly have happened in a unit constantly moving and under constant surveillance by officers and enemies, making the outlandishness of the story more plausible. The previous unit was located at a medical emergency aid station isolated from most combat and all officers, so the members had an unheard-of degree of predictability and freedom in their lives. The only other people there were South Vietnamese forces (ARVN) assigned to defend the outpost, and a small group of secretive Green Berets who kept entirely to themselves. This autonomy made it possible for one of the unit members— an eighteen-year-old with "a pair of solid brass balls"— to bring from Ohio to the station his seventeen-year-old girlfriend, Mary Anne. Her arrival was a delicious surprise to the eight other medics at the station, as Mary Anne embodied the prototypical 1960s ideal American girlfriend: white, tall, blond, and friendly, verging on flirtatious. After a trip halfway around the world, Mary Anne arrived in "white culottes and this sexy pink sweater" (102), and her clothing initially signified her mental state; Mary Anne had "a bubbly personality, a happy smile" (106). Within weeks of arriving in Vietnam, however, she wore camouflage fatigues, went out on ambush, and had "a new composure, almost serene." Cutting her hair short, wearing a green bandanna on her head, abandoning the use of makeup and learning how to fire an M-16 produced "a new confidence in her voice, a new authority in the way she carried herself" (109). Mary Anne's new confidence and firm body signified her participation in something illicit, something her "brass-balled" boyfriend could imagine only as her having sex with one of the other medics. As it turned out, however, she had been on ambush with the "Greenies," returning to camp "in a bush hat and filthy green fatigues" and with a face "black with charcoal." With the boyfriend reasserting his command over her, Mary Anne next appeared dressed like a Catholic school girl, wearing "a white blouse, a navy blue skirt, a pair of plain black flats" (113). Eventually, however, the clothing ceased to signify the inner state of Mary Anne, and, despite her clean hair and properly gendered clothing, Rat described her as "in a restless gloom" and "inside herself" (115). Mary Anne subsequently vanished with the Greenies, not reappearing for another three weeks. When she returned, Rat explains, she had become a phantom: "There was no sound. No real substance either. The seven silhouettes seemed to float across the surface of the earth, like spirits, vaporous and unreal" (115–116). The next time Rat saw her was in the Greenie hootch, where she was clothed again in the pink sweater, but barefoot and with a white blouse and skirt. She also had added a new accessory to her wardrobe: a necklace of human tongues. Mary Anne looked "perfectly at peace with herself" and declared to her boyfriend that it was he who was out of place "here," whereas she was so at home that she wanted to "*eat* this place" (120–121). As Rat continues his story he qualifies its veracity, since he only had heard the ending thirdhand, having left the unit. The Greenies reported that Mary Anne began doing things even the Greenies would not risk themselves; "And then one morning, all alone, Mary Anne walked off into the mountains and did not come back" (124). Though she left no trace, the Greenies claimed to see her, or more accurately sense her periodically in the bush: "She had crossed to the other side. She was part of the land. She was wearing her culottes, her pink sweater, and a necklace of human tongues. She was dangerous. She was ready for the kill" (125).

Critics like Milton Bates and author O'Brien read this story as about anyone's vulnerability to being corrupted by Vietnam, as Rat himself does:

"She wasn't *dumb*," he'd snap. "I never said that. Young, that's all I said. Like you and me. A *girl*, that's the only difference, and I'll tell you something: it didn't amount to jack. I mean, when we first got here—all of us—we were pretty young and innocent, full of romantic bullshit, but we learned pretty damn quick. And so did Mary Anne" [108].

Narrator "Tim O'Brien" continues later:

The wilderness seemed to draw her in. A haunted look, Rat said—partly terror, partly rapture. It was as if she had come up on the edge of something, as if she were caught in that no-man's land between Cleveland Heights and deep jungle. Seventeen years old. Just a child, blond and innocent, but weren't they all? [115].

In other words, Rat suggests that Mary Anne is no different from the rest of them in her response to Vietnam. Milton Bates agrees, as he concludes that the story "suggests that war is so alien, so unprecedented in ordinary human experience, that it can transform an innocent young woman into a remorseless killer almost overnight" (157). Author O'Brien confirms that was his intent:

"Sweetheart of the Song Tra Bong" seems to me to be an utterly feminist story. It seems to me to be saying, in part, if women were to serve in combat they would be experiencing precisely what I am, the same conflicts, the same paradoxes, the same terrors, the same guilts, the same seductions of the soul. They would be going to the same dark side of the human hemisphere, the dark side of the moon, the dark side of their own psyches [McNerney 21].

While I do not want to contest O'Brien's intent, I question his use of the word "same" in the quote above, because Mary Anne is not the "same." If she resembles anyone, it is Rat, who, as he tells the story, always has a "dark, far-off look in his eyes, a kind of sadness, as if he were troubled by something sliding beneath the story's surface" (108). Rat also appreciates the "terror" and "rapture" Mary Anne feels about the land; however, not only is Rat unreliable as a storyteller, having a "reputation for exaggeration and overstatement" (101), he also does not follow through on the terror and rapture in the way Mary Anne does, by leaving the company of "normal" men for the jungle. Instead, in "Night Life," another story in *The Things They Carried*, Rat shoots himself in the foot so that he can be evacuated to Japan and probably returned stateside (247–251). Furthermore, though Mary Anne resembles the elusive Greenies with whom she lived longer than she did the medics, she also disappears from that group. Because Mary Anne leaves both groups of men for an alternative experience, she cannot be labeled the "same." In characterizing a female in combat as excessively masculine, as O'Brien's text does, she represents things other than "same."

Katherine Kinney maintains that Mary Anne is a vehicle for illustrating how war stories are constructed, the war stories that make up the knowledge combatants (i.e., men, in this case) learn from one another. "'Sweetheart,'" asserts Kinney, "is insistently about Mary Ann's [sic] self-discovery and its effect on the masculine activity of telling war stories rather than on the lives of the men she leaves behind." Kinney astutely observes, "Rat brings to the surface the contradictory structures of war narrative that ask women to heal and absolve men of experiences they are not allowed to know" (155). The first part of Kinney's comment addresses the self-conscious story-making evident in "Sweetheart" (as well as in most of *The Things They Carried*) as Rat twice interrupts his narration to ask what the listeners think of the story. The second part of her comment also is a valid method of addressing Rat's explanations that one of the important things about Mary Anne was that she had been in Vietnam. "There it is," Rat exclaimed, "you got to taste it, and that's the thing with Mary Anne. She was *there*. She was up to her eyeballs in it. After the war, man, I promise you, you won't find nobody like her" (123). Despite her discernment in reading the short story, however, Kinney does not adequately address Mary Anne's difference from the men.

Lorrie Smith comes closer to naming this difference in "Sweetheart," what she calls "the book's most disturbing story" ("The Things Men Do" 31), when she suggests that Mary Anne's excessive masculinity casts her as "monstrous and unnatural" (32). According to Smith, the monstrosity of Mary Anne's inner peace and her identification with the land construct her as inhuman (34). Furthermore, the necklace of tongues ascribes to Mary Anne both her own language and "a multiplicitous sexual charge, suggesting both male and female genitalia, hetero and homoerotic sexually" (35). Smith concludes that Mary Anne is always the object of the men's attention, never the subject, so that "Mary Anne's savagery and monstrousness function to solidify male bonds and validate the humanity of the more 'normal' soldiers. She carries to the furthest extreme the book's [*The Things They Carried*] pattern of excluding women from the storytelling circle" (36). Though I agree with most of what Smith contends, she does not explore the mental changes indicated by Mary Anne's physical changes, outlined above. Instead, Smith asserts that Mary Anne's changes are motiveless, making her that much more mysterious and enigmatic to the men and the reader. Any changes Mary Anne does experience, suggests Smith, exist only to "register the men's reactions to her," both the players in Rat's inner story and the men in the framing "Tim O'Brien" story.

Smith's reading does not capture the liminal space that I believe Mary Anne disappears into, a mental space that Rat characterizes as "partly terror, partly rapture," and a space that has no language the men can identify. This reading, of Mary Anne deliberately stepping outside of gender and sexuality and human contact, is signified by the clothing she is said to be wearing at the close of the story: the white culottes, pink sweater, and necklace of tongues. The necklace does carry sexual signification, as Smith argues, but the tongues (as opposed to the ears in many Vietnam War texts) also suggest language. In other words, the clothing Mary Anne is expected to be wearing and that the men appreciate is augmented by an accessory of her choice, one that symbolizes multiple sexualities and ways of communicating and that, combined with the pink sweater and white culottes, defies standard gender roles which must occur outside the purview of "the normal." In this sense, then, Mary Anne occupies a liminal area that could be construed as "monstrous," but is one that David Jarraway refers to as a "healthful space" as she engages in "losing her self" (701). This redefinition of herself as crossing gender and language boundaries, I believe, is where Mary Anne enters the realm of the female masculine.

Though O'Brien claims his intent was to demonstrate Mary Anne's similarity to any of the men in combat in Vietnam, he ensures instead that she is other than they are. But she is also other than she was when she first arrived at the medical station. That otherness is outside of traditional gender roles as the pink sweater and white culottes are not "masculine," nor is the necklace of tongues a "feminine" accessory. That otherness, what Rat describes as "unnamed terror and unnamed pleasure" (123), is also outside of normal sexuality, as Mary Anne first leaves her boyfriend's bed to go "out on fuckin' *ambush*" (113) with the Greenies, and then even leaves them for the solitude of the mountains.

Whereas the two texts I analyze in Chapter One reflect their seven-year-long 1980s historical period paradoxically in trying to obviate racial difference by making it overt, the four texts investigated in this chapter reflect their greater historical span from 1967 until 1990 by illustrating the mutability of gender, sex, and sexuality. The texts analyzed here do not display the same kind of genre discipline about these identity positions that the texts analyzed for their depictions of race did. It appears, therefore, that these Vietnam War novels and films more readily connect sex and sexuality to questions of masculinity. The two texts written during the War, Norman Mailer's *Why Are We in Vietnam?* (1967) and Joe Haldeman's *The Forever War* (1974), emphasize sexuality as an integral component to making up gender; several texts published or produced after the War, Bobbie Ann Mason's *In Country* (1985), its 1989 Norman Jewison film adaptation, and Tim O'Brien's short story, "Sweetheart of the Song Tra Bong," on the other hand, display how changes in conceptions of gender roles have impacted enactments of sexuality. Both periods, before and after the War, mark the mutability of these identity positions, sex and sexuality, in their relationship to gender as military attitudes towards gender altered. Given the official military policy against homosexuality and Randy Shilts' voluminous history of the treatment of homosexuals in the military since Vietnam, it is peculiar that the military, which presumably has served as a venue for the development of (heterosexual) men, also is represented by writers of Vietnam War narratives as a venue for developing non-heterosexual sexualities.

Randy Shilts also points out two indicators of changing attitudes towards traditional gender roles during the War era. First, because the Selective Service needed so many men to conduct the War, it had to disregard its own rules by ignoring the sexualities of military members and inductees. Second, following the War, women, who previously had been segregated into their own corps, were integrated into the regular armed forces. The texts I examine illustrate how these military changes found their way into broader changes to American attitudes toward sex, gender, and sexuality. Bolstered by historic changes enacted by the Women's and Gay Liberation Movements which came to fruition in the 1970s, "sex roles," or gender, replaced sexuality as the primary concern for the military. Thus, Bobbie Ann Mason's *In Country*, Norman Jewison's film version of Mason's novel, and Tim O'Brien's "Sweetheart of the Song Tra Bong" focus on females in its context, texts that foreground female masculinities as they disrupt the traditional connection between gender identity and sexuality, a requisite component of monolithic masculinity.

Just as authors of Vietnam War narratives attempting to avoid racially stereotyped versions of masculinity are stymied by the generic conventions of realistic fiction and film, so too does my analysis of gender, sex, and sexuality in this chapter suggest another problem of genre. Before the Vietnam War not only did the American war fiction genre create a universally white experience of war, but it also created an experience that was male and unquestionably heterosexual. If war is seen as the necessary rite of passage to manhood, and "manhood" implies the racial, sexual, and gendered positions I've discussed in Chapters One and Two, then war literature should be a venue for the "normal" representations of the transformation of theoretically unsexual boys into heterosexual men. My investigation indicates that, though military policy and jurisdiction has been officially homophobic since the 1950 institutionalization of the Uniform Code of Military Justice (UCMJ), texts written about the Vietnam War reflect a greater acceptance of alternative gender and sexual roles than such a policy would suggest and than literatures of previous American wars indicate. This rescripting of gender and sexuality — which war instead is supposed to brace — is an outcome of the events of the War era, including both the War itself and the Women's and Gay Liberation Movements, enabling the reformulation and pluralization of masculinities.

I find troubling, however, a conceptual change that emerged during this period that since then has resulted in a semantic switch. Both movements advocated for a change in the distinction between the biology one is born to and the subsequent behavior expected. During the 1960s and 1970s, "sex" was the word to indicate one's biology and "sex role" the words to indicate the traditional social behavior expected of that sex. The Women's and Gay Liberation movements attempted to disrupt the traditional equations of female and feminine, male and masculine. As the texts produced during the War illustrate, crossing of "sex role" boundaries did not automatically conclude a simultaneous crossing of boundaries of sexuality. That is, texts written during that period indicate that a male engaging in homosexual acts was not necessarily also feminine. However well-intentioned and useful the theoretical switch from "sex role" to "gender" is, "gender" has also been appropriated generally in American society to signify biology. Thus, as Stephanie Gutmann points out, the military now can appear to be progressive when it refers to "gender," when what the institution actually wants to know is the biological sex of a person. This semantic conflation manifests itself in the Vietnam War texts I examine in this chapter as worries about gender and sexual "treachery," and in Randy Shilts' contention that the majority of prosecutions for homosexuality have been for lesbianism. In other words, as soon as a female begins to display masculinity, or a male to display femininity, the perceived trouble is less about those gender crossings than it is about crossing boundaries of sexuality.[22]

The post–War texts analyzed in this chapter indicate that female masculinity is culturally seen as most provocative. Bobbie Ann Mason, for instance, portrays her female protagonist as crossing a gender boundary into masculinity. The difference between Mason's depiction and Norman

Jewison's film adaptation is indicative of how disquieting female masculinity is to a popular audience that has come to expect "gender" to signify both biology and sexuality; in the popular imagination, "masculine" now connotes heterosexual males and "feminine," heterosexual females. Consequently, Mason's disruptive female masculine character is reconstructed as Jewison's inoffensive female feminine character. Similarly, Tim O'Brien's Mary Anne in "Sweetheart of the Song Tra Bong" adjusts too well to the environs of Vietnam, so that she becomes not only masculine, she exceeds the bounds of gender altogether. Though O'Brien's stated intent is to demonstrate how anyone, even the most cherubic of young American women, could be corrupted by Vietnam, that this woman becomes unrecognizable even to the male characters supposed to be embodying American masculinity at war again suggests that female masculinity and male bodies behaving in traditionally feminine ways are deviant, intolerable, and threatening to monolithic masculinity.

3

Men Out of Mind
Disabilities in Vietnam War Stories

Bodies operate socially as canvases on which gender is displayed and kinesthetically as the mechanisms by which it is physically enacted. Thus, the bodies of people with disabilities make them vulnerable to being denied recognition as men and women. The type of disability, its visibility, its severity, and whether it is physical or mental in origin mediate the degree to which the body of a person with a disability is socially compromised [Gerschick, "Toward" 254].

[T]he meanings attributed to extraordinary bodies reside not in inherent physical flaws, but in social relationships in which one group is legitimated by possessing valued physical characteristics and maintains its ascendancy and its self-identity by systematically imposing the role of cultural or corporeal inferiority on others [Garland-Thomson, *Extraordinary Bodies* 7].

Vietnam War texts sometimes challenge and sometimes confirm received notions of racialized and sexualized masculinities, but rarely do they make central disabled masculinity, despite physical and mental disabilities characterizing the outcomes of the War. "[T]he central activity of war is injuring and the central goal of war is to out-injure the opponent," claims Elaine Scarry (12). Scarry argues that the objective of war is not to kill, but to inflict pain which she characterizes as "language destroying" (19). The Vietnam War silenced many hundreds of thousands of American men and women with the pain of mental and physical disabilities. Though multitudes of soldiers returned from World War II physically and mentally disabled (Michel 247), and many thousands of Korean War veterans paid the psychic wages of war as a result of being held prisoner (Severo and Milford 275), the Vietnam War was unusual as the use of helicopters both delivered men abruptly to combat and also extricated them quickly, especially severely wounded soldiers. Consequently, American lives were preserved in Vietnam that in previous wars probably were lost (Gerber, "Heroes" 73). Paul Starr reports statistics in *The Discarded Army* (1973), a study of the Veterans Administration sponsored by Ralph Nader's Center for Study of Responsive Law, that bear out the peculiar violence of the Vietnam War on its American participants:

> In World War II the ratio of wounded to killed was 3.1 to 1, in Korea 4 to 1, but in Vietnam it was 5.6 to 1. The Army, which bore the brunt of the casualties, reports that 81 percent of its wounded survived in Southeast Asia, compared with 74 percent in Korea and 71 percent in World War II.... Among wounded Army men discharged for disability, the proportion of amputees has risen from 18 percent in World War II to 28.3 percent in Vietnam.... Paralysis of the extremities accounted for only 3.1 percent of wounded Army disability separations in World War II; for Vietnam this figure has been 25.2 percent.... [T]he rate for leg amputations in Vietnam has been 70 percent higher than in Korea and 300 percent above World War II; for functional loss of the lower extremities (paraplegia), the incidence has been 50 percent higher than in Korea and 1,000 percent over World War II.... In World War II, only 5.7 percent of the amputees had multiple amputations or other major injuries. In Vietnam the proportion has been 18.4 percent.... Among patients with burns over half their bodies, nearly 60 percent formerly died, whereas now fewer than 30 percent are lost [54–55].[1]

Those are just the visible injuries; the "invisible" ones, like Post-traumatic Stress Disorder (PTSD), alcoholism and drug addiction, and complications from exposure to Agent Orange would not typically present themselves until long after the War's end. The expediency of helicopters could not compensate for the "traumatic amputation" of limbs, severed spinal cords, opiate addiction and massive burns, so many of those saved lives were thereafter marked by severe disability, a sign frequently used to mark abnormality and what Leslie Fiedler characterizes as the "freak."[2]

This chapter examines how male veterans with disabilities, already subject to the ignominy of having participated in a controversial war, are depicted in narratives about the War and how those images are mediated by a National Symbolic that says war converts boys to masculine men. Contrary to the Symbolic's stance that this conversion is to a monolithic masculinity, these depictions of disability emphasize the variability of masculinity already illustrated in the previous two chapters, further pressuring traditional, monolithic notions of masculinity to be more accountable for "extraordinary" male bodies. Moreover, just as the texts analyzed in Chapter Two trace the evolution of American attitudes about sex, gender, and sexuality, the representations of Vietnam War veterans with disabilities historically encode the need for a more just treatment of physical and mental impairment, thereby instigating legislative changes to disability law from masculinist "compensation" to humane "accommodation." Vietnam War texts indict the cultural mores that locate disability as the result of an inherent flaw when they underscore the corruption of the "normal," especially in terms of the War. As the texts spotlight the constructedness of disability, which Thomas Gerschick in the quote at the opening of this chapter points out has been so closely aligned with gender, they also problematize the traditional ways that gender, and especially masculinity, can be enacted in American society, challenging popular notions that regard sex and gender, or the body and masculinity, as synonymous entities.

By the withdrawal from Vietnam of American troops in the spring of 1973, of the more than three million Americans who had spent their military service in Vietnam, over 58,000 had been killed or were missing in action, and more than 200,000 were wounded seriously enough to have been hospitalized (Johnson 214; Severo and Milford 350). Of these wounded 6,655 lost limbs (MacPherson 320). Disabilities continued to be revealed long after the War's end, so that a report commissioned by the United States Congress in 1983 and published in 1990, *Trauma and the Vietnam War Generation: Report of Findings from the National Vietnam Veterans Readjustment Study*, concluded that nearly 350,000 veterans suffered from "service-connected physical disabilities" (Kulka et al. 273). The study also tested for the coincidence of mental disability and physical disability, concluding that veterans with physical disabilities were much more likely than those without physical disabilities to be diagnosed with Posttraumatic Stress Disorder, or PTSD (274), suggesting thereby a causal relationship between the two conditions.

Similar warnings of "readjustment" problems were issued prior to the end of World War II, when Veterans Administration advice literature urged American women especially to help the returning veterans, naturally disturbed by their participation in war, to readjust to American society. The World War II discourse reveals a belief that the disabled male veterans were femininized by their disabilities and thereby were not "normal," that their masculinity consequently had to be re-built in order for the veterans to approximate normalcy, and that women were the agents of this re-building. David Gerber argues in "Heroes and Misfits: The Troubled Social Reintegration of Disabled Veterans in *The Best Years of Our*

Lives" that World War II movies supported the work of social, psychological, military, and religious authorities as they readied the United States population for a "demobilization crisis" (72). Women were expected to return to their traditionally submissive gender roles in order to force the disabled men back into their pre-war masculine states of independence and sociability, so they could "reclaim the obligations and prerogatives of manhood" (75). The reconstruction of masculinity for these disabled and thus ostensibly feminized men relied on women relinquishing some of the (limited number of) male perquisites they had gained as a result of the men's absence and re-assimilating to their sex roles of the pre-war American world. In "Bitterness, Rage, and Redemption: Hollywood Constructs the Disabled Vietnam Veteran," Martin Norden describes the consequences for women in post–World War II movies: "These films insisted that the veterans needed to be heroized, remasculinized, and reassimilated into society at all costs, and that the women on the home front were the primary agents for these tasks" (105).[3]

Unlike Hollywood representations of World War II, film representations of the Vietnam War, the means by which a majority of Americans are tutored about the War, have fixed largely on the mental as opposed to physical disabilities of its veterans. Contrary to the conclusions drawn by the 1990 congressional study cited above, films usually depict the Vietnam veteran as a psychically maddened and violent man inexplicably subject to moments of rage, physical violence, emotional frigidity, and flashbacks, not like the World War II veteran who returns, albeit feminized, as a hero to a welcoming society.[4] Moreover, women in Vietnam War films often are depicted as unresponsive to the expectation that they remasculinize the disabled men, as they are unwilling to forgo their masculine perquisites gained, not as a result of the men's absence, but as a result of durable social change. These differences in representations of postwar homecomings raise several questions. Assuming that gender *is* altered by disability, if women are not the medium through which disabled Vietnam veterans adapt to life in the United States, how is masculine reconstruction depicted in popular representations? If men with disabilities readjust without the assistance of women, how are their recoveries explained and how are their masculinities impacted by this self-sufficiency? Finally, legislatively and culturally, physical and mental disabilities are handled differently; how do the divisions between the two categories play out in constructions of masculinity? As Vietnam War texts spotlight the constructedness of disability, which Gerschick points out in this chapter's opening quote has been so closely aligned with gender, they also problematize the traditional ways that masculinity can be enacted in American society. As disability advocate James Weisman declares, "The Vietnam War caused us to challenge traditional assumptions. That your expectations should be different because you use a wheelchair was just not acceptable" (106).

According to Disability Rights Movement historians Paul Longmore and Lauri Umansky, the United States Congress enacted laws between 1968 and 1990 that dramatically altered the legal rights of disabled people ("Disability History" 10), offering compensation to those people (especially veterans) whose disabilities prevented them from earning a living, but more importantly, shifting "from policies based on a medical or economic definition of disability to those based on a sociopolitical definition" (Scotch 383). Some of those laws enacted during the Vietnam War era included the Architectural Barriers Act of 1968, and the Rehabilitation Act of 1973.[5] However, much of the disability legislation of the last few decades has been predicated on an original state of able-bodied employability, so federal aid to people with disabilities is regarded as compensating for an "abnormal" state of affairs: their inability to work, or to make a living wage. Rosemarie Garland-Thomson challenges this gendered logic of compensation, arguing pointedly against the soldier and the industrial worker as models on which disability should be based:

> [T]he focus on war wounds and industrial accidents as definitive disabilities supports a narrow physical norm by limiting economic benefits to those who once qualified as "able-bodied" workers, barring people with congenital disabilities and disabled women from economic "compensation" because they could not lose a hypothetical advantage they never had. According to the logic of compensation, then, "disabled" connotes not physiological variation, but the violation of a primary state of putative wholeness. The logic of accommodation, on the other hand, suggests that disability is simply one of many differences among people and that society should recognize this by adjusting its environment accordingly [*Extraordinary* 49].

Though the compensatory model resulted in significant strides for the rights of people with disabilities through federal regulations since the War era, it has been only recently, through the Americans with Disabilities Act of 1990 (ADA), that federal mandate articulates two important ideas: first, that social structures have as much to do with how disability is configured as does the body of the disabled person, and so those social structures need to be adjusted to *accommodate* people with disabilities; and two, that "disability" is a stigma only as the social interpretation of a physical impairment, so the people who experience that stigma should have more voice in determining what is and is not considered a disability. As Simi Linton explains in *Claiming Disability: Knowledge and Identity* (1998), the ADA legitimates the "sociopolitical model" of disability, which maintains that "even in the absence of a substantially limiting impairment, people can be discriminated against," citing examples such as facial disfigurement, HIV, or mental illness (33). Thomas Gerschick suggests such a dilemma in terms of gender for men with physical disabilities:

> [Gender] domination [of men with physical disabilities] depends upon a double-bind: men with physical disabilities are judged according to the standards of hegemonic masculinity which are difficult to achieve due to the limitations of their bodies. Simultaneously, these men are blocked in everyday interactions from opportunities to achieve this form of masculinity. The most significant barriers they face occur in the key domains of hegemonic masculinity: work, the body, athletics, sexuality, and independence and control. Because men with physical disabilities cannot enact hegemonic standards in these realms, they are denied recognition as men. As "failed" men, they are marginalized and occupy a position in the gender order similar to gay men, men of color, and women ["Sisyphus" 189].

Despite the sociopolitical move represented by ADA legislation in 1990, Disability Rights activists and theorists contend that "compensation" still lingers culturally and is still stigmatizing, predicated on a concept of "normal" which includes only the "temporarily able-bodied."[6] Rosemarie Garland-Thomson asserts that pre–1990 disability legislation, which is based on the compensation model, envisions disability as "a loss to be compensated for, rather than difference to be accommodated. Disability then becomes a personal flaw, and disabled people are the 'able-bodied' gone wrong. Difference then translates into deviance" (*Extraordinary* 49). In "Disability and the Justification of Inequality in American History," Douglas Baynton outlines the language usage shift from "natural" to "normal." Baynton argues that twentieth-century science heralded a departure from the belief in a backward-looking, God-given, "natural" world to a progressive, man-made, empirically "normal" world. To Baynton, however, this semantic switch signified little for those with disabilities: "[J]ust as the natural was meaningful in relation to the monstrous and the deformed, so are the cultural meanings of the normal produced in tandem with disability" (35). In other words, the "disabled" serve the same cultural purposes in the "normal" world as did the "deformed" in the world of the "natural": to operate as the opposition and thereby the definition of the non-disabled. Clearly, to Baynton and many other Disability Rights activists, "[D]isability is culturally constructed rather than natural and timeless" (52). Therefore, the "normal" on which federal law rests is a constantly altered construct answering to the social needs of particular historical periods. For instance, Thomas Gerschick and Adam Miller outline how disabled men currently are able to reconstruct their masculinities based on the prevailing form of hegemonic masculinity. In a 1997 essay entitled "Gender Identities at the Crossroads of Masculinity and Physical Disability," Gerschick and Miller suggest that men with disabilities have three avenues for reconstructing their masculinity: "reformulation," or a redefinition of masculine characteristics; "reliance," or the absolute adoption of some characteristics; and "rejection," or the renunciation of these standards ("Gender Identities" 457). Though these modes are premised on the seemingly indisputable notion that disability alters a man's gender, they suggest that a man with a disability has the option to reconstruct masculinity, but only from within the confines of a particular cultural milieu. Therefore, my readings of disabled characters in Vietnam War representations are contingent on the specific historical periods in which the texts were produced.

Another factor in reading disabled characters as signifiers of particular historical periods is the existence of a hierarchy — perhaps hierarchies — of disabilities, created in the minds of both disabled and non-disabled people.[7] As Garland-Thomson points out above, those who are disabled in the line of duty — the soldier, the industrial worker — have usually served as the impetus and model for disability legislation.[8] This form of physical disability has been characterized as "heroic" disability, as the (mostly) men were regarded as deliberately "sacrificing" themselves in the course of their work for the sake of the country or the company, placing them at the top of a disability hierarchy, and, I would argue, Connell's implied masculinity hierarchy outlined in the Introduction. The relativity of Connell's terms — hegemonic, marginal, subordinated, complicit — suggests such a hierarchy. Debra Moddelmog claims that sometimes wounds mark characters as more masculine. In *Reading Desire: In Pursuit of Ernest Hemingway*, Moddelmog contends that wounds and scars on Hemingway's heroes signify the "toughness" of the men and serve as "visible marker[s] of their white, masculine heterosexuality." Paradoxically, however, the wounds also highlight the body, therefore "moving the heterosexual [male] body into the realm of the female, the feminine, and the homosexual" (121). In the case of veterans depicted in Vietnam War texts, however, the types and degrees of their disabilities usually determine the affirmation of their masculinity; wounds and scars do not automatically confer masculinity. For instance, the scar on *Platoon*'s Sergeant Barnes (Tom Berenger) does work as Moddelmog suggests, and it works especially well as countertext to the unscarred body of Sergeant Elias (Willem Dafoe). That scar does not move beer-drinking Barnes into the purview of the clearly eroticized, "feminine," and sensitive hootch of Elias and his fellow dope-smokers. However, images of paraplegic and wheelchair-bound characters, such as Luke in *Coming Home* and Ron Kovic in *Born on the Fourth of July*, do work constantly against the pathos engendered by their "tragic" characters, which also may be viewed as "feminine."

Physical disability typifies the World War II films described above, when a victorious war had to produce only heroes; mental disability is depicted as temporary and overcome with the love and attention of a "good" woman, intimating permanent mental disability's place at the bottom of this hierarchy. According to Rosemarie Garland-Thomson, then, how a disability is acquired bears on its social acceptability, with physical impairment from war or work as the least stigmatized. Even within the category of "soldier" with disability, however, there are vast differences in treatment. According to 1983 figures, Vietnam veterans were treated differently, dependent on the degree to which they were prevented from working.

> For instance, a single veteran who has lost both legs above the knees received $1,661 a month; one with both legs lost below the knees received $1,506. [Legs lost above the knee meant there was no possibility of walking since prostheses required knees.] A veteran with one leg off above the knee received 60 percent disability and an additional monthly stipend for the loss of a leg, for a total of $506. One leg off below the knee is considered a 40 percent disability, and with the monthly stipend the check comes to $311. There is a marked decrease from 100 percent to 90 percent disabled—$1,213 a month versus $729 [MacPherson 320].

From his own experience, Lewis Puller, Jr., whose memoir is discussed later in this chapter, verifies these figures, adding to his 100 percent disability (as a result of having lost both legs at the hips and the ordinary use of both hands) the full tuition costs of attending law school at the College of William and Mary. Veterans who were not disabled, however, received very little in the form of benefits. Paul Starr's study compares the aftermath of the Vietnam War to that of World War II: "At that time [post–World War II] the VA paid for tuition and fees and provided a basic subsistence allowance of $75 a month to an unmarried student. Under the

Cold War and Vietnam era GI Bill originally enacted in 1966, the VA paid only a monthly stipend of $110, out of which the student had to pay for tuition, fees, and subsistence. In 1967 the basic stipend was raised to $130 and in 1970 to $175, still far below the World War II level considering the absence of tuition payment and the inflation in the intervening period" (Starr 227). All of these figures demonstrate the hierarchy existing even within the category of "soldier."

Accidental physical disability acquired outside of the venues of war and work is judged by the degree to which the victim can be held responsible for the accident. Physical disability acquired genetically is judged by how much control the person has over the disability, so those who "overcome" their disabilities are seen as closer to the "heroic" than those who do not. In a culture that values independence and control over the body, let alone the mind, overcoming one's disability is paramount. Rosemarie Garland-Thomson notes the rhetoric of overcoming in the "traditional" narrative of disability: "[O]ne's body is the recalcitrant object that must be surmounted, often either by some physical or psychological fear of rehabilitation or by a spiritual transcendence of the anomalous body" ("Integrating" 304). Disability theorist James Overboe categorizes hierarchal formations in disability in terms of the ability to control one's body:

> The closer one's disability [is] to the normative standard (ableness) then one has greater [control]. The less one is perceived to have control over their body (i.e. spastic) the greater the abjection. Ironically, a person experiencing paraplegia might be considered in better control [than] the person experiencing spasticity because our body conveys the image of composure [personal communication].

Where self-determination is a cultural premium, as it is in the American National Symbolic, control is the measure of a disability's abjection or stigmatization. Because mental disability is so often viewed as a lack of will, it appears at the bottom of the disability hierarchy, even when it is a predominant outcome of war. Thus, though approximately 500,000 soldiers were hospitalized for mental illness following the end of World War II, mentally disabled veterans rarely appear as subjects in movies made during or after that war.

This notion of a disability hierarchy problematizes a reading of Vietnam War veterans and constructions of masculinity especially when physical disabilities occur simultaneously with mental disabilities. In American cultural mythology war is supposed to produce heroes, but it is difficult for cultural representations to sculpt heroic figures in the case of a failed war. As is the case with many Vietnam War films, when almost exclusively mental disabilities are manifest, it becomes more difficult to assign these veterans to the traditional "heroic" status of victimized warrior, since mental disabilities are so low in the hierarchy. How, then, is the veteran with a disability represented when he is the product of a war that cannot endow heroic status, and more often than not, when he will be doubly stigmatized by both mental disabilities and physical disabilities that may demonstrate lack of control? What are the narrative strategies deployed by constructors of Vietnam War texts to position the returning veteran with a disability as a masculine man?

The bodies of veterans with disabilities are constructed against a backdrop of non-disabled bodies, "constructed" because the physical and mental wounds do not by themselves connote meaning. Though I include in this analysis depictions of mentally disabled figures, my intent is not to reify the more popular representations, but instead to explore the variances among textual depictions of many types of disability as they trace the changes in attitudes towards disability and masculinity in the postwar period. These texts reveal the differences between the compensatory models of disability typifying the period until 1990 and the Americans with Disabilities Act, and accommodationist models that followed the Act. I begin with an analysis of the "bridging" text to Chapter Two, Bobbie Ann Mason's *In Country* (1985), which demonstrates the impacts of physical and mental disabilities on the masculinities of some characters. I follow that with analyses of three biographical accounts of the interactions of masculinity and disability as a result of the War. The first of these texts is Corinne Browne's wartime *Body Shop* (1973), an oral narrative of veterans with amputations in Letterman Army Hospital that clarifies differing attitudes toward the physical and mental disabilities of male officers and enlisted, and of able-bodied and disabled. The second text is an early postwar memoir, *Strong at the Broken Places* (1980), by Max Cleland, who was director of the Veterans Administration under Jimmy Carter and a triple amputee. His narrative demonstrates his compensatory interpretation of the impact of his disability on his masculinity as a gift from God. I compare Cleland's memoir to another officer's memoir, Lewis B. Puller, Jr.'s Pulitzer Prize–winning autobiography, *Fortunate Son* (1991), written when Puller was an attorney in the Department of Defense and a double amputee. Puller's text reveals the accommodationist attitudes prevailing by the last decade of the millennium. To demonstrate how one text of the Vietnam War has dealt with the problems of constructing masculinities influenced by disability, I conclude the chapter with an analysis of Larry Heinemann's novel, *Paco's Story* (1986). Noticeably, all of the texts I examine feature characters whose physical disability is colored by mental disability. But the disabilities depicted do not include paraplegia despite Starr's data that note triple the number of "nervous system disorders" in comparison to "amputations." I contend that paraplegia rarely appears in Vietnam War narratives because it is not visible enough a sign; that is, it may appear that the person with paraplegia in the wheelchair is simply sitting placidly. The person disabled by a missing limb and thereby embodying lack, however, is far more visible and tragically evocative a figure in American culture.

A reading of *In Country* that accounts for the hierarchization of mental and physical disabilities and its impact on formulations of masculinities adds a connection to the previous chapter as well as develops strategies for later analysis, especially because *In Country* is not typically read as a disability narrative but as a coming-of-age novel. Bobbie Ann Mason's story centers on Sam(antha) as she graduates from high school and, in planning for her own future, attempts to discover more about her father who died in Vietnam before she was born. As Sam realizes she is nearly the same age as her father when he died, she relies on the people around her who were her father's contemporaries and experienced the Vietnam War in direct and indirect ways to help her find herself. Those who experienced the War directly include a cadre of male veterans from their Kentucky small town, primarily her uncle, Emmett, but also his close friends, Tom Hudson and Pete Simms. People indirectly involved are Sam's mother, Irene, who wants to leave the past behind her and so resists Sam's plying her for information, Anita Stevens, a local woman who dated Emmett and knew all the men before they went to the War, and members of Sam's family from both her mother's and her father's sides. Though typically "in country" was used during the War to refer to Vietnam, the novel's title intimates that it is difficult to distinguish between the people who experienced the War directly and those who experienced it indirectly. That is, all of the characters are "veterans" of being "in country," and all have been mentally or physically disabled by the War, a suggestion reinforced by the androgynously-named Sam's seeing her reflection and finding her name on the Vietnam Veterans Memorial at the novel's conclusion.

In an American culture that interprets the physical body as a manifestation of character, Sam has difficulty comprehending the invisible, such as mental disability; the death of a character on the TV show *M*A*S*H* made her own father's death more real to her than his absence (25), and so Sam interprets the silences of those who experienced the War as physical and not mental disabilities. Emmett, for instance, suffers from flashbacks, a variety of physical ailments, and unwillingness to fulfill his gender role: to get a job and to marry. Sam is ambivalent about Emmett's malaise and does not connect Emmett's unemployed status to his gender status, nor does she recognize a connection between the mental states he experiences (such as his "cringing" and "grimacing" during the thunderstorm [31], or at Cawood's Pond when he imagines he is back in Vietnam on "Highway 1" [38]) and his physical ailments. In fact, tutored by and embracing a culture that values the hard body as a reflection of the internal self, Sam is unable to explain Emmett's behavior *except* in terms of his physical condition. To her, Emmett's bodily ailments are not a reflection of his deteriorated mental state but instead are the result of some physical exposure: Emmett's pimples are the result of exposure to Agent Orange in Vietnam and his flashbacks are the result of heartburn. Though Sam acknowledges her uncle is a different sort of veteran — "She realized that not every soldier who came back from Vietnam was as weird as Emmett" (46) — she does not want to acknowledge his disability as a mental one because it signals a loss of masculinity.[9]

Sam's inability to account for Emmett's unconventional behavior as a mental disability and her desire to account for it physically probably has to do with the prominence of the Agent Orange case against its producers in the late 1970s and early 1980s. By 1984, the year in which *In Country* is set, a class-action suit filed in 1978 by Vietnam veterans against the chemical's manufacturers had been settled, with $180 million made available to the approximately 350,000 to 400,000 veterans in the spray areas (Severo and Milford 402). Though the settlement ended the class-action suit, the chemical companies still denied Agent Orange's culpability in veterans' ailments, and so the case's conclusion did not end the controversy or the possibility that Agent Orange was a carcinogen.[10] Emmett follows the news of the class-action suit, but he rejects the notion that his problems are a result of exposure to Agent Orange (59). Sam has done some research into the topic, and, finding similarities in descriptions of Agent Orange exposure and AIDS, another scourge then in the news, fears the worse for Emmett (68). In short, given the prevalent depictions of disabled Vietnam veterans as mentally unstable, and the new way to explain disability as physical with Agent Orange, Mason could construct a community willing to see physical ailments as having a material cause: an herbicide indiscriminately used in the later years of the War. Thus, the community believes Agent Orange is responsible for Buddy Mangrum's inability to drink a single beer without getting sick (48) and his daughter's having to have surgery on her intestines (111).

Additionally, with mental illness normalized during this period as personal failure and hence unmasculine, Sam would have been unwilling to ascribe mental illness to her uncle. He is "weird" but he is not "deranged." As a result of the traumas incurred during the Vietnam War, however, in 1980 the American Psychiatric Association added "Post-traumatic Stress Disorder" to its third edition of the *Diagnostic and Statistical Manual of Mental Disorders* (DSM-III). This was a historic change in the psychiatric world, according to the current director of the National Center for PTSD, Matthew Friedman. "From an historical perspective, the significant change ushered in by the PTSD concept was the stipulation that the etiological agent was *outside* the individual (i.e., a traumatic event) rather than an *inherent* individual weakness (i.e., a traumatic neurosis)" (Friedman; my emphasis). Though Mason litters *In Country* with contemporary cultural references, including AIDs and Agent Orange, PTSD is not among those, either indicating Mason's own ignorance of such a change or her sense that emerging theories of mental illness had not made their way to a small community imbued with Freudian interpretations of mental stability. As Emmett claims, "Everything's always ten years behind here" (59). Thus, if the inability to readjust to American society cannot be interpreted as a personal, psychic flaw, it must be explained as a physical problem by those needing to see the veterans as innocent victims. Agent Orange and AIDS are the insidious agents poisoning the lives of these returned men.

Sam goes home with Tom after the veterans' dance, intent on having sex with him. It turns out, however, that Tom is unable to have an erection as a consequence of his Vietnam memories. Though he would like to have an implant which would automatically provide an erection, he cannot afford one and, he bitterly comments, the Veterans Administration provides the devices to "the paraplegics so they can get a hard-on to please their women" (128). He becomes a victim and an object of pity to Sam at this point and, as I pointed out in the previous chapter, Sam becomes the dominant member of the pair as she "enclose[s] him with her arms" and Tom marvels at her muscles (129). Sam also needs to see her father as an innocent victim, as someone who naively went to Vietnam and naively died. After she reads his journal, though, where he details the pleasures of killing "gooks," Sam hates him and all the other veterans. When she likens her father to Pete, who claims to have enjoyed being in Vietnam, Emmett destroys Sam's ability to envision any of the veterans as innocent victims (222), and she begins to accept that their wounds are psychological. The solution to Emmett's mental impairment, then, is not to blame some material agent as the cause of the veterans' anguish, but instead to visit a communal site of mourning, the Vietnam Veterans Memorial in Washington, D.C. This form of disability, with the PTSD understanding of the illness being outside of one's self instead of caused by an inherent flaw, provides a new form of victimhood.

"[T]he body," claims Thomas Gerschick, "is central to the attainment of hegemonic masculinity" ("Sisyphus" 193). Under the rubric of PTSD, mental disabilities can be accounted for outside of the body, even as it manifests the trauma in material ways. Though *In Country* displays how the masculinities of Vietnam veterans are compromised by their mental disabilities, their gender roles are not depicted as inherent and immutable. As long as the disabilities of Vietnam veterans finally are depicted as largely mental, as they are for the main characters in *In Country*, the veterans may possibly overcome their physical impairments. Rosemarie Garland-Thomson discusses this notion of the reparable body when she describes two genres of disability narrative: the "narrative of overcoming" and the "narrative of resistance." The former, similar to the compensatory model of disability rights legislation, perceives the body as a "recalcitrant object that must be surmounted." The latter, like the accommodationist model of disability rights legislation, rejects the "normal," and "claims rather than transcends the body, rejecting the traditional pronouncements of its inferiority and asserting the right of that body to be as it is" ("Integrating" 304). Similarly, Gerschick and Miller suggest that men with disabilities can rely on, reject, or reformulate the standards of hegemonic masculinity to adjust to the dictates of gender formulation ("Gender Identities" 457). The struggle to reformulate their masculinities is a dominant theme of Mason's novel, as Emmett, Tom and Sam largely experience mental disabilities whose invisibility is both punished and privileged. Though Emmett's public behavior casts him as "weird" in the community's eyes, Tom's private impotence permits him to lead a life unmarred by stigma. Once Sam is able to overcome the idea that her father embodied a physical ideal, she is freed to begin her adult life. Because the novel suggests that all their physical disabilities—their bodies—can be overcome once they resolve their psychological traumas, *In Country* is a narrative of overcoming. The standards of traditional masculinity that rely on certain body forms, it turns out, are not their problem. Instead, in the world of Mason's masculine characters, a world dominated by the Freudian belief that one is personally responsible for mental disability, their minds prevent their bodies from being cured, from resuming traditional gender roles, so their physical impairments must be the outcome of a personal mental flaw. Mason's text concludes that by sharing that personal responsibility with a collective of masculine others in visiting the Vietnam War Memorial, one willfully can overcome the mental disability that prevents physical rehabilitation.

An embrace of masculine collectivity does not guarantee that the so-called flaws in the body will be overcome, however, according to some biographical and autobiographical narratives about or by veterans with disabilities. *Body Shop, Strong at the Broken Places*, and *Fortunate Son*, narratives of the lived experiences of amputees, problematize *In Country*'s conclusion, suggesting that the wounded body cannot be "overcome" by will alone, and it also cannot be "resisted." The implications of this problem for masculinities are significant: males "overcoming" their reluctant bodies infers adherence to traditional, or hegemonic forms of masculinity. Males "resisting" stigma and formulations of the "normal," as in Thomson's "narrative of resistance," infer a rejection of monolithic masculinity. Corinne Browne's oral narrative, *Body Shop* (1973), demonstrates the difficulties of either overcoming or resisting, or even Gerschick and Miller's more nuanced methods of rejection, reformulation, or reliance. The narrative simultaneously casts the disabled veterans as victimized by the War, by the system rehabilitating them, and by the society outside of the hospital, while it also positions them as trying to transcend or deny the effects of their disabled bodies on their gender. Conversely, Max Cleland's memoir, *Strong at the Broken Places* (1980), attempts to be a "narrative of resistance" as Cleland rejects and exceeds the typical expectations for a man with a disability. But his resistance to the dictates of the "normal" is through a born-again faith, a "spirituality" that Thomson assigns to the "narrative of overcoming," and what Gerschick and Miller would term "reformulation." Finally, Lewis B. Puller, Jr.'s autobiography, *Fortunate Son* (1991), struggles to construct a "narrative of resistance," both in terms of his body and of what loyalty to one's country means, requiring a rejection of his father's influence — of masculinity in its monolithic form — to achieve that resistance. All three texts portray men with severe disabilities struggling mentally to sustain the ideals of monolithic masculinity and realizing that masculinity is a physical performance requiring bodily configurations which they no longer have.

The ironically named *Body Shop* exemplifies a hierarchy of disability as it narrates the lives of several enlisted patients on the amputee ward at Letterman Army Hospital in San Francisco from 1970 to 1971.[11] All of the enlisted men are junior enlisted, not non-commissioned officers, so they are probably very young. It is common knowledge that, while the average age for World War II enlisted was 26, the average age for those in Vietnam was 19. Thus, the men being interviewed may not even have been able to drink alcohol in some states, and also may have the views of very young men scalded by war. As Christian Appy says in *Working-Class War* (1993), "America's most unpopular war was fought primarily by the nineteen-year-old children of waitresses, factory workers, truck drivers, secretaries, firefighters, carpenters, custodians, police officers, salespeople, clerks, mechanics, miners, and farmworkers: people whose work lives are not only physically demanding but in many cases physically dangerous" (7). This is the case for all of the enlisted men interviewed for *Body Shop*; they are all from working class (or lower) families. Charles Moskos also points out in *The American Enlisted Man* (1970) a significant age discrepancy between officer and enlisted which can be accounted for by their relative educational levels (42–43).

Among these enlisted men, *Body Shop* focuses on "Woody," a white, red-haired, blue-eyed double amputee who represents the inarticulate state of most of the enlisted patients as he finds it impossible to separate his mental state from his physical condition. His story works as a contrast to those of some officer staff members: Doctor Stanley Filarsky, the chief of the ward without a known disability; Lieutenant Anders, the psychiatric nurse without a known disability in charge of the Encounter Group Program for amputees; and Chaplain Cherry, a chaplain who is a single amputee as the result of Vietnam combat. Author Browne's account suggests that the enlisted patients are less capable of articulating their new relationship to masculinity than the staff. But the "inability" of the enlisted men to voice their anguish and the "ability" of the officers to speak it is contingent on Browne's mediation of what the men say, when they say it and what ultimately appears in the text. Leigh Gilmore points out in *The Limits of Autobiography* (2001) that narrative has come to be regarded as a powerful force for healing in psychiatric research (7, n. 13), and served as the impetus for many encounter groups after the War.[12] The reader must keep in mind that, even though Browne's recordings reveal actual experience, they are not "pure" experience; they are representations. The text argues that the men who are wounded and enlisted are, as Elaine Scarry suggests, muted by their pain, and the unwounded men, officers, are fully intelligible. *Body Shop* immediately reflects a disability hierarchy: the amputees are watched as they lounge on the terrace by Captain Morrill, the amputee ward's head nurse, who comments on the growing health of the men. Juxtaposed to Morrill's comment on the growing health of the amputees, however, are the complaints of the other staff members about their difficulties with the paraplegic patients, and Morrill's loaded observation about the men who were made paraplegic from the War: "Thank God they're not on this ward.... They're interesting patients, though" (11). Only the staff see paraplegia as worse than amputation, though, since Woody says nothing is worse than amputation: "People don't look at you as strangely if you have limbs. People think the loss of both legs is the worst. They don't even think paraplegics are grotesque. It [amputation] freaks them out" (119). Woody lays the power to interpret bodies on non-disabled "people." Another patient, Mike Tyson, agrees, but suggests that those "people" outside cannot be trusted with such a power: "Shit, I've got so I think people with two feet are strange looking" (56). When Lester is required to move to another ward, since his wounds have healed and he needs to be readied to leave the hospital, he complains he is being moved to the "loony bin" where there is "no one" left (142). While there is debate about whether amputation or paralysis is worse, to all men mental impairment is the lowest of all disabilities: those who experience it are nonentities, "no-ones."

What might invalidate the opposition of officer, non-disabled=articulate//enlisted, disabled=inarticulate, however, is that Chaplain Cherry, the man *most* expressive about masculinity, disability, and their troubled interactions, is both an officer and a man with a disability. Chaplain Cherry identifies with the officers as a chaplain and with the enlisted as a man with a prosthetic leg. This unique position, where he is neither totally invested in being an officer and a medical person nor in being a man with a disability, ironically renders his ideas about masculinity and disability the most credible. Though the tenor of the enlisted narrative generally is one of overcoming the weaknesses of the *body* in order to resume normal masculine identification, and the tenor of the officers generally is one of overcoming the weaknesses of the *mind* to do so, Chaplain Cherry's narrative is one that resists altogether "normal" masculinity. In recognition of multiple forms of masculinities, Cherry rejects Thomson's "overcoming" and "resistance," and espouses Gerschick and Miller's "reformulation."

All the enlisted men feel conflicted about the War, since if the War is regrettable and meaningless, so are the physical losses they incurred as the War's outcome. This conflict is epitomized by Woody as paradoxical and sometimes contradictory notions of masculinity, when he both identifies with the traditional roles of heroic, monolithic masculinity and also recognizes the hazard of that performance. Ultimately, Woody cannot fully reject masculinity, but finds to continue performing it he must retire from society and the powerful definitions it imposes on his body. As a Ranger in the Army, Woody had been the model of heroic masculinity: white, self-sufficient, active, and powerful. He discounts that model, however, claiming that "playing hero can get you killed," as though heroism only can be either a performance or the climax of masculine behavior, not both (46). Having had both legs severed by a North Vietnamese grenade, the text intimates that Woody ought to be bitter. But he is, above all, thankful to be alive: "Wanting to live takes over everything" (97). Woody believes this positive thinking helps him to "overcome" the strictures of his refigured body, but realizes after leaving the hospital that its environment had facilitated his recovery, where "we were even more [than in combat] in the same boat" (180). The unaccommodating environment outside of the hospital assails Woody's sunny attitude; to have this wounded body now means that "[p]eople [without disabilities] think we can't do so many things. They think our lives are ruined" (175). The markings that Woody wears involuntarily on his body circumscribe his ability to function as a self-determining masculine male, and what he dislikes most is the ableist notion that he needs compensatory federal assistance. Voicing accommodationist and, I would argue, masculinist beliefs of self-determinism, Woody says: "I don't want people to get me a job. I want to get it myself. I want to compete equally. Don't hire me because I'm a vet and I lost my legs. I don't dig people feeling sorry for me" (177). Ultimately, Woody buys a house in the California mountains and becomes a photographer, enacting his desire to overcome his new body by living the life of a rugged, masculine frontiersman. That he can only reformulate his masculinity largely outside of societal definitions suggests that he cannot overcome the mental disability incurred by his physical disability. The health of his mind, in other words, is dependent on readings of his body as masculine, something "people" cannot do.

Paul, another enlisted man, regrets how the War and the Army made him an "animal" and wants to become "normal" again (63). Though he lost his leg after being thrown from and run over by an armored personnel carrier (APC), Paul is thankful not to have lost his mind, and actually sees himself as having benefited psychologically from his Vietnam experience. "I might have lost my leg, but I sure didn't lose my mind. I got a lot of wisdom over there. I've changed a lot. I used to get paranoid. Upset over things over there and worry, now I don't. Everyday things don't bother me as much now. I always thought of myself as a boy. After being there I felt like a man" (78). Paul would have been more distraught had he suffered a mental disability, since that would have prevented him from regaining the normalcy he claims to have had before going into the service. However, Paul speaks as though that "normal" boy identity he wants to reclaim was reliant on heterosexual sex. Thus, on the one hand he desires to return to his pre–Army self, but on the other hand he realizes that some of that is unachievable and so denies its worth. In other words, he no longer equates masculinity with heterosexual genital activity because, as he sees it, the latter is far less likely to happen now that he is absent a leg. "There's more to life than going to bed with every woman you see and drinking. I have a lot of friends now because my attitude is different. A person can't figure me out when he first meets me. I'm going to be more of myself than before." At the same time Paul "overcomes" his body as he invests in his mind, his attitude, his sanity, and his libidinal and alcohol abstinence, he also indicts his body and not the environment as responsible for what he claims is, using the language of the 1970s, his "handicap" (77). To Paul, his new masculinity is wholly dependent on his mind and not his body, but paradoxically, he cannot "overcome" the body which determines how his mind can operate.

Unlike the enlisted men with disabilities, the officers in *Body Shop* are explicit about two things, the impact of bodily wounding on masculinity and whether disability is the outcome of a personal flaw or the conditions of war. Doctor Filarsky, the able-bodied doctor in charge of all amputees, believes that the men need to reconstruct their masculinities physically, viewing life in a wheelchair as a failure. He organizes sporting opportunities such as golf, skiing, and basketball, stating that one of the staff's goals is "to prepare them for the change" from the hospital conditions to those outside the hospital. Filarsky recognizes that the physical change to the patients' bodies also requires mental rehabilitation, since the two forms of disability are interrelated: "Some of them will walk extremely well and will have full lives, others will stay in their wheelchairs" (38). The implication of the latter clause is that, while the physical wounds of the men are similar, how they affect the veterans' lives is all a matter of choice; either one chooses to have a full life or one chooses not to have a full life. One either simulates a coherent, masculine body by walking with prostheses or one fails at life. Though Filarsky understands the world outside of the hospital will be physically unaccommodating to the men, he wants the men to alter their attitudes about masculinity rather than attempt to alter the hostile environment. Filarsky's stance is that the recovery of masculinity can only be total: *either* one recovers the ability to and participates in sports *or* one lives a pathetic and unfulfilled life in a wheelchair.

Lieutenant Anders, who is in charge of arranging and leading encounter groups on the ward, is vocal about equating woundedness with moral and psychic failure, regarding the enlisted patients as personally responsible for their wounds because even before they were injured they had not been able to meet the standards of masterful masculinity. He characterizes the men with amputations as being destined to arrive at Letterman. According to Anders, they are from economically poor backgrounds; they have had bad family lives; they have low intelligence quotients (IQ) and have had poor educations; and they are naturally irresponsible people, "the kind of people who get into accidents — like car and motorcycle accidents — or, in combat, they're the ones who step on mines because they're not paying attention" (105). As a psychiatric nurse, Anders wants the men to accept their personal responsibility for their disabilities. "It's easy to blame the war," he argues, "but there haven't really been that many casualties in this war, partly because of our excellent medevac service, and there is a low instance of mental casualties in this war. Often a man is to blame for his injury and that's a hard thing to face" (106). According to this logic, to recover from one's wounds requires an admission not only that one caused them, but also that one could not help causing them. In other words, masculinity of any sort is already unachievable for those whose fate is to become amputees, as masculinity requires the ability to determine one's own life course and the fated amputation makes that impossible.

Chaplain Cherry reflects the thinking of the early Disability Rights Movement and the Feminist Movement as he overtly addresses the specific problems of masculinity in an amputee, suggesting that the problem of readjustment is not totally in the man's body, nor in his mind, but is also in his social and material environment. As a man of religion, Cherry wants the patients to use religion to face their new bodies, but he also accepts that different physical conditions require different approaches. For instance, Cherry claims that masculinity is independence:

> It is easier for a cancer patient to relate to the usage of prayers and words because his immediate future is death. He needs something in his mind to give him strength. An amputee's immediate future is not death. His immediate future is masculinity. What concerns him is what he can do to rebuild his masculinity. Not God, because that would further give him dependence [47].

Thus, masculinity is neither inherent to a male body, nor does it occur the same way in bodies affected by varying illnesses. To Cherry, how masculinity is configured differently for amputees depends not just on altering the minds of the veterans with disabilities, as Filarsky and Anders imply, but also on altering the minds of people without disabilities, as "people" in Cherry's discourse implies both the disabled and the non-disabled. Cherry is accorded authority on this issue by the patients not only because he is, by profession, concerned for their welfare, as are Filarsky and Anders, but more because he also lost a leg while in Vietnam. "People can be so dumb. You know, whole people don't understand what we can do if we accept what we are and what we have to work with. Girls, wives of amputees, come to me and talk about their sexual fears and worries. I tell them, 'If you love him you'll overlook his little mishap'" (54). For Cherry, then, masculinity and disability are parallel constructs, and to reconstruct masculinity requires a change of attitude about masculinity both in the person embodying the disability *as well as* those able-bodied or "whole" people in the disabled person's environment. The absence created by "the little mishap," then, becomes less significant to whether a man can enact a masculinity. This logic echoes that of disability rights scholar and activist Lennard Davis who, in his collection of essays published thirty years after Chaplain Cherry was given voice in *Body Shop*, claims:

> We might say that disability is a postmodern identity because, although one may somatize disability, it is impossible to essentialize it the way one can the categories of gender or ethnicity. That is, although disability is "of" the body, it is much more "of" the environment which can create barriers to access and communication [*Bending* 86].

Cherry's attitude anticipates the move away from compensation for the wounds of battle and toward the accommodations needed to make it possible for people with disabilities to decide how to live their lives. While Cherry does not urge the men with disabilities to resist the normalized masculinity that Rosemarie Garland-Thomson refers to in the "narrative of resistance," he does advocate for changing attitudes and conditions outside of the hospital environment. However, the text also makes clear that, though the enlisted men believe and respect Cherry, his position as a non-medical officer compromises his ability to effect such changes.

Body Shop suggests that non-disabled male medical officers like Filarsky and Anders have the power to define what it means to be disabled and masculine: to them the condition of being disabled and masculine is always a personal, not a social dilemma. This attitude of wholly personal responsibility may be inherent to Filarsky and Anders' status as officers, as officers generally are given more responsibility than junior enlisted men. It is important at this point, then, to examine first-hand accounts of disability written by officers as they struggle against the social scripts of monolithic and heroic masculinity to refigure gender by identifying their bodies with ideas or objects rather than other bodies. Both authors, Max Cleland and Lewis B. Puller, Jr., report similar injuries occurring in 1968, as Cleland was wounded by a grenade and Puller by a booby-trapped artillery round. They experienced above-the-knee amputations of both legs and severe wounds to their upper bodies, with Cleland losing an arm and Puller losing parts of both hands. Though their wounds are similar, their stories are not. Cleland's 1980 "narrative of overcoming" reflects the budding born-again Christian movement during the late 1970s and early 1980s.[13] Meanwhile, Puller's 1991 "narrative of resistance" reflects revisions of the Vietnam War experience, such as the post–Gulf War 1991 claim by President George H. W. Bush that the Vietnam Syndrome had been defeated, and anticipates the 1995 confessional by former Secretary of Defense Robert McNamara, *In Retrospect*. Both texts include photographs of the writers, relying on a visual rhetoric to reinforce the narrative sculpting of their readers' responses to their masculinities. Published more than a decade apart and many, many years after the conclusion of the war, the accounts of Cleland and Puller become historical documentation of changing attitudes about the War, about disability, and about masculinity.

Very few autobiographical texts have been published by physically disabled Vietnam veterans, yet the few that have been generally are written by men with amputations, not paraplegia.[14] This fact confounds Starr's 1973 figures that say three times as many paraplegics as amputees were discharged from active duty for disability, and supports the idea that the more visible a disability is, the more likely it is to evoke pity and sympathy from those without disabilities. Though physiological reasons may explain why fewer texts are composed by veterans with paraplegia than with amputation, I also believe that culturally amputation is more troubling to masculinity than is paralysis. That is, paralysis does not immediately suggest a tragic loss, as does amputation; paralysis suggests total loss, whereas amputation suggests partial loss. Paradoxically, the partial loss signifies a greater tragedy because it is ambiguous about a man's ability to be masculine sexually, whereas paralysis is (seemingly) unambiguous about that ability.[15]

Max Cleland's memoir is a "narrative of overcoming"; how Cleland "overcomes" his bodily limitations, however, is not ultimately a matter of personally resolving to reconstruct his masculinity but of reliance on and surrender to his God. In short, with born-again Christianity, Cleland elides the issue of gender altogether, constructing what I term a "spiritual masculinity." *Strong at the Broken Places* was published in 1980, three years after newly-elected President Jimmy Carter had appointed Cleland as director of the Veterans Administration.[16] The memoir concludes with Cleland in that position, so it covers nearly two decades, from 1963, when Cleland is a college student visiting the White House, through his initial training as an officer in the Signal Corps, his 1967 arrival in Vietnam, and his experience in April 1968 of the siege of Khe Sanh, when he experiences "traumatic amputation" as he picks up what might be his own armed grenade. It continues with his rehabilitation in the "Snake Pit" at Walter Reed Army Hospital in Washington, D.C., where he learns to walk with prosthetic legs after having been hospitalized for fourteen months.[17] Formally discharged from active duty, Cleland becomes a patient of the Veterans Administration, and, outraged by his shoddy care, testifies before Senator Alan Cranston's Labor and Public Welfare Subcommittee on Veterans' Affairs in December, 1969.[18] That appearance launches Cleland's political career, as he campaigns for and wins a seat in the Georgia state senate in 1970 and a second term in 1972. During this period, when Jimmy Carter is governor of Georgia, Cleland institutes several pieces of legislation favoring Vietnam veterans and, after a failed attempt in 1974 to become Georgia's lieutenant governor and campaigning for Senator Alan Cranston's reelection bid in 1975, he accepts a staff position on the U.S. Senate Veterans' Affairs Committee. Less than two years later, Carter appoints Cleland head of the Veterans Administration and, after several tumultuous years there, Cleland's memoir concludes.[19]

Strong at the Broken Places was published by Chosen Books, a Christian publishing house established in 1971 by editors of *Guideposts*, Norman Vincent Peale's magazine committed to "communicating positive, faith-filled principles for people everywhere to use in successful daily living" (*Guideposts*).[20] A footnote in the final chapter indicates the memoir was "based on an article which appeared in the October 1978 issue of *Guideposts*" (151). Cleland's text, therefore, is less a paean to the fortitude of a masculine man, "living life to the fullest" by overcoming his physical impairment, and more about his growing faith in a Christian God who caused that "healing." Though Cleland briefly mentions over the course of the memoir that he is a lapsed Christian, fourteen pages from the end of the 156-page memoir he has a born-again experience as he drives up Interstate 95. Cleland uses that "encounter" to color everything that had preceded it since he was wounded: "But the glow within me remained. And with it came a revelation. Though I had departed from God, He had never abandoned me. Though I had ignored Him, He continued to love me. And now when I had reached out to Him, He came to me — right here on Interstate 95" (145). It is not until that moment that Cleland intimates he has been unable to deal with his physical trauma, having painted himself as a daringly masculine "master of my fate" (18), even as he chooses to use a wheelchair instead of the terribly painful prosthetic legs (134). The born-again chapter represents both the climax and conclusion of the narrative, and yet his conversion is so abrupt and spontaneous an occurrence that it is hard to see its coloring the story preceding it.

Thus, instantaneously, Cleland transfers the responsibility for overcoming the physical impairments that his amputations caused from his personal desire to reclaim his masculinity to his Christian God. For instance, in the final chapter, Cleland tells a story which has become lore — of how he persuaded a desperate and sick veteran to release a VA doctor the veteran had been holding hostage.[21] Simultaneous to representing himself heroically for having the language to talk the vet down, Cleland also disavows personal responsibility: "Reason hadn't worked. Logic hadn't worked. Appeals hadn't worked. A simple touch of common humanity had broken down the barriers. The right words had come because I depended on the truth I discovered that dark, rainy night on Interstate 95, outside Richmond: God is always there — especially when we need him most" (155). Concluded as it is, to some power outside of himself which governs his life, Cleland's narrative becomes a "narrative of overcoming" the constraints of his new body through spirituality. It differs from the other narratives of overcoming I have already discussed from *Body Shop*, however, in that, though the narrative is always about overcoming a recalcitrant body, Cleland rejects the "machismo" that had driven him to simulating a "normal" body by wearing prosthetic legs. He does not reject masculinity per se, however. Rather than a fuller dependence on his own resilience and a rejection of the environment that deems his body as abnormal, making his a "narrative of resistance," Cleland replaces masculine self-sufficiency and mastery with a born-again "spiritual masculinity." That is, he does not submit entirely to the will of his God, but he will use his God at opportune moments. Rosemarie Garland-Thomson claims that, culturally, disability signifies a violated, un-whole, feminized body (*Extraordinary* 45). As long as Cleland purports to handle his life independently, then, he is subject to such violation: he can fall down, he can be unable to pick himself up, and he will have only himself to blame. The addition of a God who can appear with aid at any time minimizes the possibilities of such violation.

In addition to the religious discourse illuminating Cleland's attitudes towards his masculinity is a visual rhetoric. A photograph of Cleland, appended to the chapter published in *Guideposts* magazine, encourages the reader to gaze on Cleland's body and to understand him in ways the narrative is unable to convey. The photo resembles a professional government portrait, as Cleland is clothed in a three-piece suit and poses outdoors in front of a large "Veterans Administration" sign. What suggests this is not a formal photo, however, are several details pertaining to Cleland's body. The environment is "normal," but rather than seeing a standing man with an unsmiling face, the viewer sees Cleland in a wheelchair with empty trouser legs, a broad smile on his face and waving with his left arm. The visibility of the wheelchair and of Cleland's missing limbs are counterbalanced by the smile and waving, suggesting a friendliness atypical of formal government photos and, more importantly, an effort to draw attention away from the empty trouser legs and empty jacket arm and towards Cleland's welcoming face and gesture. "Visual images," claims Garland-Thomson, "especially photographic images, of disabled people act as rhetorical figures that have the power to elicit a response from the viewer" ("Seeing the Disabled" 339). In this case, Cleland is demonstrating the ability of the disabled body to conform to a "normal" environment while simultaneously living a fulfilled and happy life. There is no evidence in the photo of the presence of Cleland's God, but the photo's being appended to the chapter appearing in a faith-based magazine causes the reader to draw one conclusion: Cleland has overcome the disabilities of traumatic amputation through the grace of God, at the same time that he has retained a masculinity which encourages gazing yet discourages the stigmatized position of being stared at. As Garland-Thomson puts it, "the disabled figure in western culture is the to-be-looked-at rather than the to-be-embraced" (340). With God augmenting his position (as told in the narrative) as director of the Veterans Administration (as told by the photograph), Cleland can surmount his disabilities by redefining his masculinity as a disembodied spiritual one, a situation that does not require personal responsibility, an alteration of the physical environment or a fear of mental disability.

Published a decade later, Lewis B. Puller, Jr.'s 1992 Pulitzer Prize–winning *Fortunate Son* (1991) reflects an altered national attitude about the Vietnam War, an attitude that, post–PTSD, had become much more accepting of the mental turmoil many veterans felt after Vietnam. It also reflects "monumental masculinity," as Puller's identification with the Vietnam Veterans Memorial is what, at least temporarily, helps him to overcome the gender anguish he feels after losing both his legs.[22] Puller's memoir recounts his descent into alcoholism many years after his tour of duty as a Marine combat officer, and it is his guilt and depression over the War he must overcome to live a fuller life, not the hubris Cleland battled.[23] Unlike Cleland, whose nemesis from childhood was his own driving ambition, Puller's was the driving ambition of his father, the paragon of manly Marines, "Chesty" Puller of World War II and Korea fame. As Chesty's only son, Lewis felt pressured to become a Marine and to abide by the "calling," to fulfill a "destiny," and to embrace the "obligation" conferred on him by his father. Only days before Puller experiences his traumatic October 1968 wounding, he realizes that he does not want a career in the military, presaging the incident that will ensure his inability to have a military career. Facing alone six or seven North Vietnamese Army soldiers, Puller runs away and detonates a booby-trapped artillery round (184). That he could not be his father's heroically masculine son in the scene of battle torments Puller as much as the loss of both legs: "I came to feel that I had failed to prove myself worthy of my father's name, and broken in spirit as well as body, I was going to have to run a different gauntlet" (187).

Like Cleland, Puller endures months and months of rehabilitation, during which time his wife gives birth to their first child. While Cleland's first concern is about whether he will be able to walk (59), Puller's primary concern is for his genitalia (212). This matter of sexuality, which arises with some frequency in the first half of *Fortunate Son*, is never referred to in *Strong in the Broken Places*, a fact that might represent both the intended audiences of the two texts as well as the certainty on Puller's part that a 1991 reader would be more receptive to the image of a "sensitive" man who can simultaneously admit the "weaknesses" of his body and also claim the ability to "perform." As John D'Emilio and Estelle Freedman report in *Intimate Matters* (1997), it was the intersection of feminism, gay liberation, *Roe vs. Wade*, and pornography that fueled the resurgence of Cleland's 1980 morally conservative "born-again" audience (346). Sexuality, however, is especially pertinent to the person with a disability, who is often read as asexual. As a result, early in the narrative Puller protests that sexuality is still a significant element of his life, even when he also describes himself as "grotesque" (206) and "crippled and deformed" (277). Interestingly, his sexuality is connected to his new son, as he feels his first sexual urges when he sees his wife nursing the baby: "I was aroused and as much in need of Toddy as the baby at her breast" (209). The parallel between father and newborn son continues, as Puller describes the corresponding developments in his male child and in his own recovery and rehabilitation. This discourse suggests not only a man who sensitively discovers an integral connection with his child. It also asserts Puller's willingness to dispel "popular notions of disabled masculinity [that] focus obsessively on perceived impotence and lack of manhood" (Shakespeare et al. 97) by "reformulating" masculinity on his own terms (Gerschick and Miller 458).

But the discourse of sexuality drops from Puller's narrative once his wounds heal, he is able to concentrate on his physical rehabilitation, and he begins to drive. This attention to his own recovery and away from the developments of his firstborn signal his ability to reclaim the prerogatives of a man, to which his wife agrees: "From the beginning of my driving I always felt less helpless and more like a man when I was at the wheel, and Toddy, sensing my need to be in control, was always willing to let me drive" (267). Thus, Puller's "reformulation" of masculinity is contradictory, as he desires to be a sensitive man but also feels the conflicting urges to be "like a man" and "in control." Puller's new masculinity is also assaulted by his growing sense that he had been used by his country, and that "I had lost my legs and several good friends for nothing" (291). So Puller feels that within the bounds of his immediate family he may "reformulate" his masculinity, but in terms of his country and in terms of the paragon of masculinity, the military that wants to discharge him from active duty to save money, he feels "alienated and separate" (272). Puller then resorts to alcohol to dull the anguish of the conflict between these two venues for masculinity, even as he completes law school. But he cannot rid himself of the idea that, through loyalty to the traditional model of masculinity his father had represented, Puller had been complicit in the conduct of an unscrupulous war: "I felt used up and discarded, and as I tried to dispel with alcohol the magnitude of the obscene fraud of which I had been a willing victim, I was assailed by conflicting and unresolved emotions" (308). Puller's pre-disability "willingness" had been motivated by an adherence to his father's model of monolithic masculinity that required mastery, decisiveness, domination of women, and physical strength, but also loyalty to male peers and, by extension, to one's government. When Puller discovers that all of those qualities still must be accessed and he no longer has the tools — his legs, but also how they signified what it meant to be manly — to access them, he despairs. Having tried and failed to reformulate his public masculinity, Puller grieves because it is the only model of non–domestic masculinity he knows succeeds.

After Puller serves on President Ford's Clemency Board in 1974 and 1975, works for the Paralyzed Veterans of America, campaigns for and loses a seat in the U.S. Congress representing Virginia (1978), gains a position as general counsel in the Department of Defense, and admits his alcoholism, he follows in the media the development of plans for and building of the Vietnam Veterans Memorial in Washington, D.C. Just as Puller saw parallels between his initial recovery and rehabilitation and his infant son's development, so does he see a parallel between his recovery from alcoholism and the progress of the memorial:

> As my recovery [from alcoholism] progressed, I focused my attention more sharply on events leading to the construction of the memorial, and in a sense I came to believe that its progress and my own progress were twin facets of a divine plan and not mere circumstance. The healing process that was at work within me, I felt, also inhabited the granite and concrete that were going to take form in the memorial, and I was immensely hopeful about what was taking place [421].

Ironically, what I am calling Puller's "monumental masculinity" results in his identification with a memorial whose design had been severely contested as a gendered "black gash of shame and sorrow" and, more evocatively, as a vaginal counterpoint to the Washington Memorial's phallus. Tom Hudson, one of the characters with a disability in *In Country* (1985), reflects this attitude when he suggests to Sam such a comparison: "A big black hole in the ground, catty-cornered from that big white prick." But then Tom follows his derogatory comment about both the Vietnam Veterans Memorial and the Washington Monument with "Fuck the Washington Monument. Fuck it" (80). This indictment of memorials per se, but of the Washington Monument especially, confounds Tom's gendering of the two memorials, since a reader expects Tom, who is confused about and frustrated by his own altered sexuality, to be antagonistic towards the vaginal/feminine/passive Vietnam Veterans Memorial, not the phallic/masculine/active Washington Monument. Yet Tom's comment also reflects an alteration or "reformulation" of what it means to be masculine as he identifies more closely with the "big black hole in the ground" than with the "big white prick."

Fred Turner also cites this gendered attitude about the Wall:

> [E]x-soldiers and civilians alike saw the Memorial [Jan] Scruggs had intended to honor veterans as a black granite symbol for the entire Vietnam War. Some called its V-shaped wall a peace sign. Others saw it as a vagina set to match the phallic Washington Monument (a cultural articulation of the belief that American soldiers in Vietnam "got screwed by Washington") [179].

Turner discusses the controversy over the memorial's differences from those for other wars, attributing the main difference to the degree of activity the memorials display: "The big-chested vigor of the men on the Marine Corps Memorial [the Iwo Jima flag-raising memorial] or the Seabees Monument reminds a viewer that America actively — vigorously — waged the Second World War. Looking at the names on the wall, on the other hand, a visitor might think that the Vietnam War was a plague that befell Americans against their will" (241). The language Turner uses to describe the memorials signifies *masculine* displays of *activity* in the World War II models and *feminine* displays of inactivity or *passivity* in the Vietnam memorial. Even referring to the memorial as a "wall" suggests a quotidian, as opposed to monumental, nature of the structure. Puller's identification with the memorial reflects similar gender ambiguity, especially because Puller expects the identification to make him whole/masculine, but in a new way.

The visual rhetoric of the 16 photographs included in Puller's text confirms this altered gender state. Included are a few pictures of Puller as a boy, and two during his pre-wound military days. Several depict Puller, always a thin man but now skeletal, shortly after he had been returned to the United States. One photo in particular reinforces the legacy of masculinity bequeathed by his father, as three generations of male Pullers pose together: Puller is in uniform, holding his infant son, while "Chesty" stands behind the wheelchair in dress uniform. More images follow, confirming that Puller was, indeed, a political figure: as a Clemency Board member, with President Gerald Ford in 1975; on the telephone during his unsuccessful 1978 run for Congress; in 1978, at the White House with President Jimmy Carter; at the 1983 Marine Corps ball, as Puller cuts the cake; in front of the Vietnam Veterans Memorial in 1991; and, finally, in an easy chair, casually dressed in shorts and T-shirt and surrounded by his family.

In "Seeing the Disabled: Visual Rhetorics of Disability in Popular Photography," Garland-Thomson outlines four "rhetorical figures that have the power to elicit a response from the viewer" (339). Suggesting that images of disabled people are almost always from the perspective of the non-disabled spectator, she names these four rhetorical categories "the wondrous," "the sentimental," "the exotic," and "the realistic" (341–344). Because Thomson singles out "the sentimental" and "the exotic" as appeals typically used for garnering financial contributions, I examine here how "the wondrous" and "the realistic" work in the Cleland and Puller images to reconstruct their masculinities, as both modes reflect the standards of control and physical strength expected of male masculinity. The "wondrous" image emphasizes the extraordinary accomplishments of what Garland-Thomson refers to as the "supercrip," or the disabled person who physically accomplishes feats such as climbing a mountain in a wheelchair. The (able-bodied) viewer is positioned at a distance to look up in awe at "difference framed as distinction" (340). "The rhetorical purpose of this contemporary figure," she contends, "is less to humble viewers who imagine themselves as nondisabled than to invoke the extraordinariness of the disabled body in order to secure the ordinariness of the viewer" (341). The securing of "ordinariness" simultaneously is engaged in establishing what are the current, culturally accepted gender modes or, in this case, masculinity. Normal, monolithic masculinity, in other words, is in the "ordinary" viewer, and the "supercrip" deviates from that normalcy. Garland-Thomson's "realistic" mode, on the other hand, minimizes the distance between viewer and viewed in order to create a relation of sameness. As Garland-Thomson puts it, "The rhetoric of the realistic trades in verisimilitude, regularizing the disabled figure in order to encourage a nonhierarchical identification between seer and seen" (344). Like Mary Anne in O'Brien's "Sweetheart of the Song Tra Bong" discussed in Chapter Two, this category appears to diminish difference through a semblance of sameness, all the while maintaining difference. While popularly both Cleland and Puller would be read as masculine because they are men, and because they both are men with amputations in wheelchairs they would be read as less masculine, Garland-Thomson's model helps us to discriminate between the masculinities constructed by their images, with the "wondrous" mode applying to Puller's and the "realistic" mode applying to Cleland's.

    The photo of Puller in front of the Vietnam Veterans Memorial most closely approximates the single photo included in Max Cleland's text. Puller is dressed in a dark, pin-striped suit and has his hands in his lap. His hair, which is dark and slightly long, is brushed to one side, and he looks sternly through his wire-framed glasses at the camera, as one side of his face is cast in shadow. Puller is situated at the apex of the memorial, but the shot is taken from such an angle that the viewer can see, receding in the distance, one full side of the two-sided monument with its thousands of engraved names. Like Cleland, Puller is not passively posed; his arms are bent and his hands are poised as though waiting for a signal from his brain to spring into action. At eye level of the non-disabled viewer, Cleland's "realistic" image asks viewers to identify with his spiritual masculinity, as he diverts our attention away from his empty trouser legs and wheelchair and towards his smiling face and waving arm. Puller, on the other hand, looks down on the viewer from his viewpoint of monumental masculinity, daring us not to look at his "incomplete" body as it fills nearly the entire frame, or at the names on the wall behind him. While Cleland's smile works to minimize the mark of disability and thereby to assure the viewer that what is being looked at is as "normal" as the viewer, Puller's gaze indicts viewers who are not like those depicted, either those severely wounded, like himself, or those dead whose names are on the Wall. In this sense, then, Puller physically demonstrates his newly formulated masculinity in an environment that has altered to accommodate him, while Cleland insists that no physical change to the environment is necessary.[24] Refusing to be the stereotypical stared-at disabled man who is regarded as passive, indecisive, and inactive, Puller obdurately suggests his dominance and self-determination, seeming to dare the viewer to regard him as otherwise.

As autobiographical texts, Cleland's *Strong at the Broken Places* and Puller's *Fortunate Son* focus more on the writers than on the environments in which they live. But because Puller's text was not aimed at the born-again Christian audience Cleland's was, and because Puller's text was published during a period when it had become more acceptable for veterans to voice their criticism of the War and for advocates of people with disabilities to be openly critical of policies and people obstructing disability rights, his text is forthcoming about both those issues. The result is that, unlike Cleland, Puller is not content to be the silent, normal disabled man, and so his text challenges the gender status quo. Vietnam War fiction sometimes engages in a similar endeavor. Unlike films of the War which often depict veterans with disabilities as the angry activist or the defeated and despairing man in a wheelchair,[25] Vietnam War fiction's rare moments of foregrounding disability as a significant outcome of the war indict the cultural mores that locate disability as the result of a personal flaw and underscore the corruption of the "normal." As these few texts spotlight the constructedness of disability, they both problematize traditional enactments of masculinity and also challenge the ease with which reformulation, reliance, or rejection can occur, as they attempt to account for the historically ambiguous feelings towards the War itself. Unlike the depictions of previous wars, disabled men of Vietnam War narratives rarely can be reassimilated, not only because the communities refuse their re-entry, but largely because the men with disabilities refuse personal responsibility for their disabilities, creating a tension between the men with disabilities and the society that created the conditions where disability was possible.

As one of the few canonical pieces of Vietnam War literature foregrounding disability, Larry Heinemann's *Paco's Story* (1986) portrays fictionally what has been manifest thus far in all of the texts analyzed in this chapter: a visual trope that defines masculinity. According to Gerschick, disability is falsely judged by its visibility ("Toward" 254); according to Judith Butler, gender is also subject to inaccurate judgements based on its visibility (*Gender Trouble* xxiii). Heinemann's text uses a visibly marked disabled male character to denote the outlines of *non*-disabled American society, thus accentuating the social nature of disability and masculinity. Published in the mid–1980s, this novel anticipates the changing concept of disability from medical to social model, implying that disability is not limited to those with marked bodies or "un-wholeness." As I have demonstrated in my previous two chapters, where the dominant race and dominant sexuality define the terms of value, it is not the undervalued races or sexualities that need exploring, it is the race and sexuality of the subjects defining the terms that especially require analysis. Jenny Morris claims in "Gender and Disability," "It is not disabled people who have defined the experience, neither have they had control over medical treatment or the social consequences of impairment. Thus, if disability is to be made sense of, it is the non-disabled society and its institutions which should be the subject of study" (87). In the remainder of this chapter, then, I examine how Heinemann's fiction uses a disabled figure to indict monolithic notions of American masculinity.

When it features disabled characters, Vietnam War fiction employs the disabled figure to indict the complacent vision of American family values and to condemn the society at large that permitted its young men to be sent to war.[26] Told by everyone *but* Paco, *Paco's Story* illustrates how a physically and psychologically scarred veteran is muted and stigmatized in a prototypical American town, Boone, by a wide group of people who appear not to be marked by race, sexuality, or disability. But those who narrate Paco's story are only able to tell his story through their own life filters, so the disabled man's story is always secondary, marginalized, and evocative of the failure of American monolithic masculinity. *Paco's Story* features a character whose disabilities offer a way for the community to redeem itself from its gender prejudices and preconceptions, but the town finally cannot tolerate Paco's disruptive influence. Though Paco uses a cane, it is his scars, his haircut, and his "1,000-meter stare" that make him visible as a Vietnam veteran to various members of the community. This physically vulnerable and thus un-masculine position is reproduced narratively, as most of *Paco's Story* is related by everyone but him, including the ghosts of his dead Vietnam buddies, placing him out of control of his own life. Because it is popularly accepted that after the War its American veterans were treated poorly, one has to inquire why Paco needs to be physically distinguished; his status as a veteran alone already would have set him apart from non-veterans and would have evoked the same minimal degree of sympathy for his homelessness and joblessness. Perhaps the mark of disability as a narrative device is meant to secure a greater amount of compassion for Paco's plight. As signs of disability, however, Paco's scars are ambivalent, since they are not the unequivocally tragic markers of blindness or amputation.[27] Moreover, though Paco's wounds are the result of "friendly fire" and thus signals of his victimization, the external, visible markings are to the narrator the physical expressions of Paco's internal wound, the guilt and shame of his having participated in the gang rape and murder of a female member of the "Viet Cong" (173–185).[28]

In other words, Paco is marked physically for two complex and possibly contradictory reasons. First, the external, un-tragic wounds are meant to elicit and validate the already ungenerous attitudes of the early 1970s Boone townspeople toward Vietnam War veterans in general, who must be seen as responsible for their own pain. But the scars also put the 1986 reader, aware of PTSD, Agent Orange, the maltreatment of veterans by the Veterans Administration and the atrocity of My Lai in the uncomfortable position of understanding the causes for the atrocious gang rape and murder, and viewing Paco's scars as penance for such an act. As a penitent, Paco emblematizes the complexities of the lived experience of disabled masculinity. That he ultimately leaves Boone indicates that, as Gerschick asserts in "Sisyphus in a Wheelchair," a physically disabled man can only live outside of (apparently) non-disabled society. Paco's particular difficulties as a disabled veteran fall in the areas of "work, the body, athletics, sexuality, and independence and control" ("Sisyphus" 189) since the townspeople make it impossible for him to meet the standards of hegemonic masculinity as they are practiced in the prototypical American town.

Paco arrives by bus in a small town called Boone, a name evoking the pioneer and frontier spirit of American lore. He has spent the last of his money to travel as far as it will take him, and aims to get a job wherever he can, moving from small business to small business, where he finally is offered a job at the local greasy spoon. Two stories are being told, but they are equally prominent. The Boone setting opens the novel, but it and the Vietnam story together drive the narrative. Disabled and in constant pain as a result of his participation in the Vietnam War, Paco walks with a cane, is disfigured by the scars covering his body, and relies on prescription drugs and alcohol to dull his constant pain. Ultimately, Paco feels abjectified in Boone and leaves. The first story is narrated from the points of view of the townspeople by an omniscient narrator; the second story is a commentary on the "normalcy" of life in Boone, rendered by the ghosts of Paco's comrades in Vietnam as his memories and dreams. While in a firefight there, Paco's lieutenant called in firepower that killed all of the other eighty-some men in his company but left Paco wounded and lying on the battlefield for nearly two days. As a result of the burns, fragment injuries and surgeries to repair his body, Paco is left scarred and pinned together; memories scar his mind.

Though ostensibly the story is his, very little is revealed about Paco or his background. His anonymity lends itself to the tenor of the story in general, as Paco is a non-entity, a commodity, an object of pity and disgust, "a piece of meat on the slab," and emblematic of not just Vietnam War veterans, but especially Vietnam War veterans with disabilities who have been objectified and emasculated by their participation in the War. Aiming for an anonymity embodied by the nameless, homeless, and historyless Paco, the text does not reveal where Boone is located, is not forthcoming about Paco's last name or the location of his home, is ambivalent about who is the oft-referred to "James,"[29] and is vague about who is the narrator. Even Paco's Vietnam story is not, in fact, told by him; instead, it is told by the ghosts of the men from his company who were killed at Firebase Harriette. This ironic positioning of Paco as the object of the story, rather than the subject or even its narrator, places him in a powerless, unmasculine position. Even when Paco has in the past told his story, the telling is framed by the filters of the ghosts:

> He has dwelt on it with trivial thoroughness, condensed it, told it as an ugly fucking joke (the whole story dripping with ironic contradiction, and sarcastic and paradoxical bitterness); he's told it stone drunk to other drunks; to high-school buddies met by the merest chance (guys Paco thought he was well rid of, and never thought he'd see the rest of his natural life); to women waiting patiently for him to finish his telling so they could get him into bed, and see and touch all those scars for themselves. There's been folks to whom he's unloaded the whole nine yards, the wretched soul-deadening dread, the grueling, *grinding* shitwork of being a grunt (the bloody murder aside); how he came to be wounded, the miracle of his surviving the massacre — as good as left for dead, you understand, James [72–73].

A reader senses that perhaps both inner and outer stories are relayed by the ghosts, who construct the story less around Paco than around the way in which they continue to create his life through story. Not only do they control how Paco may be understood by other people, they also shape how he can imagine himself, through the stories of his dreams: "And when Paco is most beguiled, most rested and trusting, at that moment of most luxurious rest, when Paco is all but asleep, *that* is the moment we whisper in his ear, and give him something to think about—a dream or a reverie" (138). Consequently, Paco is silenced from telling his own story, reflecting what Simi Linton terms the "medicalization" of disability, where society "colludes to keep the issue within the purview of the medical establishment, to keep it a personal matter and 'treat' the condition and the person with the condition rather than 'treating' the social processes and policies that constrict disabled people's lives" (11). A "medicalized" reading of a disabled character de-centralizes him, except in so far as the character is the *object* of study. This is an unmasculine position, to be out of control of one's own story. Milton Bates echoes this logic when he says about *Paco's Story*: "Paco is not so much the subject of the story as he is an occasion for telling it. The 'story' in Heinemann's title refers to a process or a performance rather than a product. When we attend to the storytelling rather than the story told, character and plot become less important than the political drama played out between the narrators and their implied audience" (128). As long as Paco's story is told by everyone but him, he will be subject to their "treatment," and will not be seen as having any masculine control over his own life. But to suggest that the story is only or even largely about the narrator and his audience limits the agency of the character with a disability.

Paco lives a circumscribed life in Boone. He washes dishes in the Texas Lunch, a tiny diner, and lives in an 8'×10" room in the boarding hotel across the alley from the restaurant. He works every day of the week but Sundays from 6:00 A.M. until midnight, hobbles back to his room, takes his pain-killing medications and alcohol, and collapses into bed. He is an enigma to the townspeople, revealing nothing about his past except that he was "wounded in the war." The focus on Paco's work enables some critics, notably Milton Bates and Katherine Kinney, to read the text as one primarily concerned with work and social class, and others like Susan Jeffords to see the novel through the lens of gender. Bates draws a parallel between the "work of war" and the labor of the working class, and another parallel between menial labor and sodomy, both of which he calls "a form of sustained assault on mind and body" (122–123).[30] Susan Jeffords focuses on the gang rape and murder, claiming that the novel's primary theme is the destructive male collective at work in Vietnam War narratives, so that "individual violence in *Paco's Story* happens in only one direction, in the collective rape of women by men" (71). Kinney agrees with Bates that issues of social class pervade the novel, especially in terms of the rape scene: "What Paco reads on her [the victim's] body is not gender but class," as the memory of seeing her back echoes the pain of his own (169). But Kinney simultaneously allies her class argument with Jeffords' gender argument and argues against Jeffords as she reads the rape scene, moving her analysis from one about identification through social class to alienation through gender: "If, in general terms, the representation of the rape is emblematic of Heinemann's drive toward an embodied realism that seeks to destroy the comfortable images of familiar war stories, it is also a deliberate disruption of the gendered boundaries of those stories" (174). Though all of these critics treat Paco's body as a legible text, none of them reads it specifically as disabled, and so all are nearly locked into a singular position: his body can be read through the lens of social class or the lens of gender or the lens of a combination of social class and gender. But to follow Jenny Morris' prescription that non-disabled people be examined in order to understand how disability is constructed, I use Gerschick's outline of "work, the body, athletics, sexuality, and independence and control," focusing on everything but athletics to examine how Paco's disability influences the construction of his masculinity through his experiences with four presumably non-disabled characters: Ernest Monroe, Paco's employer (work); the aging woman on the bus (the body); Cathy, the college student who lives in the room next to Paco's (sexuality); and Jesse, the veteran and drifter (independence and control). That Paco's masculinity is constructed through these non-disabled characters demonstrates Jenny Morris' argument that disabled people have not been the ones to define their own experiences (87). Additionally, these relationships are founded on the visibility of Paco's external scars, not the scars inhabiting his mind, and so how Paco's masculinity is constituted by the non-disabled characters is dependent on whether they identify with, or "recognize" Paco.

When Paco arrives in town, he immediately begins looking for a job, work being the first of Gerschick's areas that are problematic for the construction of disabled masculinity. Paco apparently has been homeless for some time, and comments that he wants a steady job, not day labor (91). He has walked from place to place in the very small town, but is rejected by people who are unable to see past the signs of disability and their impact on his masculinity. Before arriving at the Texas Lunch diner, Paco first tries Elliot's Goods, a junk-cum-antiques store owned and operated by an aging Russian emigré who mistakes, rather than recognizes, Paco as a young Dmitri from his Russian Revolution days. After leaving that store, Paco walks to the barbershop. On his way, all of the people in the barbershop watch him and comment on his appearance, but once he is in the shop, they hardly acknowledge his presence. These are both instances of mistaken recognition, rather than recognition. When he enters the Texas Lunch, however, the owner, Ernest Monroe, a scarred World War II veteran, immediately "sees" Paco: "He watches Paco virtually burst in the place and make a straight wake for the middle of the counter. He fully recognizes Paco's 1,000-meter stare, that pale and exhausted, graven look from head to toe" (95). As a result of the recognition, Monroe offers Paco a job washing dishes, even though it means he will have to fire the man he already employs. Monroe offers Paco $2.25 an hour for his labor, more than he had paid the previous dishwasher who presumably was not a veteran, and before affirmative action for veterans was put into place with the Vietnam-era Veterans' Readjustment Assistance Act of 1974 and the Rehabilitation Act of 1973. Though Paco's situation might have been regarded as peculiar by the people of Boone, it appears to have been more typical than not. As Paul Starr points out, "those veterans who could least afford to be without work have been without it most often, and those who bore the largest share of the fighting in Vietnam have also borne more than their share of the economic dislocations at home" (201). According to the U.S. Department of Labor in 1975, disabled veterans were twice as likely to be unemployed as non-disabled veterans (5), and among disabled veterans, those with "neuropsychiatric disorders" had the most difficulty finding work (9). Furthermore, those veterans with low educational levels "have more difficulty finding a job, tend to become discouraged in their job search, and have to accept lower-paying jobs." The Department of Labor authors go on to point out that those most severely disabled with low educational levels have the most difficulty finding employment because the types of work for which their educational levels suit them — unskilled or semi-skilled labor — are also the ones most reliant on non-disabled bodies. The authors follow up by saying that "for veterans who are college graduates, we see that the employment effects of severe disability are minimal" (10). These conditions help to explain why Paco would be willing to take any kind of work offered: his physical disabilities and probable lack of education prohibit his being discriminating.

Monroe's ability to "see" Paco stems from Monroe's experiences and wounding on Guadalcanal and Iwo Jima, and is contingent on his being able to place his experiences within Paco's, to "see" Paco as an extension of his own past. While Monroe's recognition is initiated by a physical connection — he displays the scar from his belly wound — his recognition is based more on a psychic connection than a physical one. That is, Monroe recognizes the "1,000-meter stare" as the result not of the evident physical wounds on Paco's body, but of the psychic wounds that manifest themselves as the stare. Though Mr. Hennig, the town barber and apparently not a veteran, bitterly has lumped Paco into a group who "think you owe them something," Monroe's psychological recognition of Paco minimizes Paco's physical disabilities but marks his mental ones, which then places Paco at the bottom of the disability hierarchy. This un-masculine position evokes pity from Monroe, and so Paco is offered a job not because he is especially well-suited to it but because Monroe has recognized him.

The second area where Gerschick asserts disabled men cannot meet hegemonic masculinity's standards is "the body." Though Paco's body proves inadequate as a model of masculinity throughout the novel, one of the most notable instances of it occurs early in the novel when Paco's bus pulls into town and he and "a frail old black woman" (35) are the only passengers remaining. Drugged, Paco finds it difficult to rouse himself; the woman hugs "a dilapidated carpetbag crammed with odds and ends of knitting skeins, half-crocheted knickknacks, and a small polyethylene bag of warm plums" (35). There appears to be no connection between these two people. After Paco leaves the bus and it resumes its travels, however, this woman "recognizes" Paco:

> Then the old black woman — who's been snuggling up to her carpetbag, napping and daydreaming all afternoon — suddenly opens her eyes. She sees Paco for only an instant ..., his cane as thin as a pencil and his eyes the points of pins, and instantly, vividly remembers her own son coming home from the Korean War in nineteen and fifty-three, standing in the doorway of their old shotgun house in those baggy, travel-dirty khakis of his; who said not a word about the war; who was ever morose and skittish, what folks round miscalled lazy and no-'count; who had ever since lapsed into a deep and permanent melancholy [42].

This is another moment of what I call "recognition" or identification. As a black woman, this character is like Paco because both are outside the bounds of "normalcy," making it possible for her to "open her eyes" to Paco, but only in relation to his physical resemblance to her son returning from the Korean War.[31] That the son had participated in the Korean

War is significant, since that was a moment when black soldiers, like Vietnam War veterans, were stigmatized as between being fully integrated into and fully segregated from the Regular military.[32] It is the mental state enacted by Paco's body that the black mother recognizes; the woman sees him as a person related to her own son — not marked by physical disability — but damaged mentally by the toll of war. As with the diner owner, Paco's body is recognized for its mental difference, not a physical one.

Young white women do, however, read Paco physically, as a sexual object. The first example of this is Betsy Sherburne, who is in the Texas Lunch when Paco first enters and, fetishizing his scars, fantasizes getting him drunk and taking him to bed. Paco's allure is his scars: "She sees herself drawing on his scars as if they were Braille, as if each scar had its own story" (101). The fuller example, however, is Cathy, the college student who secretly watches Paco from her apartment window when he is at work. While Cathy's looking might be termed a reverse "gaze"— where instead of the dominant male's looking at and objectifying a woman, she is dominant and looking at him — this case is also a good example of what Rosemarie Garland-Thomson calls "the stare."[33] Though both gazing and staring are visual and thus based on the body, Thomson interprets the difference between the two as a matter of intensity and purpose. The male gaze "makes the normative female a [desirable] sexual spectacle," while the stare "sculpts the disabled subject into a grotesque spectacle" (*Extraordinary* 26). The two acts differ also in how much of the body is encompassed by the looks:

> Gazing — which has been highly theorized as the dominant visual relation in patriarchy between male spectators and female objects of their gaze — differs from staring in that it usually encompasses the entirety of the body, even as it objectifies and appropriates that body. Staring at disability, in contrast, intensely telescopes looking toward the physical signifier for disability ["Seeing" 347].

Cathy watches Paco from her darkened window for weeks before he sees her sexually "gazing" at various parts of his body, writing in her diary that he is "good-looking, with nice tight buns" (202). Cathy's language changes, however, when Paco spies her watching him and returns her look, after which Cathy refers to Paco as "the gimp" (148). Any recognition of Paco on Cathy's part ultimately is based on her ability to objectify him, just as she is objectified: "All those guys staring at me. The men teachers, too. Makes me feel like a piece of meat" (201). But ultimately Cathy regards her objectification by men at school as empowering, and it does not prohibit her from sexually objectifying Paco as she writes in her diary about his attractiveness and gazes at him from a distance. Moreover, she invites his gaze as she deliberately walks around her apartment with the lights on and hardly clothed, knowing Paco will see her, while secretly she observes Paco with the lights in her apartment turned off. When Paco first discovers that she has been watching him, her actions are referred to by the narrator as a "game," one that Paco hopes to continue but instead ends by returning the gaze. This shifting of the gaze — from him, to her, back to him, back to her — suggests some mutuality in their relationship, and the possibility for a moment of recognition to occur. That moment passes, however, when Cathy instigates a new game of staring, a relation that Thomson calls a "dynamic [that] constitutes the starer as normal and the object of the stare as different," thereby shifting control entirely to Cathy ("Seeing" 347).

In this new visual "game," there is no reciprocity. Cathy stares into Paco's bedroom window without his knowing it; she stands in the doorway of her second-floor apartment, daring Paco with her eyes to make it up the stairs and into her apartment before she closes the door, even when she knows he always will fail. The dynamics of the relationship clearly are not about recognition or identification, but instead ironically are about marking Cathy as gender normal (dominant) and able-bodied, and Paco as gender abnormal (submissive) and disabled. Paco does not understand this change in the game as a power move on Cathy's part until he imagines himself in her role and reads her diary. One early morning, when Cathy is not in her room and Paco is able to go in to read her diary, he stands briefly on the landing, occupying Cathy's position as the starer and imagining seeing himself "standing at the foot of the stairs next to the phone booth, sweat-filthy, stinking from work, leaning on his black hickory cane — half drunk some nights, his back always killing him, tired as hell" (189). This position provides for Paco a vision of how he appears to others, the stigmatized image he had tried to avoid by remaining so reclusive. But the moment also transforms him into his old body as the "booby trap man" of the company, feeling "enveloped in an alien ease ..., as if he's been turned inside out and rendered invisible" (197). To avoid being stigmatized by "gimp-ness," then, Paco must return to the way in which his body was understood before Firebase Harriette was destroyed: "alien" and "invisible." In other words, for Paco to perform as monolithically masculine and therefore the subject of the gaze and not the object of the stare, he must conceive of himself — recognize himself — as existing outside of his current body; the only masculinity that had ever worked for Paco was the masculinity of secrecy, stealth, and control as the booby trap man.

As Paco is going to enter Cathy's room, the ghosts recall an incident when he was out setting booby traps, and a VC man came close to him. Knowing there were other VC in the area, and to protect himself, Paco silently killed the man with a knife. What stays with Paco is the way the man pleaded with him; Paco knew enough Vietnamese to understand the man saying "I will never see forever" (196). Another episode from his past life that intrudes on Paco's present has to do with the rape of the VC girl. After fantasizing about having forced sex with Cathy, Paco "cannot choose but remember" (174) the gang rape. That the first episode is retold by the ghosts and the second reluctantly remembered by Paco suggests that he is more affected by the second than the first, in so far as it colors how he can conceive of himself in his current life. To some extent, the two instances reveal that Paco was previously under the illusion of his physical unmarkedness; now he cannot work under that illusion.

When Paco reads Cathy's diary, at first he is pleased with the way in which she sexually objectifies him: she describes him in subsequent entries as "good-looking, with nice tight buns," "cute, you know, but covered with scars," and her boyfriend as "[n]ot as good-looking as that guy Paco" (202–204). Once the game has changed and Paco has returned her gaze, Cathy's entries become critical, and she stops gazing at him at work and begins staring at him through his bedroom window. Not only does her handwriting in the diary change from script to print with this alteration to their relationship, her assessments of Paco are based on scrupulous note-taking as she observes him in the privacy of his room. No longer is he the belabored "cute guy" working at the greasy spoon; the ugliness and squalor of his embodied life turns him into "a dingy, dreary, smelly, shabby, *shabby* little man" (205). From that point, her entries record him giving her "the creeps," as a "ghost," "this guy," "pasty," "crippled," "like he was someone back from the dead," and "obscene." As the starer, Cathy is locked into seeing Paco only as Thomson's "grotesque spectacle," a man devoid not only of masculinity but of humanity.

Missing the moment for recognition, Cathy sees Paco no longer as *object* but as *abject*, recorded as the last entry Paco reads in her diary. She dreams that she and Paco make love, and when they are finished, Paco begins to peel off his scars and to drop them all over her body; for each scar, Cathy hears a scream, and as they are dropped, they burn and suffocate her. Having read this entry, Paco "feels as if he's met his wraith" (209). Faced with the portent of his own death, Paco concludes: "Whatever it is I want, it ain't in this town; thinking, Man, you ain't just a brick in the fucking wall, you're just a piece of meat on the slab" (209). That

Paco sees himself as a "piece of meat" echoes Cathy's complaint of being looked at by men on her campus as "a piece of meat." It might have been on this basis—both being objectified—that recognition would have occurred. However, Cathy viewed her objectification as an advantage to her in sexual relationships with men, while because of the dictates of hegemonic masculinity, this objectification of Paco's disabled body makes him less recognizable to Cathy as a sexual partner or even as a friend. Moreover, to be "a brick in the wall" recalls the rape scene in Vietnam, when the VC girl is taken into a "brick-and-stucco hootch," gang-raped and then killed. Paco's part in the rape is vague, but his role clearly is participatory (174–183). To be a brick in the wall, then, would still be to take a dominant (i.e., raper) position. In this case, though, the echo of being a brick is that he was not just a part of the group participating in the rape—he became the "meat on the slab," the person *being* raped. To be "meat" as a man, therefore, is to be seen as body and not mind, as feminine, as submissive, as penetrable. Paco recognizes this and so leaves town, looking for the place which might offer "whatever it is I want." Paco is conflicted; what he wants above all, according to the execution dream, is to have his full name called, to be a whole man (with both first and last names) with the ability to embody traditional masculinity, and so to be rescued from the threat of imminent and grisly death (145). Just as in the dream his name is never called, so will the towns of the United States not offer sanctuary from the demands of hegemonic masculinity on a male body with disabilities.

The most promising moment of recognition occurs when Jesse, another male Vietnam War veteran, arrives at the diner late one night, just as Monroe and Paco are closing up. However, Jesse's non-disabled body and subsequent embrace of hegemonic masculinity prohibit his recognizing Paco and also prevents Monroe from identifying with Jesse. Monroe is resentful of the man's "waltzing in two minutes before closing" (149), especially because Jesse orders a large amount of food. Jesse, too, spent time in combat in Vietnam: "Did *my*self a tour with the 173rd *Airborneski*! Iron fucking Triangle, Hobo Woods, the Bo Loi Woods. Lai Khe, An Loc, Cu Chi—back in the days when Ben Suc was still a ville. You heard a Ben Suc!" (152). Paco had already identified Jesse as a veteran from his backpack and bindle, and knows the names of all of these places, but as the veteran with a disability, his moment of recognizing is less powerful than when he is recognized. That Monroe does not recognize Jesse in the same way he immediately recognized Paco suggests that Monroe is unable to see past Jesse's body in the way he could Paco's, emphasizing the particularity of the way in which Monroe does recognize Paco. Except for being described as "a big man, his own best customer" (97), Monroe may be the only character in the novel who is not more fully physically described. He is a World War Two Marine veteran, and though he insists he will not fly the American flag because of the horrible experiences that were Guadalcanal and Iwo Jima, he still refers to himself as a patriot (126). The botched haircut on Paco bespeaks the botched way in which he was treated by the military's medical establishment and the botched World War Two military maneuvers Monroe called Guadalcanal and Iwo Jima. Because he is not described physically, the reader can only judge him based on what he says. It is interesting, therefore, that he recognizes Paco as a veteran, but not Jesse. This inability of Monroe to see Jesse as a veteran may be based on Jesse's unscarred physical wholeness, perhaps manifested by his ponytail (155). Paco, on the other hand, has a "severe" haircut. Hennig, the barber, is anxious to point out his discriminating taste in haircuts with Paco's: "When Paco ducked into Elliot's Goods, Hennig took one look at the severe, amateurish cut of his hair and nailed him for a GI without so much as a second glance, you understand" (77).

But there is a mental connection between Paco and Jesse that does not exist between Paco and Monroe. Once Paco is hired by Monroe, he reveals very little about himself, plodding through his daily schedule without conversing. When Jesse arrives, however, and admits that he had heard about the Vietnam episode involving Paco, Paco is more willing to discuss his past; Monroe listens to the conversation, hoping he will learn something more about the enigmatic man (151–152). Jesse and Paco experience mutual recognition as masculine people who have endured the same maddening experiences, but Jesse's non-disabled status keeps them separated. Jesse's recognition of Paco has to do with his having heard of the episode: "'Heard about Harriette [the name of Paco's blown-up firebase],' Jesse says, arch and astonished at the same time, but talking easy" (152). Paco's recognition of Jesse is as another man who has endured "humpin' the boonies" in Vietnam. Their mutual recognition does not suffice, however, to pull Paco out of his stigmatized status, because even though there is a connection between the two men, and Paco urges Jesse to hang around awhile, Jesse is more a drifter who desires independence and control than he is a man who wants to secure the bonds of friendship by staying in one place. Therefore, even recognition that is the outcome of common experience cannot overcome the differences of bodies.

Paco's Story demonstrates how disability and masculinity are described and defined by non-disabled people. The trope of vision is used repeatedly to emphasize this powerlessness, as Paco has to bear the telltale markings of "friendly fire" but is prohibited from speaking that story himself. Instead, he is reliant on the "reading" skills of other non-disabled characters to decipher the meanings of his body. *Paco's Story* points out what the analyses of the texts in this chapter have elucidated, that resisting the expectations of monolithic masculinity is especially difficult for a disabled veteran of the Vietnam War *because* it was the Vietnam War in which he served. Gerschick and Miller suggest that disabled men can rely on, reject, or reformulate the standards of hegemonic masculinity ("Gender" 457). Because the very nature of the non-fictional texts is to focus on the growth of the individual disabled man and not especially on the environments in which he lives, those texts are more successful at suggesting new masculinities can be devised. What my analysis of some Vietnam War fiction suggests, however, is that the ease with which reformulation, reliance, or rejection can occur is problematized by its having to account for the ambiguous environment created by the War itself, a circumstance that confounds the dictates of monolithic masculinity.

4

A Litmus Test for Masculinity
The Vietnam War at the Turn of the Twenty-First Century

Americans cannot seem to let the sixties go gently into the night. While the 1970s disappeared before they even ended and the 1950s succumbed to a nostalgic fog, the 1960s stay hot. <u>We make [male] politicians take a decades-old drug test and scrutinize their position on the Vietnam War</u>*— though few of us are sure what makes for a passing grade in either case* [Farber 1; emphasis added].

As David Farber indicates above in his 1994 publication, *The Age of Great Dreams: America in the 1960s*, thirty years after the conclusion of the War Vietnam remained a cultural signifier in the American vocabulary. Now, nearly forty years since the end of the War in Vietnam and in the midst of another American war that has proven equally unpopular and contentious, Vietnam persists as code for the tests and subsequent failures of monolithic masculinity. As the previous chapters have demonstrated, this code pervades cultural narratives explicitly concerning the Vietnam War or post–War era, but it also leaves its traces in late twentieth-century and early twenty-first-century cultural narratives less patently about the War. These narratives include American presidential campaigns, military recruiting advertisements, campaign and War memoirs, films, and publications about the current war in Iraq.

The gender discourses appearing in these texts is a legacy of the Vietnam War, as the uneasy pursuit of monolithic masculinity is played out repeatedly decades after the War's end. The American presidential elections at the close of the twentieth and outset of the twenty-first centuries continue to register anxieties about this self-reflexive connection between masculinity and Vietnam; that these anxieties resurface periodically demonstrates their import. During the 1992, 1996, 2000 and 2004 campaigns, the candidates' military experiences were made an issue, especially their involvement in or attitude toward the decades-earlier Vietnam War.[1]

Who won these elections is relatively immaterial; that Vietnam War participation was raised repeatedly — and still is — is relevant to this study's argument. Overtly, a connection has been made in the American public imagination between a man's experience in war and his ability to act as the commander-in-chief of the United States armed forces. However, as historian Farber points out in the excerpt above, the issue for politicians and their inquisitors is not about military or combat experience in general; it is especially "Vietnam" inhabiting the imaginations of the American public. One might postulate that, though 1992 Republican incumbent George H. W. Bush was a decorated fighter pilot of the Second World War and had led the United States and its allies into winning the 1991 Gulf War, his breadth of combat military experience and command could not, in the eyes of the electorate, counterbalance the fact that his vice-presidential running mate, Dan Quayle, had avoided Vietnam combat by spending those years in the National Guard.[2] The 1992 Democratic presidential contender and winner of the election, Bill Clinton, also evaded the draft but argued that he legitimately had not been drafted, and explained his early response to not being drafted as youthful indiscretion, not faulty character.[3] Clinton's running mate, Al Gore, the son of a U.S. senator and therefore one who easily could have found a way to evade the draft, had volunteered to serve in Vietnam after graduating from college, thus assuring voters that, at least for this pair of candidates, "Vietnam" was covered. So, while it was not the campaign's most decisive factor, Vietnam played a significant part in the 1992 election and resurfaced less extensively in the 1996 campaign, which pitted the more youthful Clinton and Gore against an aging World War II veteran with a disability, Bob Dole, and his running mate, Jack Kemp, a professional football player in the American Football League (AFL) during the Vietnam era. More recently in the 2000 election, two candidates — Senators Bob Kerrey and John McCain — in particular related their combat experiences in Vietnam to developing their "character," resurrecting the question of a candidate's moral and physical ability to lead the country's armed forces in a time of war. Both Kerrey and McCain served in combat, ostensibly making them in the eyes of the public the best possible prospective commanders-in-chief.[4] However, the winning candidate in 2000, George W. Bush, is reported to have avoided going to Vietnam by gaining a scarce place in the Texas Air National Guard.[5] Finally, in the 2004 campaign, Democratic candidate John Kerry's combat experience was challenged by the Swift Boat Veterans for Truth through their manifesto, *Unfit for Command* (O'Neill and Corsi), while Dan Rather on CBS alleged that incumbent

President Bush's military records reflected a less-than-honorable fulfillment of his National Guard obligation ("New Questions"). The 2004 campaign made clear that what was being challenged about both men was their masculinity, as "fitness" for command is measured by a person's adherence to masculinity's monolithic form.

The link between Vietnam and masculinity also arose in the "character" debates of the 1992 and 1996 election campaigns, with Vietnam subsequently being used as shorthand for "masculinity" by Kerrey and McCain in 2000 and invoked fully in 2004. In the 1992 election, Democratic candidate Bill Clinton was accused of having had a long-term extramarital affair and having prevaricated about his draft deferment during the 1960s. Regardless of whether or not Clinton did these things, they weighed equally in the public's mind: infidelity to one's wife or to one's country both signified an inadequate "presidential character," or the ability to "re-present the American people to themselves" (Jay Rosen 24), earning Clinton the moniker "Slick Willie." In 1992, "Slick Willie's" potential "presidential character" was compromised by the suggestion that he had engaged in activities the American public refused to see as a reflection of itself. Though the sexual and military elements of this debate never were connected explicitly to Clinton's ability to enact a particular type of masculinity as president, it does appear that when "character" is referred to, it can be understood as code for "masculinity." In the public imagination, Clinton's dodging military participation in the Vietnam War indicates a lack of "character" which is not just about integrity and truthfulness, but is also about the physical daring and domination that are typical of the traditional form of American masculinity. The rhetoric around Clinton indicated that his ability to avoid participation in the War demonstrated not just wiliness and conniving on his part, but also, simultaneously, cowardice. This euphemistic link between "character" and "masculinity" was more evident in the 1996 election, when Republican candidate Bob Dole made "character" the dominant thrust of his campaign message by emphasizing his military experience. Like other commentators on the Clinton years, John Hohenberg points out that Dole paired his military service and Clinton's lack of military service to the character issue as a matter of course, as though military service alone could act as the conduit to or proof of "good" character.[6] But, like the measure of passing a Vietnam test that Farber describes in the quote above, the meaning of "character" also was seen as incalculable at this time. For instance, in a 1996 *Christian Science Monitor* article, Everett Carll Ladd suggests that presidential "character" is fluid:

4. A Litmus Test for Masculinity   147

>The public's thinking about "character" is often read too narrowly. Each president has personal attributes that together define his style of leadership and capacity to lead. When Americans assess the personal side of a president, they do so primarily against the backdrop of their proper concern with the quality of his leadership. *Many different elements, of course, feed into the latter judgment* [18; emphasis added].

Masculinity is, then, a principal element in Americans judging the "character" of their national leaders, an element on which Dole capitalized as he rhetorically compared the fact of his military experience to Clinton's non-experience in order to masculinize himself and de-masculinize Clinton (Feldman 1).

Journalists also discerned an equation between masculinity and character during these election campaigns. For instance, Mary Leonard of *The Boston Globe* suggested during the 2000 campaign that Al Gore was not seen as a viable president because he was "someone who doesn't take strong positions and basically is not a very masculine guy" (A1). During the 1996 campaign, Peter Canellos, also of *The Boston Globe*, described a speechwriter for Bob Dole, Mark Helprin, as believing that "combat makes a man strong and wise," that "men who avoid military service are cowards," and that combat has a role in forging character (A30). Thus, to the primary representative of Dole, not only does participating in war translate into masculinity, it also has a role in developing character. Joe Hallett, a writer for *The Columbus Dispatch*, intimated during the period before the United States preemptively invaded Iraq in 2003 that he was without character for inadvertently criticizing veterans (B5). All of these reports suggest that "character" is part and parcel of "masculinity" and both are connected to leadership. Robert Dale Dean contends in "Manhood, Reason, and American Foreign Policy: The Social Construction of Masculinity and the Kennedy and Johnson Administrations" that it was a lack of character instantiated by forms of inappropriate masculinity that led the United States into and kept it in Vietnam. This same paradox is evident in the comments of the Swift Boat Veterans, who condemn on the one hand what they see as John Kerry's cowardice and on the other, his aggressiveness (O'Neill and Corsi 185).

Given the repetition of the Vietnam War card in the campaigns at the end of the twentieth century and the beginning of the twenty-first, it is clear that a significant measure of "presidentiality" during these campaigns was a candidate's willingness to engage in combat, or to sacrifice himself in the country's service, especially during a controversial war.

Further, a candidate's displaying this willingness was a measure of his ability to behave in a "masculine," or presidential, way, problematizing the idea that anyone who was seen as feminine (i.e., a woman, or a man who had no military service) could be president, or that one must be masculine to go to war.

So, recent presidential campaigns suggest that currently in America combat participation is an indicator of a man's "character," some essential and foundational quality that can be used not just to validate his ability to be the commander-in-chief of the U.S. armed forces, but also to measure his ability to act presidential, both roles believed to typify American masculinity. Given the controversial nature of the War and the antiwar sentiments of the American public after 1968, it is ironic that three or four decades later the War should be invoked as a litmus test of monolithic masculinity when what the War's narratives reflect is a fragmenting of a singular masculinity into multiple masculinities. Words like "character," "honor," "integrity," and "duty" have been deployed as euphemisms for "masculinity," and these turn-of-the-century presidential campaigns revolved around the "politics of gender" discussed in my Introduction.[7] That is, gender is an identity that is responsive to current social needs. Thus, the question about presidential candidates' participation in Vietnam is both about the candidate's personal stance on the War and about masculinity, euphemistically termed "character" or "honor."

Though military experience always has played a part in determining which men have been chosen by the American electorate to lead the nation, in the case of the last several presidential elections a notable element of the debate has been not just whether or not a male presidential candidate participated in the Vietnam War, but also whether through that participation he demonstrated the appropriate masculinity.[8] As Farber points out in the opening of this chapter, however, the gauge to measure appropriateness itself is incalculable: "We make politicians take a decades-old drug test and scrutinize their position on the Vietnam War —*though few of us are sure what makes for a passing grade* in either case" (1; emphasis added). In other words, we Americans are willing to test men on their ability to enact monolithic masculinity by participating in war, but we also are not quite sure how that masculinity should look. It is not especially significant that neither combat veterans Kerrey nor McCain won their bids in 2000 to represent respectively the Democratic or Republican Parties, or that National Guard vet Bush did win. What is most pertinent to how Americans imagine Vietnam at the turn of the century is not the substance of these arguments—who volunteered, who was in combat and what was the quality of that experience, who was reported to have deliberately avoided being drafted by pulling strings, who avoided it by having a high draft number.

Rather, the crucial point is that the argument concerning the impact of the Vietnam War on these now middle-aged male candidates for president of the United States was raised so vociferously decades after the United States had unceremoniously left Vietnam, and, moreover, following a resounding "victory" in the 1991 Gulf War which supposedly put the Vietnam legacy to rest as it defeated the "Vietnam Syndrome."[9] Following the rout of the Iraqi forces in Operation Desert Storm, President George H. W. Bush was quoted as saying, "By God, we've kicked the Vietnam syndrome once and for all" (Cloud 26). Given the emphasis on the Vietnam War in subsequent presidential elections, however, including one in which Bush was defeated, it appears that the "syndrome" has not been left in the detritus of the 1991 war or the current one in Iraq. What is most disturbing is how the Vietnam War and masculinity are intertwined in the American sense of itself through the National Symbolic, a project that continues to this day.

In this Symbolic mode, the War has been interpreted variously, depending on how the nation needs to imagine itself; the War and its aftermath continue to be revised for national consumption through this interpretive activity. For instance, the Vietnam Syndrome variously has been defined as a form of isolationism (Shepard, Rotter), as a post–Vietnam national malaise or depression (Gitlin), as "the unwillingness to tolerate atrocities and aggression" (Chomsky), as a mistrust of American foreign policy (Weisbrot), and as "not just a nightmarish memory of a bloody and unjust war but a continued unwillingness of the US population to accept the possibility of its repeat" (Sharon Smith).[10] Though these interpretations could be said to overlap, their differences also propose that the interpretations of the war itself are not unanimous, nor has the specter of Vietnam — and its relationship to the way in which gender is formulated in the War's representations— been erased from the American National Symbolic. This is evident in the discourse about the current war in Iraq.

Furthermore, the manifest desire to correlate a president's military experience with his competency to serve as commander-in-chief, as made clear in the presidential elections closing the twentieth and opening the twenty-first centuries, has been generated by the National Symbolic despite empirical evidence that military experience or lack thereof does not significantly affect an American leader's willingness to use military force or to act in favor of the military. For instance, a 1999 paper entitled "Vanishing Veterans: The Decline in Military Experience in the U.S. Congress" concludes that, though the number of congressmen (the study deliberately excludes women) with military experience had dwindled from approximately 75 percent during the Vietnam War to 25 percent in 1999, there was no evidence to suggest that the group of representatives was more or less willing to approve the use of military force or to align themselves with the outcomes desired by military leaders. The authors cite two then-recent votes in Congress, Clinton's 1994 "don't ask, don't tell, don't pursue" policy about gays in the military, and continuing draft registration. According to the authors' analysis of voting records, "veteran status has at best a modest impact on vote decisions and policy outcomes" (Bianco and Markham 18). The results of this study indicate that the popular association at election times made between military experience and a willingness to act on the behalf of the military—to behave in a masculine way, as leaders apparently should—cannot be supported by recent governmental data. That is, although men (and women) in Congress have not had military experience, they are nonetheless willing to vote in favor of deploying the armed forces, such as in the case of the 2003 invasion and subsequent occupation of Iraq. Furthermore, a 1996 United States Information Agency (USIA) position paper entitled "The Foreign Policy Factor in Presidential Campaigns" asserts that "most elections are determined by domestic considerations, notably by the state of the economy," and that "foreign policy becomes a dominant campaign issue only when it has reached the raw nerve of the electorate" (Hess). What both these studies suggest is that, first, the majority of the United States' national leaders has no military experience yet is willing to endorse and use military force, and second, the electorate is concerned with a candidate's foreign policy attitude only when the country already is in a foreign policy crisis. As a result of these conclusions, that the American electorate employs Vietnam as one mechanism for evaluating a candidate's ability to act as commander-in-chief suggests that Vietnam both has been fully integrated into the American ethos and also is part of the discourse used to interrogate a person's masculinity.

Despite President George H. W. Bush's exhortations that the Vietnam Syndrome had been dispelled by 1991, Vietnam continues to disrupt the nation's understanding of itself as the world's best representative of democracy. These disruptions can be seen readily in film and fiction, evident in films as early as 1978 when the "Four Horsemen" were produced (Devine 130): two relatively ignored films, *The Boys in Company C* and *Go Tell the*

Spartans, and the canonical *Coming Home* and *The Deer Hunter*. The American sense of its function in the Vietnam War has continued to be formed by films such as *Apocalypse Now* (1979), *Platoon* (1986), *Full Metal Jacket* (1987), and *Rescue Dawn* (2007), and has persisted through late-twentieth-century cinematic revisions of World War II.[11] Television shows such as *Miami Vice* (1980), *China Beach* (1989), *Magnum P.I.* (1982), and *Tour of Duty* (1989) all contribute to the national significance of the American role in Vietnam during the war era. These popular film and television representations have been bolstered by the publication of innumerable novels, short stories, memoirs, autobiographies, oral narratives, and histories about the War.

Still, patently popular culture representations like films and books are not the sole way to gauge the continuing impact of the Vietnam War on current American national and gendered self-conceptions. For instance, since July of 1973, when the draft was put into hibernation and the military converted to an all-volunteer force, recruiting rhetoric stayed relatively consistent, typified by the U.S. Army's slogan, "Be All You Can Be." This slogan had the effect of distracting potential recruits from the actual purpose of the military — to kill, whether in defense or on offense — toward self-development and -fulfillment. However, 2001 marked a noticeable departure from the post–Vietnam War recruiting strategy, a move signaling a changing national consciousness and attendant recruiting rhetoric well before the September 11, 2001, terrorist attacks on the New York World Trade Center and the Pentagon. The "Army of One" motto that the United States Army embraced early in 2001 is ambiguous enough to confuse whether the "one" addresses a single person or a collective.[12] Images accompanying the slogan are equally ambiguous. As Harold Jordan, the founder of the American Friends Service Committee's National Youth and Militarism Program, points out, since the Gulf War, "the military could no longer be presented as a place where one received money for training and education, but never went to war," so that "[m]ilitary images (such as the uniform and military equipment) still figured into the equation, but they were presented increasingly as props for a demonstration of the intangible benefits of serving."[13]

An "Army of One" advertisement featured in the September 17, 2001, edition of *U.S. News and World Report*, for instance, pictures a single pair of uniformed and booted legs climbing and nearing the top of a set of painted cement stairs. A word or phrase appears in white letters stenciled on the front of each of the stairs: personal courage, integrity, honor, selfless service, respect, duty, and loyalty. The sepia-colored image of the stairs and legs is framed in a thin line of mustard yellow; this color scheme is unusual to military recruiting ads which, since the end of Vietnam, featured primary colors, and so visually calls attention to the difference of this recruiting rhetoric. Around the frame is the name of the legs' presumed owner ("SSG Calvin Garrett, Drill Sergeant"), and what is represented as a quote by Garrett ("These values are at the Army's core. In order for me to teach them to new recruits, I don't get in their face. I get in their hearts. **I AM AN ARMY OF ONE**. And there are 1,045,690 others just like me.") The ad is addressing the commonly held fear that the military will transform a self-determining individual into a heartless automaton. Rather than emphasizing the personal, individualistic development of "Be All You Can Be," this newer ad incorporates the individual into the collective through "their hearts." The values enumerated on the stairs are not exclusively emotions, though. Any one of these "values" could be construed as rational, mindful decisions. In suggesting they are exclusively emotional responses with SSG Garrett's comment—"I get in their hearts"—the ad reconstructs unrestrained emotionality as appropriate military behavior, simultaneously reconstructing appropriate gender behavior. It is permissible, in other words, for soldiers to think of "respect" as an emotion, and not a perquisite demanded by rank. The redefinition of the words suggested by the emotional rhetoric is especially important because, as a drill instructor, SSG Garrett represents one of the military's paragons of monolithic masculinity. If he works to get into the hearts of recruits (and so do the other million or so military members, as his quote claims), then the Army must, implies the rhetoric of the ad, nurture the individual within a collective of like-*feeling* individuals.[14]

This emphasis on emotions is an important rhetorical move that challenges gender permanence. The simultaneous ambiguity of language and image reflects an uncertainty both about inclusiveness and about how the military can not just tolerate, but rely officially on an emotionality not traditionally associated with masculinity. The rhetorical appeal of this advertising campaign is challenging the truism that in-control masculinity is devoid of out-of-control emotionalism. As editors Milette Shamir and Jennifer Travis point out in the Introduction to their collection, *Boys Don't Cry?* this truism is pervasive and at the core of a "master narrative" of American masculinity (1). My study is not contending that masculinity is and always has been unemotional. Instead, it is arguing that an institution that has not constructed its appeal to recruits emotionally beforehand does now, and that cultural phenomenon is intriguing. The appeal, then, is what is intriguing, not the supposed alteration to traditional forms of American masculinity. Though narratives of war often include stories of intense male bonding, American masculinity has been embodied culturally by the lone individual in action, on *his* own, not with other people, and certainly not with emotional others. (Think of most of the film characters played by John Wayne, Clint Eastwood, or Sylvester Stallone.) The rhetorical move demonstrated by the recruiting advertisement suggests a revision of military masculinity, so that the most masculine of military members—a male Drill Sergeant—can be emotionally sensitive even as he performs his unpleasant military duties. Because the Vietnam War challenged what it means to be American, especially the strict gender ideal of monolithic masculinity, the gender ambiguity in the recruiting advertisement can be seen as a residue of the Vietnam War era.

Another recent example of how Vietnam signifies "Man Dance" masculinity in American culture are two recent and related texts: Harold G. Moore and Joe Galloway's memoir of the 1965 battle at Ia Drang, *We Were Soldiers Once ... and Young* (1992) and the 2002 film, *We Were Soldiers*, featuring Mel Gibson as then–Lieutenant Colonel (LTC) Moore. Despite their addressing the same battle with the same principal characters, these texts nonetheless are quite different, a difference revolving around how the acts of masculinities depend on their intended audience. Moore and Galloway's memoir, for instance, based on their own memories and records but also on interviews with American and North Vietnamese participants in the October/November 1965 battle at Ia Drang, is intended for an audience that not only understands military terminology but also expects masculinity to be distinctly non-domestic. On the other hand, as a "major motion picture," the film places Gibson/Moore, his family, and the families of a few of his men at the center of the narrative. Admittedly, the needs of the written memoir and film genres are distinct. But a comparison is warranted because, though the two genres narrate differently, that does not mandate they narrate altogether dissimilar stories. In this case the texts narrate different masculinities in terms of form and of race.

The memoir includes several components integral to the telling of the story and yet they are not integrated formalistically. In an 11-page list at the opening of the text, Moore and Galloway dedicate the book to the men who died at Ia Drang, organizing their names by combat unit and including their hometowns and states. In an appendix, Moore and Galloway also provide brief biographies of the combat survivors and of some of the family members of those who were killed. Inserted into the center of the text are photographs, some of which were taken during the battle and some of which were taken in the United States, thus including domestic scenes with families. Finally, a concluding section entitled "Aftermath" discusses, especially in the chapter entitled "The Secretary of the Army Regrets...," the impact of the Ia Drang battles on the family members at home. The vast majority of the memoir, however, focuses almost entirely on the two parts of the October/November 1965 battle of Ia Drang: at LZ (Landing Zone) X-Ray and at LZ Albany. LZ X-Ray was the location of a formidable battle, where Moore's First Battalion of the Seventh Cavalry was dropped bit by bit into a staging area for thousands of North Vietnamese Army regulars. Though the battalion suffered many casualties in this first battle, Moore and Galloway suggest that the unit won the conflict. LZ Albany, however, was the location of a U.S. Army disaster as two other Cavalry units, brought in to reinforce Moore's battalion and, at the end of the battle, marched to Albany to be extricated by helicopter, blundered into an ambush and were unable to organize effectively enough to fight back. But these blemishes in the memoir's construction of masculinity are instructive. As Moore and Galloway claim in a small section at the end of the book that accounts for their source material, "The first draft of all history is written in the memories of the participants and witnesses to any event" (476). In terms of masculinity, then, the memoir frames it as traditionally military: combat savvy, heroic, and forbearing in the face of failure. Therefore, the memoir, formalistically signaling that the battle is central to the narrative and that the events and people outside of the battles are appendices or part of the "aftermath," is intended for an audience that values tales of military masculinity in combat and in its monolithic form. This contention is further supported by the memoir's assumption that a reader will be familiar with Vietnamese names and places and Vietnamese and American unit, rank, and weapon designations, since few of those are explained in non-military terms.

On the other hand, as a "major motion picture" and Gibson vehicle, the film focuses on the religiousness and patriotism of the central characters, the support and anguish of the officers' wives who wait stateside, and Gibson/Moore's uncanny ability to anticipate what the North Vietnamese commander intends to do during the battle. More importantly, however, Gibson/Moore's masculinity is not depicted as solely, or even primarily, military. For instance, before leaving for Vietnam — and audience members spend a large portion of the movie stateside as Gibson/Moore prepares his new airmobile force — he is shown as domestically involved, praying with his many children and spending time with the youngest, a precocious little girl. Furthermore, the film only tells the heroic story of LZ X-Ray, the one Moore and Galloway counted a win, not the display of ineptitude and arrogance that was LZ Albany in the memoir. These differences in the film from the book — the religion, the emphasis on family, the victory in combat without a hint of failure — suggest an intended audience that would not appreciate a strictly combat film and would expect the depiction of a "sensitive man" that is Mel Gibson's character. This characterization may also be connected to the filmography of Gibson, who in recent years has appeared in many films that depict him in this way: *Signs, The Patriot, What Women Want*, any of the *Lethal Weapon* films, and perhaps his recent directorial effort, *The Passion of Christ*. Or it might suggest that depictions of fractured and multiplicitous masculinities can only appear when the battle is surely won.

The second point from which the film and memoir depart has to do with race, evident most immediately in the memoir's 11-page dedicatory list of the American men killed at Ia Drang. While the dedication lists the names of the men by the military units to which they belonged, oddly it does not include their ranks. Similarly, the National Vietnam Veterans Memorial in Washington, D.C., and the register used to find names on the Wall also include names only, without rank. Instead of rank, Moore and Galloway distinguish each man within a combat unit by his American hometown, thereby identifying the men more as residents of the United States than as members of a military hierarchy. The memoir's taxonomizing effort resonates with the subtext of "An Army of One" recruiting advertisements discussed previously: the fear of anonymity and lack of personal control that being in the military represents. Moore and Galloway's defining these dead soldiers as from specific towns and cities across America allays those fears of anonymity while glossing over the fear of lack of control in not citing their ranks in the military hierarchy. However, while Moore and Galloway signal these men as American citizens in the United States' first fully racially integrated military force, they never mention their races or ethnicities, an issue that often defines the War. One could read the entire memoir without being aware of any person's race or ethnicity. Gail Buckley, author of *American Patriots: The Story of Blacks in the Military from the Revolution to Desert Storm*, attributes the racial anonymity of the memoir to the "great" race relations prevailing in the Army at that time (1965). Buckley proceeds to name as black several of the characters in Moore and Galloway's memoir: Captain Forrest, Calvin Bouknight, Ron Barrow, and John Cash (390). One might think, however, that a much larger number of the combatants at the Ia Drang battle would have been black, given that, until 1967, about 20 percent of combat fatalities were African American.

The only potential racial suggestion in the memoir has to do with the red-haired lieutenant who makes a bad tactical decision that compromises the battle plan. Lt. Herrick led his platoon away from the rest of his company in pursuit of North Vietnamese soldiers. In breaking with the rest of the company, the platoon was surrounded by North Vietnamese Army Regulars, took refuge on a small knoll, and, as the "lost platoon" (echoing the "lost boys" in Neverland of the children's story, *Peter Pan*) relied on the rescue efforts of the rest of the battalion over the next several days. By the time the "lost platoon" was rescued after 26 hours in close combat, nine men had been killed, thirteen were seriously wounded, and seven were unwounded. This trope of rescue is a frequent one in Vietnam War narratives, where a soldier launches off on his own, and rather than fighting the enemy to gain ground, American soldiers fight the Vietnamese in order to save some of their own.

But in introducing Lt. Henry Herrick, Moore and Galloway refer to him on the same page as "red-haired" and "impetuous," as though the two were synonymous (90), thereby racially essentializing Herrick's poor tactical decision. That is, he behaves impetuously *because* he is red-haired. In the film, Herrick is pointed out as a "hard-charger," but his red hair is not apparent or remarked upon, nor is he depicted as irresponsible or incompetent. Though the film suggests it is not necessary verbally to mark Herrick as racially different in order to explain his rash behavior, the visual language of the film does mark racial difference as it depicts many people of color in a multi-racial combat unit. So the book includes a discourse linking race and behavior in Lt. Herrick, but the film's discourse concerning race is a visual one only; race never is articulated in the film as an issue in character dialogue among the male combatants, even as racial differences visually are inferred.[15] In the case of the memoir, it is clear that Herrick's race or physical characteristics influence the type of masculinity he may enact. Consequently, Herrick's behavior is depicted as brash, as an abuse of the expected aggressive form of military masculinity. The film, on the other hand, despite the probability that African Americans and Latinos had made up a disproportionate number of the fatalities during this battle, remains mute on racial difference in American combat units as though it were not an issue whatsoever. This silence contributes to the film's attempt to reconstruct Gibson-cum-Moore-cum-military masculinity as "sensitive" as it shows race through his non-discriminating eyes.

This study's argument is not with the compromises necessitated by adapting a written text to a filmic one, nor is it arguing that the collective memoir is the one true story and the fictional film only a bastard form, nor is it indicting those greedy Hollywood moguls whose cynical eye on the bottom line requires a story that appeals to a wider audience, including women with its titillating romantic elements and men with its titillating gory action sequences. Instead, it is arguing that the memoir *We Were Soldiers Once ... and Young* and its film adaptation, *We Were Soldiers*, are different and perhaps opposing texts, but both appeal to intended audiences with expectations about how male masculinity should be embodied and exhibited. Gender is the primary difference because of plural masculinities, since the Vietnam War specifically and the Vietnam War era especially challenged the truism that there is one way to be a masculine man in American culture. This is not to say, however, that the problems of masculinity have been resolved. Thus, even though the memoir was written within a decade of the film's production and so one would expect the two texts to be subject to the same pressures of identity construction, they reveal how texts—written or filmic—can be invested in constructing a particular kind or kinds of masculinities, a good part of which is dependent on the expectations of those who are watching. It's useful to be reminded here of the Man Dance: a sublimely self-conscious and self-critical performance of "steely-eyed, flat-bellied professionals" whose performances of masculinity adjust to their audiences. The ironic difference between Moore and Galloway's memoir and Gibson's film is that the text on which, according to Moore and Galloway, history rests—their memoir—is the one the most resistant to the Man Dance model of plural masculinities as it marginalizes the family and home elements of war, but at the same time problematizes monolithic masculinity with the disaster story of LZ Albany. The fictional text, however, the film, constructs a masculinity that can bear the description of thoughtful and sensitive "steely-eyed, flat-bellied" men, but *only* from within the context of victory at LZ X-Ray.

Other types of Vietnam memoirs and autobiographies continue to influence American gender constructions currently. In the past, memoirs usually have been the venue for "great men" statesmen to recount the life stories that led them to distinction.[16] Senator John McCain's *Faith of My Fathers: A Family Memoir* (1999) is instructive in how the statesman and the soldier are melded in one memoir. But it also narrates McCain's gendered struggle to claim simultaneously the power to determine his own identity and the self-revealing potency of collective effort, the conflicting subtextual elements of the "Army of One" advertisement.[17] McCain's title and subtitle themselves announce this conflict between the military masculinity of self-determination ("Faith of My Fathers") and the domestic femininity of collective action ("A Family Memoir"). While this full title appears on the hard copy book cover, where a photograph of father and grandfather is featured next to a photo of the youthful fighter pilot McCain, the subtitle never appears again. The subtitle on the book cover, then, advertises McCain's mutual commitment both to his professional career and also to his private family, but, like most packaging, is enigmatic about the product inside. Unsurprisingly, the text deals far less with McCain's "family" (i.e., both of his parents, most of his grandparents, his siblings, two wives, and many children) than it does with the heroics of his father and grandfather, both admirals in the United States Navy during, respectively, the Vietnam War and World War II. What McCain professes in the title and the Preface — that "as a prisoner of war, I learned that a shared purpose did not claim my identity"—and what McCain demonstrates in his story-telling are at odds (viii). Thus, while the title on the hard copy book cover signifies a man who is willing to regard his distinction as the outcome of an effort shared by many people in his "family," the reference to "fathers" is literal; "family" is almost exclusively "fathers." The influences of McCain's mother are limited by him to her energy, his siblings never come into focus, his maternal grandparents are mentioned only for their propriety and trying to prevent their daughter's marrying his (clearly worthy) father, and his father's mother is rarely represented, except in passing as the person who instilled in him a love for literature. The text instead focuses on the exploits of his paternal grandfather and his father, both men who McCain admits were workaholics and who subsequently did not know their family members well, including McCain. Nonetheless, the feistiness of both "fathers," which McCain largely learns through stories told to him by third parties, fuels what McCain reports was his unfailing resistance to his North Vietnamese captors from late 1967 until his release early in 1973. Therefore, while the book's title is meant to signify McCain's debt to an entire family, painting him as a sensitive "New Man,"[18] he instead engages in another Great Man tome: his military heritage and greatness were bequeathed to him genetically, and rather than being influenced so much by the behaviors of his "family," he instead has inherited through his "fathers" the destiny to be great. In *Faith of My Fathers*, then-presidential candidate McCain is not just playing politics; he's playing the politics of masculinity endemic to Vietnam War representations.

Vietnam persists as code for masculinity, as this "Man Dance" ambiguity reveals itself through narratives of the current war in Iraq. It was not long into this war before critics began comparing it to Vietnam, citing a fabricated rationale for going to war, compounded by the lack of post-invasion plans to rebuild infrastructure and to win hearts and minds. It is not uncommon now to see the U.S. occupation of Iraq referred to as a "quagmire," a term frequently used to describe the American presence in Vietnam, and dwindling popular American support for this war recalls that for Vietnam. In *Is Iraq Another Vietnam?* (2006), Robert Brigham, Shirley Ecker Boskey Professor of History and International Relations at Vassar College and noted Vietnam War expert, contends that strategically and operationally the two wars are very different. Among other dissimilarities, the two wars differ in size and scope, with far fewer American combatants in Iraq than in Vietnam and a noted absence of the use of air power in Iraq (36). Consequently, he prophesizes, unlike in the Vietnam War, American casualties will remain relatively low in the Iraq war.

Culturally, however, the wars are to Brigham frighteningly similar in their "shared illusion about the efficacy and limitlessness of U.S. power" (137), a sort of absolutist thinking that is related to the concept of an unchanging, unmitigated monolithic masculinity. In fact, though in the 2000 election campaign candidate George W. Bush promised to avoid a war like Vietnam that had "no clear goal, no clear sense of purpose, and no plan to win" (157), Brigham claims that President Bush and his administration "purposefully turned its back on the lessons of Vietnam" (xiv). These attitudes in the American government reveal a masculinist tendency similar to that that took the United States into Vietnam, one that celebrates control, power, and action. As Brigham argues, one important lesson of Vietnam is that there are limits to the efficacy of American power, a lesson apparently having to be relearned in the deserts of Iraq (165).[19]

A parallel lesson is being learned as American combatants see the ineffectuality of a masculinity relying on wholeness and coherence when they are in the midst of a maelstrom called war. Two narratives written by different men but based on the same unit and mission reveal that, to the men involved in the Iraq war, there is little similarity between the monolithic masculinity of the National Symbolic and that practiced in their war. Evan Wright published *Generation Kill: Devil Dogs, Iceman, Captain America, and the New Face of American War* (2004) about his two-month experience as a pro-war embedded reporter with the First Marine Reconnaissance Battalion, spearhead unit of the American invasion of Iraq in March 2003.[20] Wright traveled with a platoon led by Lieutenant Nathaniel Fick, who wrote *One Bullet Away: The Making of a Marine Officer* (2005). While Fick recounts the entirety of his military experiences and training as a Marine officer, both his and Wright's narratives focus on the early 2003 Iraq incursion. They often comment on the same things, such as how a scene uncannily resembles one from *Apocalypse Now* or how "hardness" is a valuable quality among the Marines, and they explore in the course of their narratives the state of military masculinity from their different vantage points. Together, what they reveal is that "Man Dance" masculinity is the governing attitude as male combatants find it difficult if not impossible to adhere to the Symbolic's monolithic masculinity.

At Fick's urging, Wright avoids field-grade officers and senior non-commissioned officers and interacts largely with junior enlisted men, the privates and corporals. Consequently, he is the mouthpiece for the normally silenced military underclass, the group that lives most intensely the contradictions in monolithic masculinity. Wright's version has these men seeing and most of the others blind to the moral chaos inherent to war and the contradiction of American culture that promotes individualism when their lives depend on the power of collectivity (42); their main objective is to stay alive and kill only if necessary (375). As Wright says, "These young men represent what is more or less America's first generation of disposable children" who, as a consequence of the Vietnam era, "almost expect to be lied to" by authorities (19–20). They also see too clearly the dangerous incompetence of many of the men senior to them, though they are comforted by the "Peter Pan quality" of just being all together (44). Though most of the platoon members are heard from in Wright's narrative, including Lieutenant Fick, Sergeant Antonio Espera's story is most telling about the contradictions of monolithic masculinity. Despite his belief that wars are fought because "white man's gotta rule the world," Espera enlisted in the Marines to "serve" the white man with his own "purity and honor" intact (242), something he couldn't retain as a man who repossessed cars from poor people in South Central Los Angeles. However, even though he aspires to be like his absent father, a "psycho ex–Marine Vietnam vet" (403), Espera doesn't like the "tough-guy shit" of combat (241), he claims that the war has caused him to lose any trace of humanity he had brought there (281), and he is cynical about the ability of American charity distributed to Iraqis to change anything (300). Finally, when he returns to the States and is fêted as a war hero at a wealthy Malibu home, Espera says to the guests who want to view him as a hero, "Guys like me are just a necessary part of things. To maintain this way of life in a fine community like this, you need psychos like us to go out and drop a bomb on somebody's house" (445). Sergeant Espera demonstrates the inadequacy of monolithic masculinity to sustain a person at war. On the one hand, he admires and desires the "psycho" legacy of Vietnam on which wealthy Americans rely and, on the other, he sees how self-destructive and dehumanizing a force it is.

Marine Lieutenant Nathaniel Fick has more invested in monolithic masculinity, as he claims before going to war a "continuity with other infantrymen stretching back to Thermopylae" (33), that the Marines are "a last bastion of manhood in American society" (45), and laments having been born too late "for a young man who wanted to wear armor and slay dragons" (4). Despite these romantic beliefs, a conviction that the Iraq war is an appropriate one, and a resolve to make the Marines his career, Fick opts to leave the military after several years in the Marines and months in Afghanistan and Iraq. He claims he left because of his own inadequacies:

> I left the Corps because I had become a reluctant warrior. Many Marines reminded me of gladiators. They had that mysterious quality that allows some men to strap on greaves and a breastplate and wade into the gore. I respected, admired, and emulated them, but I could never be like them. I could kill when killing was called for, and I got hooked on the rush of combat as much as any man did. But I couldn't make the conscious choice to put myself in that position again and again throughout my professional life. Great Marine commanders, like all great warriors, are able to kill that which they love most — their men. It's a fundamental law of warfare. Twice I had cheated it. I couldn't tempt fate again [364].

In this passage, Fick esteems the model of monolithic masculinity — the "fundamental law of warfare" — and ascribes all of the problems he experienced as a Marine Corps officer to his inability to conform to it; though he is masculine in that he enjoys combat "as much as any man did," he is also unable to send men to their deaths, as a "great commander" would. At the heart of the model as it is enacted in Iraq, as reported by both Wright and Fick, however, is this very paradox: repeatedly, commanders who must have accomplished missions in order to have been promoted to commander status vow that their first priorities in combat are to protect their men, to ensure their survival. Were they to do that, however, they might not accomplish their next missions. This is not the only paradox in Fick's narrative, however, suggesting that the problem is not with Fick or his inability to match the contours of monolithic masculinity; the problem is in the monolith itself, in the "fundamental law of warfare."

Throughout his text, Fick demonstrates the contradictions inherent to the model, all in terms of some qualities or components traditionally viewed as masculine: the inviolability of history, sports, credibility, and seizing initiative. In each case, rather than war confirming those qualities of monolithic masculinity, it is the experience of war that alters Fick's attitudes, demonstrating their changeability. First, he extols history as the "religion" of the Marine Corps: "Past deeds are a young Marine's source of pride, inspiration to face danger, and reassurance that death in battle isn't consignment to oblivion" (72). Only a few pages later, on hearing of the September 11, 2001, attacks and presuming his unit will be sent to war, however, history becomes a violation: another officer, Jim Beal, claims "[f]ellas, history just bent us over" (74). Clearly, history is neither all good nor all bad, nor is it something to rely on uncritically.

Second, Fick initially objects to the use of sports analogies to describe combat, even when they were regularly a part of Marine officer diction during training:

> OCS [Officer Candidate School] was a game. Taking advantage of unrealistic details on field exercises at TBS [The Basic School] was "gaming the game." Winning. Losing. Code words like "touchdown" and "foul ball." But sitting in that CH-53 [helicopter], racing north into Pakistan, it didn't feel like a game. It felt like the most serious thing I'd ever done [97].

Later, however, in Iraq, "game" seems a more appropriate moniker for what he is doing: "This was becoming a game. I was starting to look forward to missions and firefights in the way I might savor pickup football or playing baseball. There was excitement, teamwork, common purpose, and the chance to demonstrate skill" (261). War itself has altered his notions of proper semantics.

Third, after some time in Iraq, Fick learns while choosing whether to treat an injured Iraqi girl or to look for fedayeen that decision-making is not as straightforward as monolithic masculinity would have Americans believe. On reflection, he comments that he is "learning that choices in war rarely are between good and bad, but rather between bad and worse" (339). This anguish is reflected earlier when, after Espera worries about killing people, Fick contemplates how each combatant agonizes over the decisions he must make in the midst of combat (261). Later, however, after leaving the Corps and having to justify his departure from "a last bastion of manhood," Fick reverses himself, remarking that while there was no pride simply in having been in Iraq, "The pride was in our good decisions, in the things we did right" (368). This amnesia is forgetful at best, contradictory at worst, but reflects how masculinity is at its most vulnerable during war when it cannot uphold decisiveness.

Fourth, Fick reports Espera's misgivings that a concern for credibility, whether personal or national, will bog down American forces, just as it did in Vietnam.

> If these people don't want for themselves what we want for them, then this *will* be Vietnam. We'll get our pride and our credibility involved, and then we'll keep throwing money and men down the pit long after everybody else knows we're fucked. We'll leave, and Iraq will be even worse than the shit hole it was a month ago when we kicked down the door [318].

While Fick does not indicate whether he agrees with Espera, the lesson silences them all, suggesting Fick is mulling over the idea. Nonetheless, not long later and contrary to Marine regulations, Fick opts to disarm some unexploded ordnance for the sake of credibility: "Not personal pride — that sort of immaturity got people killed — but the credibility of the U.S. Marines as a force for good in these people's lives" (330). It is Fick's desire to reinforce monolithic masculinity that compels him to establish the credibility of the Marines. Fick's distinction that one type of credibility-seeking would get people killed and another not seems false in this instance: Marines and Iraqis both could die were the ordnance to explode. Clearly, Fick is motivated by pride in being a Marine.

Finally, Fick is divided when it comes to activity, initiative, and productivity, three elements of monolithic masculinity. Not knowing that his unit's mission is to act as a feint for the force's main thrust (oddly, journalist Wright does know this), he is frustrated that they always are encountering Iraqi ambushes rather than establishing ambushes themselves. He longs for control of this unruly and unpredictable situation, and when his platoon is stationary for a number of days, Fick "craved action" and "needed a fix" (279, 322). He is "aggressive, almost euphoric" when they do seize the initiative and, when they finally arrive in Baghdad, feels purposeful with the prospect of making changes in Iraqi lives (256, 316). Once the euphoria and illusion of making change wear off, however, Fick is willing to forgo his masculine ideals about honor and glory, about the Marines being the last bastion of American manhood. Instead, he re-arms some Kurdish fighters opposed to the Hussein regime because "I preferred to have as many proxies fighting for us as possible if that meant more killing and dying done by them and less by my Marines" (346). Calling the peshmerga "proxies" instead of "allies" is instructive: Fick defies the "fundamental law of warfare" because, as he points out, "war makes for rational choices that are hard to understand in more reflective moments." Thus, rather than war providing an emotional venue to test and prove one's masculinity on the battlefield, war rationally forces having others fight one's fights. Just as Espera saw himself and other "psychos" as proxies for wealthy Americans, American combatants view peshmerga as proxies for themselves.

Wright's and Fick's narratives make clear that the meanings of masculinity are not absolute, and especially not so where they are supposed to be most secure. "Combat," Fick declares, "is a form of vertigo. I was trained to thrive on chaos, but nothing prepared me for the fear of doubting my own senses. Frequently, I found that my memory of a firefight was just that — mine. Afterwards, five Marines told five different stories" (219). The persistence of this view of war into the early twenty-first century verifies the durable change to the masculinity of men and women in combat. All of these late twentieth- and early twenty-first-century cultural products—presidential campaigns, recruiting ads, films, political studies, and memoirs—some more apparently than others, mark the traces of the Vietnam War and its connection to masculinity. As Todd Gitlin claims in "Unforgettable Vietnam and Its Burdens," "The afterlife of the Vietnam War has lasted longer now than the war itself. Time makes new wounds. A host of legends clamor to make the disaster mean something." The "legends" to which Gitlin refers appear both in popular culture forms, such as film, television, and fiction, and also in national culture, such as military recruiting advertisements and campaign strategies. What the profusion of Vietnam War traces intimate is that some factor is at work in the national imagination, a factor these texts urge is the evolution of gender.

Chapter Notes

Introduction

1. I thank David Arnold for identifying this former officer as LTC Hank Kiersey, a one-time Army officer and West Point instructor. Kiersey is featured in David Lipsky's 2003 *Absolutely American: Four Years at West Point* as the well-loved "huah of huahs" (74) who took the fall for a junior officer's homophobic faux pas and was then asked to retire. In 2007, Kiersey could be found as the military advisor for an Xbox game, "Call of Duty" (Team XBox).

2. Equally important to the development of theories of masculinity are the anthologies and applications of masculinity theory that have been published since the early 1990s. These include: *The Changing Fictions of Masculinity* (David Rosen, 1993); *Gendering War Talk* (Miriam Cooke and Angela Woollacott, eds., 1993); *Running Scared: Masculinity and the Representation of the Male Body* (Peter Lehman, 1993); *Theorizing Masculinities* (Harry Brod and Michael Kaufman, eds., 1994); *Constructing Masculinity* (Maurice Berger, Brian Wallis and Simon Watson, eds., 1995); *Messages Men Hear: Constructing Masculinities* (Ian M. Harris, 1995); *Are We Not Men? Masculine Anxiety and the Problem of African-American Identity* (Philip Brian Harper, 1996); *Race and the Subject of Masculinities* (Harry Stecopoulos and Michael Uebel, eds., 1997); *Black Men on Race, Gender, and Sexuality: A Critical Reader* (Devon W. Carbado, ed., 1999); *Citizen-Soldiers and Manly Warriors: Military Service and Gender in the Civic Republic Tradition* (R. Claire Snyder, 1999); *Taking Care of Men: Sexual Politics in the Public Mind* (Anthony McMahon, 1999); *Genders* (David Glover and Cora Kaplan, 2000); *"I Will Wear No Chain!" A Social History of African American Males* (Christopher B. Booker, 2000); *Manly States: Masculinities, International Relations, and Gender Politics* (Charlotte Hooper, 2001); *The Masculinities Reader* (Stephen M. Whitehead and Frank J. Barrett, eds., 2001); *Masculinity: Bodies, Movies, Culture* (Peter Lehman, ed., 2001); *Racial Castration: Managing Masculinity in Asian America* (David L. Eng, 2001); *Boys Don't Cry? Rethinking Narratives of Masculinity and Emotion in the U.S.* (Milette Shamir and Jennifer Travis, eds., 2002); and *Handbook of Studies on Men and Masculinities* (Michael S. Kimmel, Jeff Hearn, and R. W. Connell, eds., 2005).

3. In *Manipulating Masculinity: War and Gender in Modern British and American Literature* (2006), Kathy Phillips includes a chapter about the American War in Vietnam.

4. Homoeroticism is often referred to in criticism of Vietnam War narratives, though rarely is homosexuality dealt with at length. This element of masculinity has not been totally obscured in histories of the Vietnam War era, however. Randy Shilts' 1993 history of homosexuality in the U.S. military from the Vietnam through the Gulf War details multiple examples of gay and lesbian people in uniform. In his mainstream history of the 1960s, David Farber also points out that the "Gay Power Movement," openly initiated by the Stonewall Riots in 1969, was fueled by the voices of other civil rights and liberation movements of the era. Moreover, he points out that the movement was successful at having homosexuality depathologized with its 1973 removal from the American Psychiatric Association's list of diagnoses, and that "the gay rights movement was the most controversial civil rights or liberation movement to emerge out of the 1960s" (*Age of Great Dreams* 261). Michael Kimmel elaborates on the construction of masculinity as homophobia in "Masculinity as Homophobia: Fear, Shame, and Silence in the Construction of Gender Identity." Another important anthology is Wilbur J. Scott and Sandra Carson Stanley's *Gays and Lesbians in the Military: Issues, Concerns, and*

Contrasts (1994). This collection of essays provides information contextualizing the early 1990s conflict over openly gay and lesbian people serving in the American military.

5. In *The Scar That Binds: American Culture and the Vietnam War*, Keith Beattie discusses at length this pervasive belief, that only people — no, men — who were in Vietnam have the authority to speak about it. See his chapter, "The Vietnam Veteran as Ventriloquist," 58.

Chapter 1

1. For an example of this disproportion, consider an analysis of the Department of Defense database, "Southeast Asia, Combat Area Casualties File," which reveals the following percentages of enlisted casualties in the U.S. Army during the Vietnam War: "Whites" (83.5 percent); "Blacks" (15.1 percent); "American Indian" (.4 percent); Asian (.7 percent); and "Unknown" (.07 percent). At the time, however, African Americans made up 11 percent of the U.S. population, and 14.1 percent of casualties in all four branches of the armed forces. The database does not contain information on Latino American casualties; the analysts deduced from census data and surnames of those killed that between 5 and 6 percent were Latino American, when Latino Americans made up approximately 4.5 percent of the total U.S. population. Casualties among officers in all branches, however, were overwhelmingly white, reflecting the fact that the vast majority of officers were (and are) white: "White" (96.4 percent); "Black" (1.8 percent); "American Indian" (1.3 percent); "Asian" (.08 percent); "Unknown" (1.3 percent). See "American War Library" for more data and analysis.

2. After the racial tumult of 1968, and the ensuing radicalization of many black soldiers, the armed forces instituted reforms aimed at quelling racial tensions. One of the effects of this reform effort was to reduce the number of African Americans assigned to especially hazardous duty, such as Rangers, Airborne, and Green Berets, and to increase the numbers of black officers. By 1971, the numbers of casualties among blacks were reduced from over 20 percent in 1965 and 1966 to 11.5 percent in 1969 (American War Library), with an average casualty rate of 12.6 percent by War's end (Westheider 13). According to a 1971 report issued by the Equal Opportunity Office of the Department of Defense, "Negroes" made up 11.9 percent of the Army, 4.5 percent of the Navy, 9.7 percent of the Marine Corps, and 13.2 percent of the Air Force. The same document reported that "Negroes" made up 13.2 percent of casualties in the Army, 2.4 percent in the Navy, 12.4 percent in the Marine Corps, and 2.6 percent in the Air Force. Clearly, African Americans still made up a disproportionate number of casualties in the two groups most responsible for ground warfare: the Army and the Marines (U.S. Department of Defense [Equal Opportunity]).

3. For more about African Americans, the Civil Rights and Black Nationalist Movements, and the Vietnam War, especially in terms of assimilation and separatism, see the following: Christopher Booker, Colburn and Pozzetta, "Statement on Vietnam," Clyde Taylor, James Westheider, Colin Powell, and David Parks.

4. For more about the racial status of Latino Americans before the War and the Chicano Movement, see F. Arturo Rosales, Juan Gómez Quiñones, and Ignacio M. Garcia.

5. For more about American Indians and the Vietnam War, see Tom Holm. For more about the American Indian Movement, consult the following: Peter Matthiessen, *In the Spirit of Crazy Horse* (1980); Rex Weyler, *Blood of the Land: The Government and Corporate War against the American Indian Movement* (1982); Paul Chaat Smith and Robert Allen Warrior, *Like a Hurricane* (1996); Philip J. Deloria and Neal Salisbury, *A Companion to American Indian History* (2002); and Chadwick Allen, *Blood Narrative: Indigenous Identity in American Indian and Maori Literary and Activist Texts* (2002).

6. Both are veterans of the War, Del Vecchio as a combat correspondent with the 101st Airborne (Airmobile) Division, and Duncan as an infantryman in the highlands of I Corps, whereas the author of the third possible text, John Williams, is black but never served in the military. Moreover, as Jeff Loeb points out in his Afterword to Terry Whitmore's re-published memoir, *Memphis-Nam-Sweden* (1997), only three African American veterans have written novels about Vietnam: George Davis, *Coming Home* (1971); A. R. Flowers, *De Mojo Blues* (1985); and John Carn, *Shaw's Nam* (1984) (Whitmore 202). Both Bates and Kinney discuss Williams' text, *Captain Blackman* (1972).

7. For instance, in texts concerning the

post-Civil War battles with Native Americans, black "buffalo soldiers" often were used to fight the battles. As a contemporary example of the depiction of "buffalo soldiers" in the Ninth Cavalry during the "Ghost Dance Wars" of 1890, see Charles Alexander Eastman, "From the Deep Woods to Civilization" (1916). It is well known, too, that blacks in the Navy have most often been permitted to serve only in the messman's branch, as cooks and stewards (Moskos 112-113). See Moskos, *The American Enlisted Man* (1970) for a contemporary analysis of the racial situation in the United States military during the Vietnam War era. See Buckley, *American Patriots* (2001) for a historical account of black soldiers in the American military. See also Graham, *The Brothers' Vietnam War* (2003) and Lanning, *The African-American Soldier* (2004) for detailed analyses of experiences of some African Americans during the Vietnam War.

8. According to Moskos and Butler (29-30), under the threat of civil disobedience by the Brotherhood of Sleeping Car Porters and the Committee against Jim Crow in Military Service and Training if racial segregation were not ended in the military, President Truman signed Executive Order 9381 on July 26, 1948, ending segregation in the military. It reads: "It is the declared policy of the President of the United States that there shall be equality of treatment and opportunity for all persons in the Armed Forces. This policy shall be put into effect as rapidly as possible, having due regard to the time required to effectuate any necessary changes without impairing efficiency or morale."

9. See Moskos and Butler, pages 15-36, for a concise history of the African American presence in the American military from the American Revolutionary War to the 1992-93 incursion into Somalia. See also the American War Library at http://members.aol.com/WarLibrary for a close look at the demographics of the racial and other identities of the people involved in America's wars. Clyde Taylor's introductory essay to the collection *Vietnam and Black America*, entitled "Then and Now," provides a contemporary (1973) perspective on the experiences of African Americans in the United States military.

10. See U.S. Department of Defense for the link to the electronic National Archives. See http://members.aol.com/WarLibrary/vwc20.htm for a comprehensive analysis of this database. In this summary, the author (William F. Abbott, Vietnam Veteran) says: "Of all enlisted men who died in V'nam [sic], blacks made up 14.1 percent of the total. This came at a time when blacks made up 11 percent of the young male population nationwide. However, if we add officer casualties to the total then this over-representation is reduced to 12.5 percent of the casualties. [The officer corps was predominately white. Christian Appy says in *Working-Class War* that 2 percent of officers were black (22). Adding officers to the dead, then, reduces the proportion of the black dead to the total dead.] Of the 7262 blacks who died, 6955 or 96 percent were Army and Marine enlisted men. The combination of our selective service policies, our skills and aptitude testing of both volunteers and draftees (in which blacks scored noticeably lower) all conspired to assign blacks in greater numbers to the combat units of the Army and USMC." Abbott continues by qualifying the numbers cited above: "Early in the war, when blacks made up about 11 percent of our Vietnam force, black casualties soared to over 20 percent of the total (1965 and 1966). Black leaders, including Martin Luther King, protested and Pres [sic] Johnson ordered that black participation in the combat units should be cut back. As a result, the black casualty rate was reduced to 11.5 percent by 1969."

11. Anti-miscegenation laws were also in place that stipulated "one drop" of "black" blood would categorize a person as black and not white. See Siobhan Somerville's Introduction to *Queering the Color Line* (2000) for an outline of these laws. Werner Sollors points out that a result of the use of "race" by the NAZI Party, preceding and during World War II, was the revival of the "obsolete English noun [ethnicity]." "'Race,'" he says, "[...] is, in current American usage, sometimes perceived to be more intense, 'objective,' or real than ethnicity. As in the cases of 'the Irish race' or 'Jewish race,' the word was, however, the eighteenth- and nineteenth-century synonym for what is now, after the fascist abuses of 'race' in the 1930s and 1940s, more frequently discussed as 'ethnicity'[...] that seems to have served as a more neutral term than the one in the name of which the National Socialists shaped their genocidal policies" (Sollors 289).

12. David Roediger argues in the introduction to *Towards the Abolition of Whiteness* (1994): "[T]hat race is socially constructed broadly 'works,' by helping powerfully to clarify important issues, but that [constructivist idea] does not, by itself, settle the question of what political direction to take in matters of race and class." He elaborates on

this, suggesting that "the central political implication arising from the insight that race is socially constructed is the specific need to attack *whiteness* as a destructive ideology rather than to attack the concept of race abstractly" (3). In a chapter entitled "Whiteness and Ethnicity in the History of 'White Ethnics' in the United States," Roediger examines the specific way, in the first half of the twentieth century, ethnic groups in the United States from areas such as Italy, Ireland, and Poland constructed themselves (and were constructed) as specifically white *ethnic* groups, not just as white. Race became the presiding factor — distinct from ethnicity — when who was "foreign" needed to be determined (189). As an example, Roediger analyzes a passage from William Attaway's 1941 novel, *Blood on the Forge*, which illustrates what Roediger terms a "recasting" of the distinctions between a black man and some Irish immigrants. When the black man behaves nobly in the eyes of the Irish men, the Irish therefore confer on the black man the accolade "Black Irish." Roediger reads this scene as a painful example of the way race lines may appear to be broken down, but it is a temporary and superficial break, one which will not bridge the gap in status between white ethnics and blacks. It seems to me that the same simulation of breaking down boundaries is occurring in *The 13th Valley*: the "bridging," between lower class whites and blacks is, in fact, superficial and temporary, though the centrality of characters of color intimates otherwise.

13. Both of these text-producers make claims to authenticity as a result of first-hand experience. John Del Vecchio was a combat correspondent in Vietnam with the 101st Airborne Division (Airmobile) from 1970 to 1971. He says in his "Author's Note" that the story is "a composite of events from several operations" occurring during the battle he depicts in the novel. Furthermore, he is deigned the truth-teller and granted further authenticity by another soldier in that battle: "You can do it, Man. You write about this place. You been here a long time. People gotta know what it was really like" (Acknowledgements). Though all reports confirm that Patrick Duncan served in the Vietnam War, the dates of that service conflict. One report says he served for 15 months (1968-1969) in the 173rd Airborne Brigade (the same unit that Larry Heinemann's "Paco" of *Paco's Story* served in when he was hit by friendly fire) and that the experience changed his life, from that of a young working-class man in and out of jail to a college graduate and upstart filmmaker ("Patrick S. Duncan"). Another source states that Duncan "enlisted in the US Army in 1965 to qualify for the G.I. Bill; his tenure included a 15-month tour of duty in Vietnam, which formed the basis for several of his later film projects" ("Celebrities"). The differing dates in these two reports could be significant, since the 173rd may have been engaged in dissimilar missions in those years, thereby calling into question Duncan's "eye witness" account.

14. See the on-line American War Library at http://members.aol.com/WarLibrary/vwc20.htm. Author William F. Abbott concludes from his analysis of Department of Defense data: "During the V'nam [sic] War, the Navy and USAF [United States Air Force] became substantially white enclaves. Of the 4953 Navy and USAF casualties, both officer and enlisted, 4736 or 96 percent were white. Officer casualties of all branches were overwhelmingly white. Of the 7877 officer casualties, 7595 or 96.4 percent were white; 147 or 1.8 percent were black; 24 or .03 percent were Asian; 7 or .08 percent were Naive[sic] Amer [sic] and 104 or 1.3 percent were unidentified by race." Because of these minuscule percentages of officers of color, it seems highly significant that Del Vecchio would choose to make his central character black, and that he would have his central character at the center of a multi-racial company.

15. Other Vietnam War novels which are notable in their dependence on names to signify something important about characters' identities include: most of James Webb's novels, especially *Fields of Fire*; most of Tim O'Brien's work, including *If I Die in a Combat Zone*, *Going after Cacciato*, and *The Things They Carried*; William Eastlake's *The Bamboo Bed*; and a variety of other texts like Michael Herr's *Dispatches*, the film *Full Metal Jacket*, and narratives and memoirs such as *Bloods*, *No Shining Armor*, and *We Were Soldiers Once ... and Young*.

16. Judith Butler problematizes the significance of names in *Bodies That Matter*. Footnote 18 to Chapter Eight (280) raises the issue of naming and how names may substitute for descriptors of people. Citing Saul Kripke's contention in *Naming and Necessity* (1980) that names are not identical to the descriptions of a person, Butler wonders whether a person's name is assigned as the result of already existing characteristics, or if the name, once assigned, constitutes the person's identity. She concludes that names, not

descriptions, are the things that guarantee a person's identity. "Hence, even if descriptions are invoked in naming, in the primal baptism, those descriptions do not function as rigid indicators: that is the sole function of the name. The cluster of descriptions that constitute the person prior to the name do not guarantee the identity of the person across possible worlds; only the name, in its function as rigid indicator, can provide that guarantee" (280). In this sense, then, when soldiers are named in a military context, they are not re-born but their identities are re-made in the "rigidity" of the new designator. This, it seems to me, is part of the masculinizing effort that war precipitates.

17. In discussing the genre of the World War II combat film, Thomas Schatz emphasizes how these films were used as propaganda devices by the United States government. In his discussion of *Bataan* (1943) as a prototypical combat film, Schatz points out that an element of the "propaganda" of these films was their "democratic ethnic mix" (116).

18. A battalion is a tactical-level unit. From strategic to tactical, Army units are: *Division*, made up of many brigades, and commanded by a one- or two-star general; *Brigade*, made up of many (at least four) battalions, and commanded by a colonel; *Battalion*, made up of (at least four) companies, and commanded by a lieutenant colonel; *Company*, made up of three platoons plus a command post, and commanded by a captain; *Platoon*, made up of three squads plus a platoon command post, and commanded by a first or second lieutenant; *Squad*, made up of between seven and ten people, and commanded by a senior non-commissioned officer; *Team*, made up of three or four people.

19. In his history of the anti-war movement, *The War Within*, Tom Wells cites many major anti-war demonstrations in the Berkeley area during this time, beginning with the spring 1965 "teach-ins" (24) which included 30,000 people during a 36-hour period; another large teach-in in the autumn (57); an April 1966 anti-war demonstration in response to the Buddhist uprising in South Vietnam (71); the autumn 1967 "turn-in" of draft cards and subsequent demonstration at the Oakland induction center (192-193); and in April 1970, thousands of protestors laid siege to the Berkeley ROTC building (406). In *Antiwarriors*, Melvin Small adds that "[a]t Berkeley alone during the 1968-69 school year [nine months after Brooks had left graduate school], there were six major confrontations between students and the police, which resulted in twenty-two days of street fighting, 2,000 arrests, 150 suspensions or expulsions, and twenty-two days of occupation by the National Guard" and that San Francisco State University experienced a 134-day strike beginning in December 1968 (87). Nationally, ROTC numbers were large in 1966 at nearly 200,000, but by 1973, only 72,000 students were enrolled and many ROTC programs had been discontinued (Small 71). The number of ROTC programs at historically black colleges increased during the War, however, from 14 in 1970 to 19 by 1972 (Westheider 123).

20. In *Paco's Story*, a novel I analyze in Chapter Three, a loathsome character named Russell is telling others the story of how a pair of black men mistakenly tried to rob a bingo club attended by sheriffs. Russell uses many racist terms for the robbers: "shines," "nigger," "soul brother," "jitterbug." He also uses names to signify black race, among them, "Rufus": "This Jasper–name of Rufus or Zebedee or Snowflake, or some lamebrained affair as that–must have been a busboy or dishwasher around back in the kitchen someplace" (80). This usage indicates how the name "Rufus" is deliberately used by Del Vecchio for what it suggests about race.

21. In *Deep Talk: Reading African-American Literary Names*, Debra Walker King claims that names, as they are conceived by black authors for black characters, are ways to engage in "deep talk," a talk which suggests meanings beyond the literal ones used to distinguish characters, and that provide, in a positive sense, the resources for characters to resist the oppressive forces in their lives. Though Del Vecchio's use of names might be considered "deep talk," the talk is not liberating for the characters of color, but is just the opposite.

22. For examples of early Men's Movement literature, see Pleck and Sawyer, Goldberg, and Farrell.

23. Colburn and Pozzetta liken "ethnic activism" to African American cultural nationalism. They cite Italian Americans especially, who organized extensively to redefine what it meant to be Italian American. These efforts resulted not just in an embrace of cultural expression, but also in lobbying for representation in government and labor. This "renaissance" was an attempt to "rewrite American history" in order to "remake the group's image" (133-134).

24. These are among a list of what H. Bruce Franklin calls "fantasies" of Vietnam in *Vietnam and Other American Fantasies* (2000). He argues that "the necessary therapy [to help the United States out of its "Vietnam Syndrome"] would have to include some confrontation with the fantasies that made the war possible as well as those myths, celluloid images, and other delusory fictions about 'Vietnam' that in the subsequent decades have come to replace historical and experiential reality" (3).

25. In *Film, Form, and Culture*, Robert Kolker defines shot/reverse shot as a filmic method of incorporating, or "suturing," the spectator into the narrative: "A character is seen talking or registering a response to something (this is the shot). Cut to the person being spoken to or the person or object that caused the character to respond (the reverse shot)" (37). In this way, "We [spectators] are connected to a filmic story largely through the orchestration of looks" as the gaze of the spectator is worked into the narrative through the invisibility of editing.

26. "Seeing Is Not Believing" is the title of Robert Kolker's first chapter of his book, *Film, Form, and Culture*. He claims "[r]eality is not an objective, geophysical phenomenon like a mountain. Reality is always something *said* or *understood* about the world. The physical world is 'there,' but reality is always a polymorphous, shifting complex of mediations, a kind of multifaceted lens, constructed by the changing attitudes and desires of a culture. Reality is a complex image of the world which many of us choose to agree to. The photographic and cinematic image is one of the ways we use this 'lens' (here in quite a literal sense) to interpret the complexities of the world" (9).

Chapter 2

1. The co-authors of this essay are described in the "Contributors" section as midlevel officers (captain and major) in the U.S. Army, stationed at the Defense Attaché's Office in Venezuela. Not only do their ranks and location suggest they represent a particular strata of service member, aspiring young officers who have made the "first cuts," they might also have more invested in asserting sexuality as an ethical choice. This hypothesis may apply especially in light of events such as Tailhook 1991, when many junior Navy officers were found "ethically lacking,"

and in the U.S. Air Force Academy rape scandal of 2003.

2. Homoeroticism is often referred to in criticism of Vietnam War narratives, though rarely is homosexuality dealt with at length. This element of masculinity has not been totally obscured in histories of the Vietnam War era, however. Randy Shilts' 1993 history of homosexuality in the U.S. military from the Vietnam through the Gulf War details multiple examples of gay and lesbian people in uniform. In his mainstream history of the 1960s, David Farber also points out that the "Gay Power Movement," openly initiated by the Stonewall Riots in 1969, was fueled by the voices of other civil rights and liberation movements of the era. Moreover, he points out that the movement was successful at having homosexuality depathologized with its 1973 removal from the American Psychiatric Association's list of diagnoses, and that "[t]he gay rights movement was the most controversial civil rights or liberation movement to emerge out of the 1960s" (261). Michael Kimmel elaborates on the construction of masculinity as homophobia in "Masculinity as Homophobia: Fear, Shame, and Silence in the Construction of Gender Identity." Another important anthology is Wilbur J. Scott and Sandra Carson Stanley's *Gays and Lesbians in the Military: Issues, Concerns, and Contrasts* (1994). This collection of essays provides information contextualizing the early 1990s conflict over openly gay and lesbian people serving in the American military.

3. One of the key queer theorists is Eve Kosofsky Sedgwick, whose books *Between Men* (1985) and *Epistemology of the Closet* (1990) set out the parameters of the debate. Another key theorist is Judith Butler, especially her book, *Gender Trouble* (1990). Other important theorists include Michel Foucault, Gayle Rubin, Michael Warner, Gloria Anzaldua, David Halperin, and Marjorie Garber.

4. See Berubé, Scott and Stanley, Williams and Weinberg, and D'Emilio, in addition to Shilts, for historical accounts since World War II of these actions against alleged homosexual military members. Berubé deals especially with the war era, Scott with the period following World War II (the "Cold War"), and Williams and Weinberg with the social and mental health implications for service members who were discharged with less-than-honorable discharges. D'Emilio argues that the World War II period was essential for creating a sense of a national gay culture. Shilts records specific

cases of discharge from 1954 to 1990. All five sources advocate for homosexuals serving, and serving openly.

5. These documents can be found assembled in one volume, *Homosexuality and the Military*. See also a brief of the legal situation following the enactment of the National Defense Authorization Act of 1993, "Homosexuals and U.S. Military Policy: Current Issues." Reports conducted by the United States military, however, continue to find that homosexuals serving openly in the U.S. forces would be detrimental. See, for instance, a report issued in 1998, following the institution of President Clinton's "don't ask, don't tell, don't pursue" law of 1993: "Report to the Secretary of Defense: Review of the Effectiveness of the Application and Enforcement of the Department's Policy on Homosexual Conduct in the Military." This document was produced in 1998 by the Department of Defense's Office of the Under Secretary of Defense (Personnel and Readiness), the DoD unit responsible for ensuring the Defense Department is adhering to federal laws. The study concludes that discharges for homosexuality since the enactment of the law had risen noticeably but that those numbers did not indicate "witch hunts" on the part of the military. However, the study found that "women have been discharged under the policy at rates that exceed their representation in the force. Women made up just over 13 percent of the military strength of the Services but accounted for 29 percent of the homosexual conduct discharges in Fiscal Year 1996" ("Office"). While this study provides substantial evidence of continued ignorance concerning the 1993 law and its subsequent enactment into military regulations—"a lack of familiarity with the policy"— it does not conclude the law itself is at fault. Instead, there is a continued desire in the military to punish homosexual identification.

6. See Skaine, *Women at War: Gender Issues of Americans in Combat*, for a brief history of women serving in the United States military.

7. Perhaps the scene has not been analyzed because, as Jeffords puts it, "Vietnam narratives are replete with sexual encounters, pornographic images, and sexually motivated vocabularies" (*Remasculinization* 72), and so this one is only one among many. While *The 13th Valley* is recognized as part of the canon based on the number of passing references to it (i.e., Turner, Jason), only a few critics have given it substantial attention, including an article-length treatment of the novel by Pauline Uchmanowicz, entitled "Vanishing Vietnam: Whiteness and the Technology of Memory." References to *The 13th Valley* appear in John Hellmann's *American Myth and the Legacy of Vietnam*, where he discusses Del Vecchio's novel as "a journey of American heroes into a frontier where they find themselves stranded from their society" and as "a mythic representation of the living American ideal" (133). Thomas Myers devotes a whole chapter to comparing *The 13th Valley* to Herman Melville's *Moby Dick* in *Walking Point: American Narratives of Vietnam*. Milton Bates mentions Del Vecchio's novel in passing, as an illustration of the rhetorical use of documents in fiction (229) in *The Wars We Took to Vietnam*, while Katherine Kinney's *Friendly Fire* does not reference the novel.

8. In "The Creation of Army Officers and the Gender Lie," Billie Mitchell discusses the labels applied to women in the military. "Paula Coughlin — the whistleblower of the [1991] Tailhook scandal — has been recast as 'slut,' the role of bitch having been taken to its limit. At first, she was condemned in testimony for her abrasive manner (uncontrollable), foul mouth (too masculine), and unattractiveness as a woman and an officer (dyke). Recent testimony has placed her on the scene at Tailhook, having her legs shaved by men in the main lounge (willing whore). On the day her multimillion-dollar victory in court was announced, a colleague of mine [at West Point, where Mitchell was on the faculty] referred to her as 'the babe.' But even people who are not vested in any particular outcome to her case and are not easily duped by the Navy's typecasting of her are honestly perplexed by her and women like her" (Stiehm 38).

9. I was on active duty in the U.S. Army during this period, 1979–1983, serving in the 3rd Armored Division in West Germany. As one of perhaps 100 women among thousands of men in a tactical unit (one that would be in direct combat during war), and one of a handful of female officers, I felt intensely the silent accusation against women: that we were strange people, abnormal women, for being in the military, and that our sexuality was always suspect. (I was married, but to a non-military man, which made me still somewhat suspect and him, very suspicious.) As one of the few female officers, especially when I was re-assigned from the Division Headquarters to the Division Artillery, I sometimes was sought out as a confidante by

enlisted women who were not in my chain of command. One episode which highlights how the identity of "lesbian" could invalidate a female soldier occurred when one confided to me that a male soldier had raped her. Her story was that his girlfriend lived in the room directly above hers in the barracks, and his room was directly below hers. One hot summer night he was visiting the girlfriend beyond curfew, so he had to scale the outside wall to return to his room without being detected. He ended up entering the confider's open window, and she was wakened to his raping her. Though the event had happened months before the soldier told me, she had been unwilling to report it to anyone earlier because she was afraid the accusation would rebound on her. She intimated to me that she was a lesbian, so if she were to report the assault, her claim would be minimized because she would not be seen as "attractive enough" to warrant raping. She could not bear that the male soldier would get away with this crime, so, with my support, she made her accusations against him to the Criminal Investigative Division (CID). I attended the meetings she had with the investigators, and though they did not challenge her sexuality, it was apparent to me that they were unwilling to believe her story because of her appearance as a very physically strong young woman who worked in an armored artillery unit. Complicating the case even further was the fact that the young man was African American and everyone else involved — I, the accuser, and the male and female investigators — were white. Nothing ever came of the case.

10. R.W. Connell's work exemplifies this recent switch from indifference/ignorance to interest in female masculinity. For instance, though Connell had published several books on masculinity before 2000, it was only in *The Men and the Boys* (2000) that he recognized the exigency of female masculinity. "Masculinity *refers* to male bodies (sometimes directly, sometimes symbolically and indirectly), but is not *determined* by male biology. It is, thus, perfectly logical to talk about masculine women or masculinity in women's lives, as well as masculinity in men's lives" (29).

11. Both Milton Bates' *The Wars We Took to Vietnam* (1996) and Philip Beidler's *Re-Writing America: Vietnam Authors in Their Generation* (1991) ascribe to the "lost frontier" reading of *Why Are We in Vietnam?* Another study that includes a discussion of *Why Are We in Vietnam?* is Michael K. Glenday's historicist study of Norman Mailer's work. Glenday contends Mailer's work needs to be considered in a historical context and in relation to previous work by Mailer. However, Glenday reaches a conclusion similar to those of Hellmann, Bates, and Beidler: "The intimation received is in the end not one of transcendence, but of sorrow, inescapable and endemic. That is the meaning of the North American wilderness in Mailer's late-century reworking of its myth. The nation has slimed its very foundation in its embrace of technology for destruction" (114).

12. Norman Mailer's 1948 *The Naked and the Dead* and James Jones' 1962 *The Thin Red Line* both depict the war in the Pacific during World War II, yet the two diverge in their depictions of homosexuality, even though the official word on homosexuality during World War II was that it was a mental illness subject to hospitalization or discharge, not imprisonment (Berubé 128-148). Mailer's text intimates that General Cummings is homosexual, but never demonstrates his acting on that desire (403-427), demonstrating the World War II era's attitude that homosexuality was shameful but not criminal. James Jones' 1962 rendering, however, depicts two enlisted men, Fife and Bead, engaging in homosexual acts without consequence, demonstrating a loosening of military policies in the 1960s, even as homophobia during the Cold War era was escalating (Corber 5).

13. The birth of the Gay Liberation Movement is usually cited as the June 27, 1969, raid of the Stonewall Inn in Manhattan (D'Emilio, *Sexual Politics* 231), though that date is also interpreted as an outcome of building tensions as opposed to the beginning of tensions. In fact, in an essay published after *Sexual Politics* (1983), D'Emilio suggests that pinning the beginnings of the Gay Liberation Movement only to the Stonewall Inn riot and, consequently, to what he terms the "bad 60s" is hazardous, since when "the country is spinning out of control, historians inevitably imprison homosexuality and gay liberation in a narrative of decline" ("Placing" 211). D'Emilio instead wants to position the Gay Liberation Movement as the "echo" of the 1960s and a "harbinger" of the progressive politics that have since occurred in the late twentieth century. Justin David Suran also posits in "Coming Out against the War: Antimilitarism and the Politicization of Homosexuality in the Era of Vietnam" that the War and the anti-war movement were central to "the emergence of the Gay Liberation Movement"

(452) and, in fact, preceded Stonewall. "In reality," says Suran, "a socially constructed persona was central to the initiation of Gay Liberation as a mass protest movement; Gay Liberationists constituted an identity as revolutionist-homosexuals in the culture of antiwar protest" (479). Suran's assertion supports my contention that the era openly was suffused with changes to the concepts of gender and sexual identity and fear of that change, evident in Mailer's and Haldeman's texts.

14. In the Author's Note to the 1997 "definitive edition," Haldeman outlines the difficulties he had getting the novel published in the early 1970s. The novel was rejected by eighteen publishers, but in the meantime was being serialized in the science fiction *Analog* magazine. One section was omitted from the serialization as a result of its being "too downbeat," but that section was restored in the 1997 edition, and appears as the "Sergeant Mandella" section, Chapter Six through the section's conclusion. During this section, William and Marygay return to Earth, where they find life intolerable. One of the moments most disturbing to William is his discovery of his mother's homosexual relationship. In terms of the growing evidence of failed approaches to the actual Vietnam War, Christian Appy and Alexander Bloom assert in their 2001 essay that the War was continued because "policy makers were more concerned merely with the effect of defeat on the U.S. image as a world power." The outcome of the War was also seen as a reflection on the President then in office: "No one was willing to be the first president to lose a war, regardless of the cause or the cost" (52).

15. Mason suggests that Sam reflects the era, though Mason is not explicit about Sam's sexuality. Further, Mason expresses appreciation for the film version, but insists that changes were made that "lost some of the motivation from the story" (Schroeder 178). I contend that what is missing from the film is Sam's female masculinity.

16. For a reading of Jewison's adaptation, see Lauren Berlant's "Theory of Infantile Citizenship" in *The Queen of America Goes to Washington City: Essays on Sex and Citizenship* and Barbara Tepa Lupack's "History as Her-Story: Adapting Bobbie Ann Mason's *In Country* to Film." For gender in Mason's *In Country*, see Blais, Graybill, Timothy D. O'Brien, and Carton.

17. In *Vietnam at 24 Frames Per Second*, Jeremy Devine records the 1980s evolution of the Vietnam vet image. Devine refers to films made in the period from 1980 to 1985 as "delusionary escapist adventures" (198), films made in reaction to films like the "accusatory" *Apocalypse Now* (1979) and *The Deer Hunter* (1978). Devine claims the 1986-1987 period initiated depictions of the victimized Vietnam vet, with films serving as "celebrations of the sacrifices of the foot soldier, the grunt" (237). Once Devine gets to the 1988-1989 film-making period, he argues that the "nation's collective psyche," damaged by Vietnam and Watergate, was experiencing a "rebirth," "rendered with more drama and less adventure" (275). Thus, the emphasis in the 1989 film is on the *rebirth* of Emmett, who had "died" as a 19-year-old numbskull in Vietnam, rather than on Sam's 1985 *birth* as a feeling and thinking 18-year-old. As Susan Jeffords claims about the whole of the 1980s "remasculinization" project, however, "Vietnam veterans are portrayed in contemporary American culture as emblems of an unjustly discriminated masculinity" (*Remasculinization* 116).

18. Devine includes Willis in the list of "stars" who made Vietnam War films during the 1988-1989 period. However, Willis was not star enough to drive the success of the film in Europe; Devine says, "*In Country* relied on Lloyd's star power in Britain for its marketing" (304), even though Lloyd, as a teen actress, had only been in two films before this one: *Cookie* (1989) and *Wish You Were Here* (1987).

19. This is a particularly nebulous passage, because Emmett was looking at the memorial for the names of the men he knew had been killed as well as for the name of a friend he had hoped was still alive. Though he does display pleasure at what he sees—"his face bursts into a smile like flames"—it is unclear whether he is seeing names (of those he knew had died) or seeing the absence of a name (the friend about whom he was uncertain) (245).

20. In an astute analysis of the rhetoric of masculinity in 1970s and 1980s men's liberation discourse, Sally Robinson concludes that the discourse exemplifies a paradox that I find pertains to the Willis character. In "Men's Liberation, Men's Wounds," Robinson argues: "Men *must* restrain their dangerous impulses, but men *cannot* restrain them; men *must* release their blocked emotions, but men *cannot* release them. It is in the space between the 'must' and the 'cannot' that the physically and psychically wounded man emerges, *not* as a pathological, or even 'failed' man, but as the norm of a masculin-

ity that can only attempt to be 'healthy'" (225-226).

21. The version I am working with is published as one of the longer stories in O'Brien's *The Things They Carried* (1990). According to Milton Bates and Lorrie N. Smith, however, five of these stories previously were published in *Esquire* magazine from 1986 to 1989. As Smith claims, reading these texts sequentially from the point of view of the *Esquire* audience clarifies the stories' "increasingly misogynist narrative of masculine homosocial behavior under fire" ("The Things Men Do" 20).

22. Though women in the military had been, prior to the end of the Vietnam War, regarded as lesbians, the War's closure and the institution of a volunteer military forced a change in that attitude. With the switch to a volunteer Army after the War, the military had difficulty enlisting enough male soldiers to fill its ranks, and so targeted females. Randy Shilts details that change in *Conduct Unbecoming*:

> The 1972 predictions about recruitment shortfalls were the realities of 1973.... Opportunities for women exploded. The Army announced it would double the size of the Women's Army Corps by 1978. WAC uniforms would be restyled "to make them more feminine"; and the number of Military Occupational Specialties for which women qualified would increase from 139 to 436 out of the 484 MOS's [sic] in the Army. The Air Force more than doubled its jobs open to women, freeing up all but five of its 242 MOS's [sic] to WAFs. In January 1973, the Navy put its first woman in pilot training. And Admiral Elmo Zumwalt, the Chief of Naval Operations, stunned sailors nationwide when he said that if the Equal Rights Amendment passed, women would be allowed to serve on warships.... [Inequities continued, but] the military still offered women more opportunities than much of the civilian world did, and the number of women enlisting soared. By 1973, the women in the Air Force program, for example, had grown to 17,000–compared with 7,000 just five years earlier [182-183].

Chapter 3

1. Starr's 1973 report also presents evidence that the majority of those disabled by the War's events were "psychiatric" cases which could include, among other conditions, drug abuse, alcoholism, clinical depression, suicidal tendencies, and other behaviors that eventually would fall under the heading of Post-traumatic Stress Disorder. "Since the war began," claims Starr, "the VA [Veterans Administration, the institution which cares for the disabled veterans after they are discharged from the services] has received about 20,000 men directly from the military [i.e., their symptoms were manifest immediately during service, not years later], nearly all of them totally disabled. About 30 percent of the cases have been psychiatric, another 30 percent with nervous system injuries [like paraplegia], 10 percent amputees, and 8 percent with tuberculosis" (56). Starr's source for this data came from the 92nd Congress, which, because Starr's research began in 1971, means the War was not ended and that the total number of disabled soldiers had not yet been counted. For information on PTSD, see the National Center for Post-traumatic Stress Disorder at http://www.ncptsd.org. See Fontana and Rosenheck for another, less comprehensive study comparing the effects of the three different wars. This study focuses on the differences in military service in the three wars and calculates the effects of "traumatic exposure and psychiatric symptoms" (27). It concludes that suicide is more prevalent among Vietnam War veterans, that Vietnam veterans feel guiltier than those of the other two wars, that there is a causal relationship between PTSD and the quality of the homecoming, and that the single most traumatic event of war is not being wounded but being responsible for the death of another human being.

2. See Norden, *The Cinema of Isolation*, for a history of the use of the disabled image in cinema. He also cites Leslie Fiedler's *Freaks: Myths and Images of the Secret Self* as a source to explain the psychic appeal of people with disabilities.

3. See also Sonya Michel, "Danger on the Home Front: Motherhood, Sexuality, and Disabled Veterans in American Postwar Films," for a larger discussion of the reintegration problem.

4. Films that focus on the mental disability of the Vietnam veteran as opposed to his physical disability include the following: any of the Billy Jack films (*Billy Jack* [1971], *Trial of Billy Jack* [1974], *Billy Jack Goes to Washington* [1977]); any of the Rambo films (*Rambo: First Blood* [1982], *Rambo: First Blood II* [1985], *Rambo III* [1988]); *Taxi Driver* (1976); and *In Country* (1989). Interestingly, in the index to Jeremy Devine's *Vietnam at 24 Frames a Second*, under "Vet-

erans" depicted in films are sub-categories such as "as criminals," "as filmmakers," "and mental illness," "as politicians," "as scapegoats," "as vigilantes," but nothing referring to physical disability (399).

5. The Architectural Barriers Act of 1968 "requires that buildings and facilities that are designed, constructed, or altered with Federal funds, or leased by a Federal agency, comply with Federal standards in new and altered buildings and in newly leased facilities." The Rehabilitation Act of 1973 "prohibits discrimination on the basis of disability in programs conducted by Federal agencies, in programs receiving Federal financial assistance, in Federal employment, and in the employment practices of Federal contractors" (U.S. Department of Justice).

6. Saying that "almost everyone will experience a disability before death," Thomas Gerschick suggests using the term "temporarily able-bodied" to signify people who have not yet experienced their disability ("Sisyphus" 208, n. 2).

7. In a personal communication, Wendy Harbour suggests there are probably multiple hierarchies: "Personally, I don't believe a single hierarchy exists. I think there are several happening at once, and they happen to overlap somewhat. One hierarchy is 'Visibility,' as in how visible, distracting, or abnormal does this person appear? Another has to do with 'Severity,' meaning how severe is the disability — people often say things like 'well, at least she can still walk' or 'at least it's not life-threatening.' And I think we are all familiar with the term 'chrome mafia' and the perception that people with chairs are controlling the Movement. Then I've seen another hierarchy related to 'Intelligence' or 'Work Ability.' Of course there are also different hierarchies among ethnic groups and between men and women. Even within subgroups, there are hierarchies, with disabled people arranging their own community members into subgroups."

8. The first act of disability legislation was the War Risk Insurance Act of 1917, which "reimbursed potential future income loss due to service-related impairment and the disadvantage it caused the veteran in the labor market" (Hickel 239).

9. The argument of Jonathan Shay's popular study, *Achilles in Vietnam: Combat Trauma and the Undoing of Character* (1994), is that the narratives of Vietnam War veterans with PTSD reproduce Homer's account of Achilles in *The Odyssey*, thus offering to psychiatrists a mode for treatment. "The thrust of this work," asserts Shay, "is that the epic gives center stage to bitter experiences that actually do arise in war; further, it makes the claim that Homer has seen things that we in psychiatry and psychology have more or less missed" (xiii). Moreover, Shay is especially concerned with how war ruins "character," and so, paradoxically, "renders one unfit to be its [a nation's] citizen" (xx). Shay advocates for the good treatment of warriors, insisting that a nation which sends its people to war has the obligation to heal those same people, especially through a Homeric form, narrative. The message of this text is important to a disabled reading of any Vietnam War narrative, as it reflects how PTSD was being culturally integrated during the late 1980s and early 1990s, even though in 1980 PTSD had been entered into the diagnostic tool for psychiatry, the third edition of the *Diagnostic and Statistical Manual of Mental Disorders* (DSM III).

10. The controversy over the effects of Agent Orange continue into the twenty-first century, two and a half decades after the conclusion of the War, and nearly two decades after Mason had Sam proposing to Emmett that his ailments were a result of such exposure. Even though the Settlement Fund had been depleted and closed by 1997 (Veterans Benefits), as late as 2000, a representative of the Disabled American Veterans (DAV) group appealed to the Institute of Medicine (IOM) of the National Academy of Sciences to hold the United States government responsible for the welfare of soldiers exposed to Agent Orange during the Vietnam War. Said Richard A. Wannemacher, Jr., the Assistant National Legislative Director of Medical Affairs for the DAV, "We call upon the IOM, and all other agencies involved with herbicide exposure to continue to seek answers to the mystery surrounding the illnesses suffered by Vietnam veterans. We also ask that you act on what is already known [that a link had been found between exposure to Agent Orange in Vietnam and diabetes], by reporting to the Secretary [of the National Academy of Sciences] expeditiously, requesting that he work to bring laws in alignment with what the studies have found" (Disabled American Veterans). The controversy over Agent Orange continued when, in February of 2003, the Supreme Court heard a case arguing that victims of Agent Orange poisoning should still have the right to sue the manufacturers of Agent Orange, since the symptoms for many of those exposed had not manifested themselves when the settle-

ment fund was available (Sayre). In his history of the veterans' anti-war movement, Gerald Nicosia suggests that the VA was taken off guard by the Agent Orange allegations, as it was still reeling from the recent "delayed stress" [i.e., "PTSD"] diagnosis. "But Max Cleland [the VA administrator whose memoir I examine in this chapter] was blindsided by Agent Orange. For two years he had been fighting a pitched battle to get delayed stress recognized and to get Congress to foot the bill for at least some form of treatment. All the experts had told him it was delayed stress that was killing vets and wrecking their lives, driving them to drugs and booze and keeping them from being productive members of society. Now all of a sudden here were another group of screaming 'crazies,' only they were saying that nine-tenths of the problems with Vietnam vets—even things like lack of sex drive and kids with learning problems—were due to getting too many whiffs of a common weed spray. Cleland felt he had to draw the line somewhere, and draw the line he did" (388).

11. The different branches of the military forces finance and staff their own hospitals to serve their active-duty members. When those members are discharged from the services, their further rehabilitation occurs in Veterans Administration medical centers, which are funded and staffed by the federal government. Typically, medical service in branch hospitals, especially during the Vietnam War era, is far superior to that in VA centers, and the patients in the military branch hospitals tend to be younger than those in VA centers. With military cuts during the late 1980s, however, many military posts and bases were closed, and hospitals in those locations were deemed inefficient, since they served largely retirees and their families. Such was the case with the Letterman Army Hospital, which was deactivated in 1995. Despite Letterman Army Hospital's having been the Army's largest general hospital for most of the last century and a half, and a major research center for artificial blood, laser physics, and the treatment of trauma, the building where *Body Shop*'s narrative is set, opened in 1969 by Richard Nixon to serve the huge numbers of Vietnam wounded, was deemed "non-historic" and razed in the early part of 2003 as part of a Presidio area beautification plan. In 2005 it was replaced by the "Letterman Digital Arts Center" and is home to several Lucasfilm Ltd. companies. See http://www.presidio trust.gov/letterman/history.asp for a brief history of Letterman, and http://www.lucas film.com/press/presidio preview/ for a brief description of the plans for the Digital Arts Center.

12. Fred Turner cites one such psychiatrist in *Echoes of Combat* (2001), Mardi Horowitz. "To resolve this dilemma [of trying to deny having seen a horrific event], most people try to set the new, disruptive information aside and cling to their original beliefs....The idiom in which traumatic memory makes itself known varies, but the message remains the same: This new information somehow has to be brought together with the worldview it seems to shatter.... [O]nly when the survivor can draw new maps of the world, maps which incorporate both the horrific landscapes of the past and the comparatively well-ordered fields of the present, will the wheels of recollection and denial ground to a halt" (13). According to Turner, this "re-mapping" of the world has happened through a series of narratives that have broken the silence about Vietnam that prevailed after the War, and were occasioned in 1980 by the U.S. Congress's authorization for the building of the Vietnam Veterans War Memorial and a speech by then-President Reagan to the Veterans of Foreign Wars (15). I contend that this articulated pain was evident much sooner in cultural products such as films; it just had not been "officially" condoned.

13. Reverend Jerry Falwell founded the Moral Majority in 1979.

14. A crude analysis of several databases, including Ohio State's holdings, Amazon booksellers, and an Internet search for "disabled veterans," "paraplegic veterans," and "Vietnam War disabled veterans" came up only with the texts included in this analysis and, under the first two categories, a handful of narratives of paraplegia from World War II. There were no narratives of paraplegia from the Vietnam War.

15. See Boyle, "Phantom Pains: Disability, Masculinity and the Normal in Vietnam War Representations" for a fuller discussion of this phenomena in relation to the Vietnam War film, *Coming Home*.

16. The title is taken from Ernest Hemingway's World War I novel, *A Farewell to Arms*. In Chapter 34, Frederic Henry and Catherine Barkley have reunited and that night, Henry thinks this: "If people bring so much courage to this world the world has to kill them to break them, so of course it kills them. The world breaks every one and after-

ward many are strong at the broken places" (249).

17. According to Cleland, this accomplishment was no mean feat, since both his legs were amputated above the knee (AK). One of the primary problems for AK amputees using prosthetic legs is that, were they to fall, without the ability to maneuver that knees afford they would not be able to pick themselves up. Cleland's situation if he were to fall would be doubly difficult because he had only one arm. Additionally, knees help give our bodies balance; without that, an amputee on prosthetic legs would need to use crutches. But with one arm only, Cleland would not be able to use crutches (59-60).

18. See Gerald Nicosia's *Home to War* (2001), Chapter Four ("Invisible Wounds: Post-Traumatic Stress Disorder") for a detailed account of the Cranston committee findings and their outcome.

19. Cleland was defeated by Saxby Chambliss in his bid for reelection as a U.S. senator from Georgia during the 2002 election. Chambliss was accused of negative advertising which impugned the patriotism of Cleland. See "Notebook," Graham-Silverman, and D'Agostino for discussions of the campaign.

20. In "The History of Chosen Books," the anonymous author describes the publishing house's birth as the result of a dream, a "vision," which the husband of one of the founders had in 1971. This document also suggests that the publisher succeeded initially by riding the tide of the "charismatic renewal" or "born-again" movement in the 1970s, as it published books "with a charismatic flavor and a dramatic, first-person quality" (*Chosen Books*).

21. In *Home to War* (2001), Gerald Nicosia suggests that Cleland may have assumed someone else's story as his own, or at the least, that was the single instance of Cleland's toughness, as he used his general counsel, Guy McMichael III, as his front man. "Cleland liked to brag about how he once talked a disturbed vet out of killing a VA doctor, but the truth was he often used tough negotiators like McMichael to insulate himself from the anger of the veterans' community as well as backroom haggling and bullying on Capitol Hill" (364).

22. Only two years after receiving the Pulitzer Prize for this memoir, and 26 years after having multiple parts of his body blown off, Puller committed suicide on May 11, 1994. Reportedly, marital problems and drug and alcohol abuse had led to his taking his own life. See Witteman and Levy, Adler and Clift, and Kerrey for discussions of this event.

23. Puller suggests that he was only a social drinker before he was injured, a normal state in the military of the 1960s. Jerry Adler and Eleanor Clift, however, claim that Puller already was an alcoholic when he was hospitalized: "He was an alcoholic even before his injury, and a worse one after, until he quit drinking in 1981" (44).

24. Given Cleland's subsequent record as a Democratic advocate not only for veterans but also for other liberal causes, it is ironic that this portrait might suggest that no environmental changes are necessary. See especially D'Agostino and "Notebook" for the legislation Cleland has been engaged in as a U.S. senator. See also Gerald Nicosia for accounts of Cleland as the director of the Veterans Administration.

25. Examples of angry activists include Tom Cruise as Ron Kovic in *Born on the Fourth of July* (1989) and Jon Voight as Luke in *Coming Home* (1978). Examples of despairing men in wheelchairs include John Savage as Stevie in *The Deer Hunter* (1978) and Gary Sinise as LT Dan in *Forrest Gump* (1995).

26. Another text that focuses on the impact of disability on a young man's masculinity and the subsequent repercussions for his family is David Rabe's 1969 play, *Sticks and Bones*.

27. A U.S. Labor Department monograph published in 1975 entitled "Jobs for Veterans with Disabilities" asserts that "[t]he disabled veteran is commonly pictured as an amputee or a blind man, but only 6 percent of disabled Vietnam-era veterans fit this picture" (U.S. Department of Labor 7).

28. I write "Viet Cong" in quotation marks because that was a term applied by members of subsequent American administrations to people who referred to themselves as members of the National Liberation Front (NLF). Truong Nhu Tang, a former leading member of the NLF, defines the term this way in "A Vietnam Vocabulary": "Vietcong. A term since the late 1950s and applied generally to the insurgent forces in South Vietnam; the fighting arm of the NLF. The name is short for Viet Nam Cong San, or Vietnamese Communist. Many of the non-Communist revolutionaries [of the NLF] initially considered the term insulting" (xi).

29. Heinemann does offer a foreword, however, where he attempts to pin down who the "James" is. What he ends up doing,

though, is enumerating so many possibilities that none of them seems to apply. At the same time, the multiple interpretive possibilities of "James" suggests the interstitial space Paco may occupy.

30. Paco's employer at the Texas Lunch, Ernest Monroe, is a veteran of Iwo Jima, which he characterizes as "a sloppy, bloody butt-fuck" (128).

31. The text is unclear concerning Paco's race. His first name, which is used repeatedly, suggests he might be Hispanic. Paco's relative anonymity contributes to a reader not knowing what his race is. The text only reveals once, during one of Paco's dreams, that his last name is Sullivan, thereby complicating the reader's drawing conclusions about Paco's race based on his name(s).

32. James E. Westheider says in *Fighting on Two Fronts: African Americans and the Vietnam War*: "The Korean conflict was the first war to be affected by Executive Order 9981 [the law President Harry Truman had signed in July 1948]. Though the United States would enter the war with a still largely segregated military, the demands of combat would lead to rapid integration, especially in the combat units. In several key aspects, Korea would foreshadow the African American experience in Vietnam. As in the First World War and Vietnam, blacks would be disproportionately high numbers. Between 1950 and 1954, more than 1.7 million men were drafted and 219,128 or 12.8 percent of the total were African Americans. In both Korea and Vietnam, African Americans would also enlist in large numbers. By mid-1951 nearly one in four of the army's new recruits was black, and whether draftee or volunteer, he was more likely than the average white soldier to see combat and become a casualty, just as in Vietnam [pre-1969]" (21-22). In John A. Williams' 1972 *Captain Blackman*, the narrator makes clear that the transition to an integrated force during the Korean War was very difficult, as the characters "Blackman" and "Whittman" battle for superiority. Blackman thinks: "Now it's payoff time. Send your [black]ass across the Yalu [river between China and North Korea] to stop 700 million Chinese who don't give a shit about you anymore than you give a shit about them, just to save the world from communism for some Whitey sonofabitch who's afraid of it because maybe it'd give other people the same things he has" (240).

33. See Laura Mulvey, "Visual Pleasure and Narrative Cinema," for an explanation of the gaze.

Chapter 4

1. During the 2008 presidential primary campaign, only one of the six campaign leaders in each of the two parties had served in the military. As a young woman in the 1960s and early 1970s, Hillary Clinton would not have been expected to serve or be drafted. Barack Obama was born in 1961 and so at twelve years old was not eligible for the draft, which ended in 1973. John Edwards just missed the draft as he was born in 1953 and had a college deferment. Rudy Guiliani, born in 1944, had multiple educational and occupational deferments which concluded in 1971. Mitt Romney, who was born in 1947, was granted a draft deferment for his work as a Mormon missionary. John McCain, the only candidate with military experience, served on active duty in the Navy for 23 years and was a POW in North Vietnam for 5.5 years. Because the 2008 presidential primary campaign included a woman who came of age during the Vietnam War, the issue of serving in Vietnam — perhaps even serving in the military — seemed a non-issue, though the commander-in-chief's ability to command the military to go to combat does seem pertinent, given the current Iraq and Afghanistan wars. That military service has become somewhat of a non-issue may also be because so few of the American governmental leaders have served at all in the military.

2. According to initial reports, Quayle's being in the Indiana National Guard was the result of string-pulling: "His uncle asked Wendell Phillippi to put in a good word for Quayle. Phillippi, a former commanding general of the Indiana Guard, was at that time the managing editor of the Quayle-family-owned 'Indianapolis News' paper" ("Pulling Strings"). As part of a series of articles written by *Washington Post* staff writers Bob Woodward and David Broder in 1992, however, these initial reports were demonstrated to be inaccurate. Though Woodward and Broder concede that the principal actors were the same as those in the rumors, they assert Quayle's role in the National Guard was not conceived illicitly, but in fact there were spots in the local National Guard group for which Quayle was qualified (Woodward and Broder A1). I am not disputing the specific conditions of Quayle's Vietnam War participation; what I am arguing is that certain military roles signify greater and lesser degrees of masculinity, with ground combat at the peak of a mas-

culinity hierarchy. Most importantly, however, is that the Vietnam War *could* be employed to verify a man's masculinity.

3. Clinton gained a deferment from the draft by enrolling in ROTC, but withdrew, perhaps coincidentally, without fulfilling his commitment at a time when the threat of his being drafted was minimized. Clinton's role in the War was raised when he ran for governor of Arkansas in 1978, and was resurrected during the 1992 presidential campaign. Interestingly, it was less of an issue for his reelection campaign of 1996. For details of the 1996 campaign, see Hohenberg. For how Clinton dealt rhetorically with questions about his evasion of the draft, see Stephen A. Smith, especially chapters "Dodging Charges and Charges of Dodging: Bill Clinton's Defense on the Character Issue" and "Easy Access to Sloppy Truths: The '92 Presidential Media Campaign." For a broad discussion of all of these events, see David Maraniss' 1995 biography of Clinton, *First in His Class: A Biography of Bill Clinton.*

4. In an editorial published in the February 27, 2000, edition of *The Columbus Dispatch,* Charles Krauthammer compares the "heroisms" of Bob Kerrey and McCain: "[McCain] routed no enemy. He conquered no territory. Nor did he commit the momentary act of insane self-sacrifice in the chaos and terror of battle, as did, for example, Sen. Bob Kerrey, D-Neb., who saved his platoon in a firefight after losing a part of his leg. McCain's is not the heroism of conquest or even of rescue, but of endurance, and, even more important, endurance for principle" (3B). This comment demonstrates that even among war heroes, heroisms can be valued differently. However, Krauthammer suggests that it was McCain's memoir, *Faith of My Fathers,* that set him apart from other candidates, Kerrey in particular.

5. According to a story by the *Los Angeles Times,* "Bush easily got in the Guard and received a commission as a second lieutenant, despite lacking the credentials many other [Guard] candidates had, such as ROTC experience. He also had no previous aviation experience [but was 'fast-tracked' into an officer's fighter jet flying program]." See Crowley.

6. See also Stephen A. Smith, and Denton and Holloway. For the issue of "character," see Shenkman.

7. The best-known use of "honor," for instance, was President Richard M. Nixon's invocation of the word in trying to negotiate the end of the war: "Our broad objective, of course, is peace with honor" (Karnow 593). Two recent examples of uses of "honor" include John McCain's memoir, *Faith of My Fathers,* which I discuss later in this chapter, and *Return with Honor* (1998), a documentary film presented by Tom Hanks, about American pilots downed over North Vietnam and their stories as prisoners of war. Tim O'Brien's composite novel, *The Things They Carried* (1990), discusses how particular words are used to mean certain things. He especially focuses on a redefinition of "courage," arguing, for instance, in "On the Rainy River" that the character named Tim O'Brien could not evade the draft by running to Canada because running would have been the *brave* thing to do. "I couldn't endure the mockery [of my neighbors and family knowing I'd run], or the disgrace, or the patriotic ridicule. Even in my imagination, the shore [of the Canadian side of the Rainy River] just twenty yards away, I couldn't make myself be brave. It had nothing to do with morality. Embarrassment, that's all it was. [...] I was a coward. I went to war" (62-63). O'Brien continues this contemplation of how words typically used to describe manly behavior were reversed in the Vietnam War and its aftermath throughout the book, but especially in "How to Tell a True War Story," "The Man I Killed," and "Speaking of Courage." The meaning of "honor" similarly can be turned on its head to mean traditionally masculine.

8. This has been demonstrated most recently in the case of Senator Bob Kerrey, whose heroics during Vietnam were held up as exemplary until those same "heroics" were redefined as "atrocity." See Kerrey and Vistica for at-length discussions of this event.

9. Since Eisenhower, all presidents had military experience—usually in combat—until Bill Clinton. John F. Kennedy's exploits in the Navy during World War II are well-known. Lyndon Baines Johnson, Richard Milhous Nixon, and Gerald Ford were all engaged in politics until the United States entered World War II. Johnson was appointed "Congressional inspector of the war's progress in the South Pacific," and "went on a single bombing mission, securing the 'combat record' and a silver star for serving under hostile fire." Nixon joined the Navy as a Junior Grade lieutenant, served in air transport units in the South Pacific, and was discharged from active duty after the war with two battle stars. Ford enlisted in the Navy after Pearl Harbor and was involved in most of the major battles of the South Pacific,

reflected by the ten battle stars with which he was discharged. James Earl Carter intended to make the Navy a career, and so spent the World War II years at the Naval Academy. He resigned from active duty in 1953 after his father died and he became responsible for the family farm. Ronald Reagan was a professional actor, though he had been in the Army Reserve since the 1930s. At the outset of World War II, he was called to active duty, when he sold war bonds, narrated training films for bomber pilots, and made several military propaganda films. George H. W. Bush enlisted in the World War II Navy at 18 and became the military's youngest fighter pilot at 19. He flew 58 combat missions, was shot down once, and left the Navy after the war with a Distinguished Flying Cross, three air medals, and the rank of lieutenant. See "American Presidents."

10. Other critics weighing in on the Vietnam Syndrome include Harry G. Summers, Jr., (a colonel and veteran of the War) in "The Vietnam Syndrome and the American People," where he recites the argument that President Johnson lost the War because he did not build the support of the American people. Summers argues this in order to assert that President George H. W. Bush rightfully built American support for the 1991 Gulf War, thereby winning it. Another resonance of the Vietnam Syndrome is in Richard Falk's discussion of the case of Senator Bob Kerrey's involvement in the Thanh Piong incident. Falk, a professor of international law at Princeton, argues that the Vietnam Syndrome is a case of "too much remembering" while the "American Syndrome" is a case of "too much forgetting." Geoff Simons, a British scholar, claims in *Vietnam Syndrome: Impact on US Foreign Policy* (1998): "The horrors brought to Vietnam by American power had little influence in shaping the Vietnam Syndrome — sired as it principally was by *American* defeat, *American* pain, *American* anguish. If the United States had committed all the horrors and more, *and won the war,* there would have been no Vietnam Syndrome. It was born of nothing more than the humiliation of a massive ego" (xx; emphasis in original). Simons concludes "*that Vietnam forced the United States to refine its pursuit of global hegemony, with ethical factors continuing to weigh nothing in the scale of realpolitik calculation*" (xv; emphasis in original). However these critics define the "Vietnam Syndrome," it is always seen as a negative influence on American conceptions of itself; the difference among critics has to do with whether the Syndrome has continued to exercise a negative influence on this conception.

11. See Jeremy Devine, *24 Frames a Second*. Though the number of films directly addressing the American involvement in Vietnam has dwindled since 1993, the surplus of war movies produced at the turn of the twentieth century, especially those purportedly concerning World War II, reflects the influence of Vietnam as they focus on the psyches of individual soldiers and challenge received notions of the justness of World War II. This is especially so with two World War II stories, *The Thin Red Line* and *Saving Private Ryan*, and *The Three Kings*, set in the 1990s Middle East. Thomas Schatz's essay, "World War II and the Hollywood 'War Film,'" outlines in detail the historical influences on war films made during and after World War II. He makes clear in this tracing of the influences that the films responded to the needs of a wartime government and populace: "Never before or since have the interests of the nation and the movie industry been so closely aligned, and never has Hollywood's status as a national cinema been so vital" (89). Though many Vietnam War films did abide by the generic expectations of a (World War II) combat film, those departing from the genre are all the more marked by the uncertainties generated by the Vietnam War experience. See Westwell for more about the genre of war films.

12. The advertisement also includes a single star in the same sepia tones as the rest of the image. The star contributes to the single person/collective conundrum, as it recalls the flags of many Cold War countries, including Vietnam: the Soviet Union, China, and Yugoslavia, among others. I thank Kathleen Wallace for calling my attention to this.

13. Attempts have been made deliberately to target Hispanic-Americans and Internet cruisers through the consistent use of Spanish in hard copy material, and through the use of flash advertising and media on web sites. See the official military web sites for examples both of Spanish language appeals and flash media: http://www.goarmy.com (Army); http://www.airforce.com/ (Air Force); http://www.navy.mil/swf/index.asp (Navy); http://www.marines.com/ (Marines). For commentary on recruiting efforts, see http://www.defenselink.mil/news/newsarticle.aspx?id=41606; Suro and Waxman; Michael McCarthy; and Gersten.

14. See Sackett and Mavor for a discussion of military recruitment strategies. The

"Army of One" recruiting campaign replaced "Be All You Can Be" in January 2001. "Army of One" persisted for nearly six years, when it was replaced in November 2006 with the current Army slogan, "Army Strong."

15. Racial prejudice is an issue raised among the wives stateside, however, reinforcing the notion that skin color is immaterial in combat.

16. The publication of Vietnam War memoirs also traces Vietnam in American culture and has followed a national trend; in *When Memory Speaks* (1998), Jill Ker Conway claims that "autobiography [is] the most popular form of fiction for modern readers" (3). Opening her book, *The Limits of Autobiography* (2001), Leigh Gilmore cites a tripling in the number of autobiographies or memoirs published between 1940 and 1990, suggesting that the expectations for the genre themselves have changed. "Previously associated with elder statesmen reporting on the way their public lives parallel historical events, memoir is now dominated by the young, or at least the youngish in memoir's terms, whose private lives are emblematic of a cultural moment" (1). The shift Gilmore describes may account for the number and type of Vietnam War memoirs that have been published since the War's end, as the authors of these texts now include both statesman and soldier. Gilmore's "statesman" publications include texts like the magisterial memoir of President Richard Nixon's Secretary of Defense, Henry Kissinger. *Years of Upheaval* (1982) begins with the ending of the 1973 Paris Peace Talks, continues with an emotionally distant account of Watergate and the Middle East War, and concludes with Nixon's disgraceful exit from office in 1974. Recent "statesman" memoirs, however, are as much an emotional accounting as they are historical. Illustrative of such texts is the confessional memoir of Robert McNamara, Secretary of Defense for Presidents Kennedy and Johnson (*In Retrospect: The Tragedy and Lessons of Vietnam* 1995). In spite of these two examples, however, the preponderance of Vietnam War memoirs has been produced by soldiers, though usually by soldiers who were officers, not enlisted, and war correspondents, both military and civilian. A cross-sampling of these texts include: Philip Caputo's *A Rumor of War* (1977); David Harris' anti-war activist and draft-resister account, *Our War* (1996); Robert Mason's narrative of the helicopter war, *Chickenhawk* (1983); Harold Moore and Joe Galloway's story of the 1965 battle at Ia Drang, *We Were Soldiers Once ... and Young* (1992); Nathaniel Tripp's tome about father-son relationships in *FatherSoldierSon* (1996); Lynda Van Devanter's story of an Army nurse, *Home before Morning* (1983); and Tobias Wolff's memoir, *In Pharaoh's Army* (1994).

17. Published in late 1999, John McCain's memoir was a timely addition to the 2000 election campaign. Reviewers had mixed responses: while *The Columbus Dispatch*'s Charles Krauthammer (see endnote 4) lauded it as "without a doubt the most important campaign book in recent American history," Krauthammer's reference to the memoir as a "campaign book" does qualify the "memoir" element. Trying to disrupt the public's equation of military heroism and presidentiality, Evan Thomas of *Newsweek* concludes: "The book amply demonstrates that McCain was a brave warrior and an honorable man. Whether it shows that McCain would make a good president is a more complicated question." An editorial in *The Seattle Times* claims that, though the reader gains some insight to the flaws of McCain, "[r]eaders looking for some insight into how being a POW shaped the self-proclaimed pain-in-the-ass who wants to be president won't find it here" (Nelson). Furthermore, McCain's "family memoir" concludes with his release from prison in Hanoi, and says nothing whatsoever about the family to which he returned: his two children and his first wife, who had been irrecoverably injured and disfigured in a car accident. The story of their divorce soon after his return from Vietnam, an event that would not have played well in a "campaign book," would be left to a biography also published in 1999, Robert Timberg's *John McCain: An American Odyssey*. In his 2002 follow-up to the campaign book, *Worth the Fighting For: The Education of an American Maverick, and the Heroes Who Inspired Him*, McCain's limited discussion of family outside of his father and grandfather persists.

18. For a discussion of the "New Man," see McMahon.

19. In *Iraq, Vietnam, and the Limits of American Power* (2008), Brigham concludes: "U.S. policymakers went to war in Vietnam and Iraq with the expectation that a distinctively American story would emerge. It was not to be. One has to wonder if both wars were simply the miscalculations of a few shortsighted individuals, or if, in the words of cold war diplomat George Kennan, these wars reflect 'a certain unfitness of the system as a whole for the conceiving and executing

of ambitious political-military ventures far from our own shores.'" In either case, Brigham comments, "it is time for the United States to reorient its power and begin to rebuild relationships around the globe" (180).

20. Wright's book was published in England as *Generation Kill: Living Dangerously on the Road to Baghdad with the Ultraviolent Marines of Bravo Company*, which includes one notable difference from its American version. In the British version, a derogatory passage about "Captain America," another platoon leader in the reconnaissance battalion, is omitted. Wright's book was also televised in 2008 as a Home Box Office miniseries entitled *Generation Kill*.

Works Cited

Adair, R. D., and Joseph C. Myers. "Admission of Gays to the Military: A Singularly Intolerant Act." Robert M. Baird and M. Katherine Baird, eds. *Homosexuality: Debating the Issues.* 173–181.

Adams, Hazard, ed. *Critical Theory Since Plato.* Revised ed. New York: Harcourt Brace Jovanovich, 1992.

Adler, Jerry, and Eleanor Clift. "Death of a 'Fortunate Son.'" *Newsweek.* May 23, 1994: 44.

Allen, Chadwick. *Blood Narrative: Indigenous Identity in American Indian and Maori Literary and Activist Texts.* New Americanists Series. Durham: Duke University Press, 2002.

Ambrose, Stephen E. *Americans at War.* New York: Berkley Books, 1998.

"American Presidents." PBS series website. http://www.americanpresidents.org/Ko Train/Courses.htm July 29, 2002.

American War Library. http://members.aol.com/WarLibrary January 15, 2002.

Anderegg, Michael. *Inventing Vietnam: The War in Film and Television.* Philadelphia: Temple University Press, 1991.

Anzaldúa, Gloria. *Borderlands = La Frontera.* 2nd ed. San Francisco: Aunt Lute Books, 1999.

Apocalypse Now. Dir. Francis Coppola. Perf. Marlon Brando, Robert Duvall, and Martin Sheen. Paramount, 1979.

Appiah, Kwame Anthony. "Race." Frank Lentricchia and Thomas McLaughlin, eds. *Critical Terms for Literary Study.* 274–287.

Appy, Christian, and Alexander Bloom. "Vietnam War Mythology and the Rise of Public Cynicism." Alexander Bloom, ed. *Long Time Gone: Sixties America Then and Now.* 47–73.

Appy, Christian G. *Working-Class War: American Combat Soldiers and Vietnam.* Chapel Hill: University of North Carolina Press, 1993.

Attaway, William. *Blood on the Forge.* 1941. New York: New York Review Books, 2005.

Auster, Albert, and Leonard Quart. *How the War Was Remembered: Hollywood and Vietnam.* New York: Praeger, 1988.

Baird, Robert M., and M. Katherine Baird, eds. *Homosexuality: Debating the Issues.* Amherst, NY: Prometheus Books, 1995.

Barber, James David. "Presidential Character." James P. Pfiffner and Robert H. Davidson, eds. *Understanding the Presidency.* 445–454.

_____. *The Presidential Character: Predicting Performance in the White House.* 4th ed. Englewood Cliffs, NJ: Prentice Hall, 1992.

Baskir, Lawrence, and William A. Strauss. *Chance and Circumstance: The Draft, the War, and the Vietnam Generation.* New York: Knopf, 1978.

Bates, Milton J. *The Wars We Took to Vietnam: Cultural Conflict and Storytelling.* Berkeley: University of California Press, 1996.

Batres, Alfonso. "Readjustment Counseling Services Physically Disabled Veterans Working Group." *NCP Clinical Quarterly* 2.2 (1992). http://www.ncptsd.org/publications/cq/v2/n2/rcsbatre.html February 6, 2003.

Baynton, Douglas C. "Disability and the Justification of Inequality in American History." Paul K. Longmore and Lauri Umansky, eds. *The New Disability History: American Perspectives.* 33–57.

Beattie, Keith. *The Scar That Binds: American Culture and the Vietnam War.* New York: New York University Press, 1998.

Beidler, Philip D. *Re-writing America: Vietnam Authors in Their Generation.* Athens: University of Georgia Press, 1991.

Bell, Betty. "Gender in Native America." Philip Deloria and Neal Salisbury, eds. *A Companion to American Indian History.* 307–320.

Berger, Maurice, Brian Wallis, and Simon Watson, eds. *Constructing Masculinity.* New York: Routledge, 1995.

Berkowitz, Edward D. *Disabled Policy: America's Programs for the Handicapped.* Twentieth Century Fund Report. New York: Cambridge University Press, 1987.

Berlant, Lauren. *The Anatomy of National Fantasy: Hawthorne, Utopia, and Everyday Life.* Chicago: University of Chicago Press, 1991.

———. *The Queen of America Goes to Washington City: Essays on Sex and Citizenship.* Durham: Duke University Press, 1997.

Bernstein, Richard. "Brothers in Arms." Rev. of *84 Charlie MoPic*, dir. Patrick Duncan. *New York Times Film Reviews* 138 (Mar 22, 1989): C24.

Berubé, Alan. *Coming Out under Fire: The History of Gay Men and Women in World War Two.* New York: The Free Press, 1990.

Bianco, William T., and Jamie Markham. "Vanishing Veterans: The Decline in Military Experience in the U.S. Congress." http://www.cbrss.harvard.edu/events/ppe/papers/bianco.pdf July 8, 2002.

Bibby, Michael. "The Post-Vietnam Condition." Michael Bibby, ed. *The Vietnam War and Postmodernity.* 143–171.

———, ed. *The Vietnam War and Postmodernity.* Amherst: University of Massachusetts Press, 1999.

Billy Jack. Dir. Tom Laughlin. Perf. Tom Laughlin, Delores Taylor, Clark Howat. Warner Brothers, 1971.

Billy Jack Goes to Washington. Dir. Tom Laughlin. Perf. Tom Laughlin, Delores Taylor. Billy Jack Enterprises, 1977.

Blais, Ellen A. "Gender Issues in Bobbie Ann Mason's *In Country.*" *South Atlantic Review* 56.2 (1991): 107–118.

Bloom, Alexander, ed. *Long Time Gone: Sixties America Then and Now.* New York: Oxford University Press, 2001.

Booker, Christopher B. *"I Will Wear No Chain!" A Social History of African American Males.* Westport, CT: Praeger, 2000.

Born on the Fourth of July. Dir. Oliver Stone. Perf. Tom Cruise, Willem Dafoe, Tom Berenger, Frank Whaley, Kyra Sedgwick, Raymond Barry, Caroline Kava. Universal Pictures, 1989.

Boyle, Brenda M. "Phantom Pains: Disability, Masculinity and the Normal in Vietnam War Representations." *Prose Studies* 27.1–2 (2005): 93–107.

The Boys in Company C. Dir. Sidney J. Furie. Perf. Stan Shaw, Andrew Stevens, Michael Lembeck, Craig Wasson, and James Canning. Columbia Pictures, 1978.

Bratton, Jacky, Jim Cook, and Christine Gledhill, eds. *Melodrama: Stage, Picture, Screen.* London: BFI Publishing, 1994.

Brigham, Robert K. *Iraq, Vietnam, and the Limits of American Power.* New York: PublicAffairs, 2008.

———. *Is Iraq Another Vietnam?* New York: Public Affairs, 2006.

Brod, Harry, and Michael Kaufman, eds. *Theorizing Masculinities.* Thousand Oaks, CA: Sage Publications, 1994.

Browne, Corinne. *Body Shop: Recuperating from Vietnam.* New York: Stein and Day, 1973.

Browne, Nick, ed. *Refiguring American Film Genres: Theory and History.* Berkeley: University of California Press, 1998.

"Bruce Willis." http://us.imdb.com/Name? Willis, %20Bruce January 2, 2003.

Buckley, Gail. *American Patriots: The Story of Blacks in the Military from the Revolution to Desert Storm.* New York: Random House, 2001.

Burrelli, David F. "96029: Homosexuals and the U.S. Military Policy: Current Issues; Updated December 12, 1996." *CRS Issue Brief,* Foreign Affairs and National Defense Division and Charles Dale American Law Division. http://www.fas.orh/man/crs/96–029.htm November 24, 2002.

Butler, Judith. "Against Proper Objects." Elizabeth Weed and Naomi Schor, eds. *Feminism Meets Queer Theory.* 1–30.

———. *Bodies That Matter: On the Discursive Limits of "Sex."* New York: Routledge, 1993.

———. *Gender Trouble: Feminism and the Subversion of Identity.* 2nd ed. New York: Routledge, 1999.

Camacho, Paul. "From War Hero to Criminal: The Negative Privilege of the Vietnam Veteran." Charles R. Figley and Seymour Leventman, eds. *Strangers at Home: Vietnam Veterans Since the War.* 267–272.

Canellos, Peter S. "An Outline for a Novelist: Give Dole Some Passion." *The Boston Globe.* August 15, 1996 (Thursday City Edition): A30.

Caputo, Philip. *A Rumor of War.* 1977. 2nd ed. New York: Henry Holt and Company, 1996.

Carbado, Devon W., ed. *Black Men on Race, Gender, and Sexuality: A Critical Reader.* Foreword Kimberle Williams Crenshaw. New York: New York University Press, 1999.

Carn, John. *Shaw's Nam.* Indianapolis: Benjamin Books, 1984.

Carter, Robert T. "Is White a Race? Expressions of White Racial Identity." Michelle Fine et al., eds. *Off White*. 198–206.

Carton, Evan. "Vietnam and the Limits of Masculinity." *American Literary History* 3.2 (1991): 294–318.

"Celebrities." http://www.hollywood.com/celebs/bio/celeb/341871 October 14, 2002.

China Beach. With Dana Delany, Concetta Tomei, Marg Helgenberger, Brian Wimmer, Michael Boatman, Robert Picardo, Jeff Kober, Nancy Giles, et al. 1988–1991.

Chomsky, Noam. "Afterword." *Deterring Democracy*. Cambridge: South End Press, 1991. Qtd. at http://www.zmag.org/chomsky/dd/dd-after-s01.html July 10, 2002.

Chosen Books. "The History of Chosen Books." http://www.bakerbooks.com/bakerbooks/divisions/chosen/chosenstory February 24, 2003.

Cleland, Max. *Strong at the Broken Places: A Personal Story*. Lincoln, VA: Chosen Books, 1980.

Cloud, Stanley W. "The Home Front: Exorcising an Old Demon." *Time*. March 11, 1991: 26–27.

Clute, John. "In Defense of Science Fiction." http://www.salon.com/books/feature/1999/05/25/sfdefense July 17, 2002.

Colburn, David R., and George E. Pozzetta. "Race, Ethnicity, and the Evolution of Political Legitimacy." David Farber, ed. *The Sixties: From Memory to History*. 119–148.

Coming Home. Dir. Hal Ashby. Perf. Jane Fonda, Jon Voight, Bruce Dern, Penelope Milford, Robert Ginty, and Robert Carradine. Indochina Peace Campaign Films, 1978.

Connell, R. W. *Masculinities*. Berkeley: University of California Press, 1995.

———. *The Men and the Boys*. Berkeley: University of California Press, 2000.

———. "Politics of Changing Men." *Australian Humanities Review*. December 1996. Qtd. at: http://www.australianhumanitiesreview.org/archive/Issue-Dec-1996/connell.html January 11, 2002.

Conway, Jill Ker. *When Memory Speaks: Exploring the Art of Autobiography*. New York: Random House, 1998.

Cooke, Miriam, and Angela Woollacott, eds. *Gendering War Talk*. Princeton: Princeton University Press, 1993.

Corber, Robert J. *Homosexuality in Cold War America: Resistance and the Crisis of Masculinity*. New Americanists Series. Durham: Duke University Press, 1997.

Crowley, Candy. "Bush Says He's 'Proud' of Vietnam-Era National Guard Service." http://www.cnn.com/ALLPOLITICS/stories/1999/07/04/bush.02/ July 8, 2002.

D'Agostino, Joseph A. "Conservative Issues Boosted GOP in Hard-Fought Senate Campaigns." *Human Events* 58.42 (November 11 2002): 1.

Davidson, Phillip B. *Vietnam at War: The History, 1946–1975*. New York: Oxford University Press, 1988.

Davis, George. *Coming Home*. 1971. Washington, D.C.: Howard University Press, 1984.

Davis, Lennard. *Bending Over Backwards: Disability, Dismodernism, and Other Difficult Positions*. New York: New York University Press, 2002.

———. *Enforcing Normalcy: Disability, Deafness, and the Body*. New York: Verso, 1995.

———, ed. *The Disability Studies Reader*. New York: Routledge, 1997.

Dean, Robert Dale. "Manhood, Reason, and American Foreign Policy: The Social Construction of Masculinity and the Kennedy and Johnson Administrations." Diss. University of Arizona, 1995.

"Debunking Jack Thompson's Virginia Tech Video Game Claims." CNet News.com. April 17, 2007. http://news.com.com/8301-10784_3-6176816-7.html July 23, 2007.

The Deer Hunter. Dir. Michael Cimino. Perf. Robert DeNiro, Meryl Streep, Christopher Walken, John Savage, John Cazale, Chuck Aspegren, and George Dzundza. Universal Pictures, 1978.

Delgado, Richard, and Jean Stefancic. *Critical White Studies: Looking behind the Mirror*. Philadelphia: Temple University Press, 1997.

Deloria, Philip J., and Neal Salisbury, eds. *A Companion to American Indian History*. Blackwell Companions to American History. Malden, MA: Blackwell Publishers, 2002.

Del Vecchio, John. *The 13th Valley*. New York: Bantam Books, 1982.

D'Emilio, John. "Placing Gay in the Sixties." Alexander Bloom, ed. *Long Time Gone: Sixties America Then and Now*. 209–229.

———. *Sexual Politics, Sexual Communities: The Making of a Homosexual Minority in the United States, 1940–1970*. 1983. 2nd ed. Chicago: University of Chicago Press, 1998.

———, and Estelle B. Freedman. *Intimate Matters: A History of Sexuality in America*. 2nd ed. Chicago: University of Chicago Press, 1997.

Denton, Robert E., Jr., and Rachel L. Holloway. *Images, Scandal, and Communication Strategies of the Clinton Presidency.* Westport, CT: Praeger, 2003.

Devine, Jeremy. *Vietnam at 24 Frames a Second: A Critical and Thematic Analysis of Over 400 Films About the Vietnam War.* Austin: University of Texas Press, 1995.

Diagnostic and Statistical Manual of Mental Disorders: DSM-III-R. 3rd ed. Washington, D.C.: American Psychiatric Association, 1987.

DiClerico, Robert. "Assessing Context and Character." *Society* 33.6 (1996): 28–37.

Disabled American Veterans. "Agent Orange/Herbicide Exposure Testimony–May 23, 2000." http://www.dav.org/voters/testimony_orange_20000523_print.html February 6, 2003.

Dittmar, Linda, and Gene Michaud, eds. *From Hanoi to Hollywood: The Vietnam War in American Film.* New Brunswick: Rutgers University Press, 1990.

Draper, Ellen. "Finding a Language for Vietnam in the Action-Adventure Genre." Michael Anderegg, ed. *Inventing Vietnam: The War in Film and Television.* 103–113.

Duiker, William J. *Ho Chi Minh: A Life.* New York: Hyperion, 2000.

Dyer, Richard. *White.* New York: Routledge, 1997.

Eastlake, William. *The Bamboo Bed.* New York: Simon and Schuster, 1969.

Eastman, Charles Alexander. "From the Deep Woods to Civilization." 1916. *The Norton Anthology of American Literature, Volume 2.* 5th ed. Nina Baym, ed. New York: W.W. Norton & Company, 1998.

Edgerton, Gary R., Michael T. Marsden, and Jack Nachbar, eds. *In the Eye of the Beholder: Critical Perspectives in Popular Film and Television.* Bowling Green: Bowling Green State University Popular Press, 1997.

84 Charlie MoPic. Dir. Patrick Duncan. Perf. Richard Brooks, Christopher Burgard, Nicholas Cascone, Jonathan Emerson, Glenn Morshower, Jason Tomlins, and Byron Thames. The Charlie Mopic Company, 1989.

Ellmann, Mary. *Thinking about Women.* New York: Harcourt, 1968.

"Emily Lloyd." http://us.imdb.com/Name?Lloyd,%20Emily January 2, 2003.

Eng, David L. *Racial Castration: Managing Masculinity in Asian America.* Durham: Duke University Press, 2001.

Evans, Martin, and Kenn Lunn, eds. *War and Memory in the Twentieth Century.* Oxford: Berg, 1997.

Falk, Richard. "The Vietnam Syndrome." *Nation* 273.2 (2001): 18–23.

Faludi, Susan. *Backlash: The Undeclared War Against American Women.* New York: Crown, 1991.

Farber, David. *The Age of Great Dreams: America in the 1960s.* American Century Series. New York: Hill and Wang, 1994.

_____, ed. *The Sixties: From Memory to History.* Chapel Hill: University of North Carolina Press, 1994.

Farrell, Warren. *The Liberated Man: Beyond Masculinity; Freeing Men and Their Relationships with Women.* New York: Random House, 1974.

Feldman, Linda. "On Dole's Canvas: Clinton Portrayed As Untrustworthy." *Christian Science Monitor* 88.118 (1996): 1.

Fick, Nathaniel. *One Bullet Away: The Making of a Marine Officer.* Boston: Houghton Mifflin, 2005.

Fiedler, Leslie A. *Freaks: Myths and Images of the Secret Self.* New York: Simon and Schuster, 1978.

Figley, Charles R. "A Postscript: Welcoming Home Strangers." Charles R. Figley and Seymour Leventman, eds. *Strangers at Home: Vietnam Veterans since the War.* 363–367.

_____, and Seymour Leventman, eds. *Strangers at Home: Vietnam Veterans since the War.* New York: Praeger, 1980.

Fine, Michelle, Lois Weis, Linda C. Powell, and L. Mun Wong, eds. *Off White: Readings on Race, Power, and Society.* New York: Routledge, 1997.

Firestone, Shulamith. *The Dialectic of Sex: The Case for Feminist Revolution.* New York: William Morrow and Company, 1970.

Flowers, A. R. *De Mojo Blues: De Quest of HighJohn de Conqueror.* New York: E.P. Dutton, 1985.

Fontana, Alan, and Robert Rosenheck. "Traumatic War Stressors and Psychiatric Symptoms among World War II, Korean, and Vietnam War Veterans." *Psychology and Aging* 9.1 (1994): 27–33.

Foucault, Michel. Trans. Robert Hurley. *The History of Sexuality: Volume 1, An Introduction.* New York: Vintage Books, 1978.

_____. "Truth and Power." Hazard Adams, ed. *Critical Theory since Plato.* 1135–1145.

Fout, John C., and Maura Shaw Tantillo, eds. *American Sexual Politics: Sex, Gender, and Race since the Civil War.* Chicago: University of Chicago Press, 1993.

Franklin, H. Bruce. *Vietnam and Other American Fantasies.* Amherst: University of Massachusetts Press, 2000.

Friedman, Matthew J. "Post-traumatic Stress Disorder: An Overview." National Center for PTSD. http://www.ncptsd.org/facts/general/fs_overview.html February 19, 2003.

Full Metal Jacket. Dir. Stanley Kubrick. Perf. Matthew Modine, Adam Baldwin, Vincent D'Onofrio, R. Lee Ermey, et al. Warner Brothers, 1987.

Garber, Marjorie. *Vested Interests: Cross-dressing and Cultural Anxiety*. New York: Routledge, 1992.

Garcia, Ignacio M. *United We Win: The Rise and Fall of La Raza Unida Party*. Tucson: University of Arizona Press, 1989.

Garland-Thomson, Rosemarie. *Extraordinary Bodies: Figuring Physical Disability in American Culture and Literature*. New York: Columbia University Press, 1997.

_____. "Integrating Disability Studies into the Existing Curriculum: The Example of 'Women and Literature' at Howard University." Lennard Davis, ed. *The Disability Studies Reader*. 295–311.

_____. "Seeing the Disabled: Visual Rhetorics of Disability in Popular Photography." Paul K. Longmore and Lauri Umansky, eds. *The New Disability History: American Perspectives*. 335–374.

Gerber, David A., ed. *Disabled Veterans in History*. Corporealities: Discourses of Disability. Ann Arbor: University of Michigan Press, 2000.

_____. "Heroes and Misfits: The Troubled Social Reintegration of Disabled Veterans in *The Best Years of Our Lives*." David A. Gerber, ed. *Disabled Veterans in History*. 70–95.

Gergen, Mary M., and Sara N. Davis, eds. *Toward a New Psychology of Gender*. New York: Routledge, 1997.

Gerschick, Thomas J. "Sisyphus in a Wheelchair: Men with Physical Disabilities Confront Gender Domination." Jodi O'Brien and Judith A. Howard, eds. *Everyday Inequalities: Critical Inquiries*. 189–211.

_____. "Toward a Theory of Disability and Gender." Judith A. Howard and Carolyn Allen, eds. *Feminisms at a Millenium*. 253–258.

_____, and Adam Stephen Miller. "Gender Identities at the Crossroads of Masculinity and Physical Disability." Mary M. Gergen and Sara N. Davis, eds. *Toward a New Psychology of Gender*. 455–475.

Gersten, David. "An Army of Uno: Courting Hispanics." *National Review Online*. May 31, 2002. http://www.nationalreview.com/comment/comment-gersten053102.asp June 29, 2002.

Gerstle, Gary. *American Crucible: Race and Nation in the Twentieth Century*. Princeton, NJ: Princeton University Press, 2001.

Gettleman, Marvin E., Jane Franklin, Marilyn B. Young, and H. Bruce Franklin, eds. *Vietnam and America: A Documented History*. 2nd ed. New York: Grove Press, 1995.

Gilman, Owen W., Jr., and Lorrie Smith, eds. *America Rediscovered: Critical Essays on Literature and Film of the Vietnam War*. New York: Garland, 1990.

Gilmore, Leigh. *The Limits of Autobiography: Trauma and Testimony*. Ithaca: Cornell University Press, 2001.

Gitlin, Todd. "Unforgettable Vietnam and Its Burdens." *Dissent* 47.2 (2000). Qtd. at http://www.dissentmagazine.org/archive/sp00/gitlin.shtml July 10, 2002.

Glass, Ira. "I'm from the Private Sector, and I'm Here to Help." *This American Life*. Chicago Public Radio. Serial 266, June 4, 2004.

Glenday, Michael K. *Norman Mailer*. Modern Novelists Series. New York: St. Martin's Press, 1995.

Glover, David, and Cora Kaplan. *Genders*. New York: Routledge, 2000.

Go Tell the Spartans. Dir. Ted Post. Perf. Burt Lancaster, Craig Wasson, Joe Unger, Jonathan Goldsmith, Dennis Howard, Evan Kim, and Dolph Sweet. Avco Embassy, 1978.

Goldberg, Herb. *The Hazards of Being Male: Surviving the Myth of Masculine Privilege*. New York: Nash Pub., 1976.

Goldstein, Joshua S. *War and Gender: How Gender Shapes the War System and Vice Versa*. New York: Cambridge University Press, 2001.

Graham, Herman. *The Brothers' Vietnam War: Black Power, Manhood, and the Military Experience*. Gainesville: University of Florida Press, 2003.

Graham-Silverman, Adam. "Duo's Contentious Battle Features Patriotism and Homeland Security." *CQ Weekly*. August 10, 2002: 2174–2176.

Graybill, Mark S. "Reconstructing/Deconstructing Genre and Gender: Postmodern Identity in Bobbie Ann Mason's *In Country* and Josephine Humphrey's *Rich in Love*." *Critique* 43.3 (2002): 239–259.

Guideposts. http://www.guideposts.com. February 24, 2003.

Gustainis, J. Justin. *American Rhetoric and the Vietnam War*. Praeger Series in Political Communication. Westport, CT: Praeger, 1993.

Gutmann, Stephanie. *The Kinder, Gentler Military: How Political Correctness Affects Our Ability to Win Wars.* San Francisco: Encounter Books, 2000.

Halberstam, Judith. *Female Masculinity.* Durham: Duke University Press, 1998.

Haldeman, Joe. *The Forever War.* 1974. 3rd ed. New York: Avon Books, 1997.

Hallett, Joe. "Letters from Veterans Hits Home after Writer's Dumb Bomb Misfires." *The Columbus Dispatch.* March 30, 2003 (Sunday Edition): B5.

Halperin, David M. *How to Do the History of Homosexuality.* Chicago: University of Chicago Press, 2002.

Harbour, Wendy. Personal communication. February 1, 2003.

Harper, Philip Brian. *Are We Not Men? Masculine Anxiety and the Problem of African-American Identity.* New York: Oxford University Press, 1996.

Harris, David. *Our War: What We Did in Vietnam and What It Did to Us.* New York: Random House, 1996.

Harris, Ian M. *Messages Men Hear: Constructing Masculinities.* Bristol, PA: Taylor and Francis, 1995.

Hedges, Chris. *War Is a Force That Gives Us Meaning.* New York: Anchor Books, 2003.

Heinemann, Larry. *Paco's Story.* New York: Penguin Books, 1986.

Hellmann, John. *American Myth and the Legacy of Vietnam.* New York: Columbia University Press, 1986.

———. "Vietnam and the Hollywood Genre Film: Inversion of American Mythology in *The Deer Hunter* and *Apocalypse Now*. Michael Anderegg, ed. *Inventing Vietnam: The War in Film and Television.* 56–80.

———. "The Vietnam Film and American Memory." Martin Evans and Kenn Lunn, eds. *War and Memory in the Twentieth Century.* 177–188.

Hemingway, Ernest. *A Farewell to Arms.* 1929. New York: Scribner, 1995.

Herr, Michael. *Dispatches.* 1977. New York: Vintage Books, 1991.

Hess, Stephen. "The Foreign Policy Factor in Presidential Campaigns." *U.S. Foreign Policy Agenda.* United States Information Agency, October 1996. Qtd. at http://usinfo.state.gov/journals/itps/1096/ijpe/pj14hess.htm July 8, 2002.

Hickel, K. Walter. "Medicine, Bureaucracy, and Social Welfare: The Politics of Disability Compensation for American Veterans of World War I." Paul K. Longmore and Lauri Umansky, eds. *The New Disability History: American Perspectives.* 236–267.

Hohenberg, John. *Reelecting Bill Clinton: Why America Chose a "New" Democrat.* Syracuse: Syracuse University Press, 1997.

Holm, Tom. *Strong Hearts, Wounded Souls: Native American Veterans of the Vietnam War.* Austin: University of Texas Press, 1996.

Homosexuality and the Military: A Sourcebook of Official, Uncensored U.S. Government Documents. Upland, PA: DIANE Publishing Co., 1993.

Hooper, Charlotte. *Manly States: Masculinities, International Relations, and Gender Politics.* New York: Columbia University Press, 2001.

Howard, Judith A., and Carolyn Allen, eds. *Feminisms at a Millenium.* Chicago: University of Chicago Press, 2000.

In Country. Dir. Norman Jewison. Perf. Bruce Willis, Emily Lloyd, Joan Allen, et al. Warner Brothers, 1989.

Jaehne, Karen. "Company Man." Rev. of *84 Charlie MoPic*, dir. Patrick Duncan. *Film Comment* 25 (March/April 1989): 11–15.

Jagose, Annamarie. *Queer Theory: An Introduction.* New York: New York University Press, 1996.

Jarraway, David R. "'Excremental Assault' in Tim O'Brien: Trauma and Recovery in Vietnam War Literature." *Modern Fiction Studies* 44.3 (1998): 695–711.

Jason, Philip K. *Acts and Shadows: The Vietnam War in American Literary Culture.* New York: Rowman & Littlefield Publishers, Inc., 2000.

———. "Vision and Tradition in Vietnam War Fiction." Owen W. Gilman, Jr., and Lorrie Smith, eds. *America Rediscovered: Critical Essays in Literature and Film of the Vietnam War.* 75–86.

Jeffords, Susan. *The Remasculinization of America: Gender and the Vietnam War.* Bloomington: Indiana University Press, 1989.

———. "Telling the War Story." Judith Stiehm, ed. *It's Our Military, Too!* 220–234.

Johnson, Loch. "Scars of War: Alienation and Estrangement among Wounded Vietnam Veterans." Charles R. Figley and Seymour Leventman, eds. *Strangers at Home: Vietnam Veterans since the War.* 213–227.

Jones, James. *The Thin Red Line.* 1962. New York: Delta Paperbacks, 1998.

Jordan, Harold. "The New Face of Military Advertising: Behind the Army of One." *Y&M Magazine Online.* May/June 2001. http://www.afsc.org/youthmil/200106/adface.htm July 1, 2002.

Karnow, Stanley. *Vietnam: A History.* 2nd ed. New York: Penguin, 1997.

Kauffmann, Stanley. "Fact-facing: *84 Charlie Mopic.*" Rev. of *84 Charlie MoPic,* dir. Patrick Duncan. *New Republic.* April 24, 1989: 24–25.

Kerrey, Robert. "For Lew." *New Republic.* June 6, 1994: 12–14.

"Kicking the 'Vietnam Syndrome.'" *The Washington Post.* March 4, 1991: A1.

Kimmel, Michael. *Manhood in America: A Cultural History.* New York: The Free Press, 1996.

_____. "Masculinity as Homophobia: Fear, Shame, and Silence in the Construction of Gender Identity." Harry Brod and Michael Kaufman, eds. *Theorizing Masculinities.* 119–141.

Kimmel, Michael S., Jeff Hearn, and R. W. Connell, eds. *Handbook of Studies on Men and Masculinities.* Thousand Oaks, CA: Sage Publications, 2005.

_____, and Michael A. Messner. *Men's Lives.* 4th ed. Boston: Allyn and Bacon, 1998.

King, Debra Walker. *Deep Talk: Reading African-American Literary Names.* Charlottesville: University of Virginia Press, 1998.

King, William M., ed. *Vietnam Generation.* 1.2 (1989).

Kinney, Katherine. *Friendly Fire: American Images of the Vietnam War.* New York: Oxford University Press, 2000.

Kirkham, Pat, and Janet Thumin, eds. *You Tarzan: Masculinity, Movies, and Men.* New York: St. Martin's Press, 1993.

Kissinger, Henry. *Years of Upheaval.* Boston: Little, Brown and Company, 1982.

Kleinhans, Chuck. "Realist Melodrama and the African-American Family: Billy Woodberry's *Bless Their Little Hearts.*" Jacky Bratton et al., eds. *Melodrama: Stage, Picture, Screen.* 157–167.

Kolker, Robert. *Film, Form, and Culture.* New York: McGraw Hill College, 1999.

Krauthammer, Charles. "War Experience Sets McCain Apart in Eyes of Voters." Editorial. *The Columbus Dispatch.* February 27, 2000 (Sunday edition): 3B.

Kripke, Saul. *Naming and Necessity.* Cambridge, MA: Harvard University Press, 1980.

Kulka, Richard A., William E. Schlenger, John A. Fairbank, Richard L. Hough, B. Kathleen Jordan, Charles R. Marmar, Daniel S. Weiss, and David A. Grady. *Trauma and the Vietnam War Generation: Report of Findings from the National Vietnam Veterans Readjustment Study.* Brunner/Mazel Psychosocial Stress Series 18. New York: Brunner/Mazel Publishers, 1990.

Ladd, Everett Carll. "To Voters Picking a President, Character Does Matter." *Christian Science Monitor* 88.166 (1996): 18.

Lanning, Michael Lee. *The African-American Soldier: From Crispus Attucks to Colin Powell.* New York: Citadel Press, 2004.

_____. *Vietnam at the Movies.* New York: Fawcett Columbine, 1994.

Lehman, Peter, ed. *Masculinity: Bodies, Movies, Culture.* New York: Routledge, 2001.

_____. *Running Scared: Masculinity and the Representation of the Male Body.* Philadelphia: Temple University Press, 1993.

Lehrack, Otto J. *No Shining Armor: The Marines at War in Vietnam.* Modern War Studies Series. Lawrence, KS: University Press of Kansas, 1992.

Lemons, Stephen L., and Patrick Sweeney. "Veterans Vocational Rehabilitation: A Program in Transition." *The Personnel and Guidance Journal* 12 (1979): 295–297.

Lentricchia, Frank, and Thomas McLaughlin, eds. *Critical Terms for Literary Study.* 2nd ed. Chicago: University of Chicago Press, 1995.

Leonard, Mary. "Campaign 2000: Gore Falls into the 'Marriage Gap.'" *The Boston Globe.* May 28, 2000 (Sunday Edition): A1.

Letterman Digital Arts Center. "Inside LucasFilm." http://www.lucasfilm.com/inside/letterman/ July 30, 2007.

Linton, Simi. *Claiming Disability: Knowledge and Identity.* New York: New York University Press, 1998.

Lipsitz, George. *Time Passages: Collective Memory and American Popular Culture.* Minneapolis: University of Minnesota Press, 1990.

Lipsky, David. *Absolutely American: Four Years at West Point.* Boston: Houghton Mifflin, 2003.

Livneh, Hanoch. "Disability and Monstrosity: Further Comments." *Rehabilitation Literature* 41.11–12 (1980): 280–283.

Loeb, Jeff. Afterword. *Memphis-Nam-Sweden*. By Terry Whitmore. Jackson: University Press of Mississippi, 1997.

Longmore, Paul K., and Lauri Umansky. "Disability History: From the Margins to the Mainstream." Paul K. Longmore and Lauri Umansky, eds. *The New Disability History: American Perspectives*. 1–29.

———, and ———, eds. *The New Disability History: American Perspectives*. The History of Disability Series. New York: New York University Press, 2001.

Lupack, Barbara Tepa, ed. "History as Her-Story: Adapting Bobbie Ann Mason's *In Country* to Film. Barbara Tepa Lupack, ed. *Vision/Re-Vision: Adapting Contemporary American Fiction by Women to Film*. 159–192.

———, ed. *Vision/Re-Vision: Adapting Contemporary American Fiction by Women to Film*. Bowling Green: Bowling Green State University Popular Press, 1996.

MacPherson, Myra. *Long Time Passing: Vietnam and the Haunted Generation*. New edition. Bloomington: Indiana University Press, 2001.

Magnum P.I. With Tom Selleck, John Hillerman, Roger E. Mosley, Larry Manetti. 1980–1988.

Mailer, Norman. *The Armies of the Night: History as a Novel, the Novel as History*. New York: Penguin Books, 1968.

———. *The Naked and the Dead*. New York: Rinehart, 1948.

———. *Why Are We in Vietnam?* New York: Henry Holt and Company, 1967.

Maraniss, David. *First in His Class: A Biography of Bill Clinton*. New York: Simon & Schuster, 1995.

Martin, Andrew. *Receptions of War: Vietnam in American Culture*. OK Project for Discourse and Theory 10. Norman: University of Oklahoma Press, 1993.

Mason, Bobbie Ann. *In Country*. New York: Harper and Row, 1985.

Mason, Robert. *Chickenhawk*. New York: Penguin Books, 1983.

Matthiessen, Peter. *In the Spirit of Crazy Horse*. 1980. New York: Viking, 1991.

McCabe, David. "Character Counts." *Commonweal* 124.7 (1997): 10–12.

McCain, John, with Mark Salter. *Faith of My Fathers: A Family Memoir*. New York: Random House, 1999.

——— with ———. *Worth the Fighting For: The Education of an American Maverick, and the Heroes Who Inspired Him*. New York: Random House, 2002.

McCarthy, Cameron, and Warren Crichlow, eds. *Race, Identity and Representation in Education*. New York: Routledge, 1993.

McCarthy, Michael. "Army Enlists Net to Be All It Can Be." *USA Today*. http://www.usatoday.com/life/cyber/tech/cth756.htm June 29, 2002.

McIntosh, Patricia. "White Privilege and Male Privilege: A Personal Account of Coming to See Correspondences through Work in Women's Studies." *Working Paper No. 189*. Wellesley: Wellesley College Center for Research on Women, 1988.

McMahon, Anthony. *Taking Care of Men: Sexual Politics in the Public Mind*. New York: Cambridge University Press, 1999.

McNamara, Robert S., with Brian VanDeMark. *In Retrospect: The Tragedy and Lessons of Vietnam*. New York: Random House, 1995.

McNerney, Brian C. "Responsibly Inventing History: An Interview with Tim O'Brien." *War, Literature, and the Arts* 6.2 (1994): 1–26.

Meyer, Leisa D. "Creating G.I. Jane: The Regulation of Sexuality and Sexual Behavior in the Women's Army Corps during World War II." Martha Vicinus, ed. *Lesbian Subjects: A Feminist Studies Reader*. 66–84.

Miami Vice. With Don Johnson, Philip Michael Thomas, Olivia Brown, Saundra Santiago, Michael Talbot, Edward James Olmos, John Diehl. 1984–1989.

Michel, Sonya. "Danger on the Home Front: Motherhood, Sexuality, and Disabled Veterans in American Postwar Films." John C. Fout and Maura Shaw Tantillo, eds. *American Sexual Politics: Sex, Gender, and Race since the Civil War*. 247–266.

Millett, Kate. *Sexual Politics: The Classic Analysis of the Interplay between Men, Women, & Culture*. 1969. New York: Simon and Schuster, 1990.

Moddelmog, Debra A. *Reading Desire: In Pursuit of Ernest Hemingway*. Ithaca: Cornell University Press, 1999.

Moore, Lt. Gen. (Ret.) Harold G., and Joseph Galloway. *We Were Soldiers Once ... and Young*. New York: HarperCollins Publishers, 1992.

Morris, Jenny. "Gender and Disability." John Swain et al., eds. *Disabling Barriers— Enabling Environments*. 85–92.

Moskos, Charles. *The American Enlisted Man: The Rank and File in Today's Military*. New York: Russell Sage Foundation, 1970.

———. "From Citizens' Army to Social Laboratory." Wilbur J. Scott and Sandra Carson Stanley, *Gays and Lesbians in the Military: Issues, Concerns, and Contrasts.* 53–65.

Moskos, Charles C., and John Sibley Butler. *All That We Can Be: Black Leadership and Racial Integration the Army Way.* New York: HarperCollins Publishers, 1996.

Moynihan, Daniel Patrick. "The Negro Family: The Case for National Action." Office of Policy Planning and Research of the Department of Labor. Washington, D.C.: U.S. Government Printing Office, 1965.

Mullen, Robert W. *Blacks and Vietnam.* Washington, D.C.: University Press of America, Inc., 1981.

Mulvey, Laura. "Visual Pleasure and Narrative Cinema." *Screen* 16.3 (1975): 6–18.

Muse, Eben J. *The Land of Nam: The Vietnam War and American Film.* Lanham, MD: Scarecrow Press, 1995.

Myers, Thomas. *Walking Point: American Narratives of Vietnam.* New York: Oxford University Press, 1988.

Nalty, Bernard C., and Morris J. MacGregor, eds. *Blacks in the Military: Essential Documents.* Wilmington, DE: Scholarly Resources, Inc., 1981.

Neilson, Jim. *Warring Fictions: Cultural Politics and the Vietnam War Narrative.* Jackson: University of Mississippi Press, 1998.

Nelson, Robert T. "McCain's Profile in Courage: Autobiography Offers Candor without Insight." Rev. of *Faith of My Fathers*, by John McCain. *The Seattle Times.* October 1, 1999: E4.

"New Questions on Bush Guard Duty." CBS News on-line. September 18, 2005. http://www.cbsnews.com/stories/2004/09/08/60II/main641984.shtml June 14, 2007.

Newsinger, John. "'Do You Walk the Walk?': Aspects of Masculinity in Some Vietnam War Films." Pat Kirkham and Janet Thumin, eds. *You Tarzan: Masculinity, Movies, and Men.* 124–136.

Nicosia, Gerald. *Home to War: A History of the Vietnam Veterans' Movement.* New York: Three Rivers Press, 2001.

Norden, Martin F. "Bitterness, Rage, and Redemption: Hollywood Constructs the Disabled Vietnam Veteran." David A. Gerber, ed. *Disabled Veterans in History.* 96–114.

———. *The Cinema of Isolation: A History of Physical Disability in the Movies.* New Brunswick: Rutgers University Press, 1994.

———. "Hollywood's Disabled Vietnam Vet Revisited." Gary R. Edgerton et al., eds. *In the Eye of the Beholder: Critical Perspectives in Popular Film and Television.* 179–190.

———. "Portrait of a Disabled Veteran: Alex Cutter of *Cutter's Way.*" Linda Dittmar and Gene Michaud, eds. *From Hanoi to Hollywood: The Vietnam War in American Film.* 217–225.

"Notebook." *New Republic.* December 2, 2002: 8–10.

O'Brien, Jodi, and Judith A. Howard, eds. *Everyday Inequalities: Critical Inquiries.* Malden, MA: Blackwell Publishers, 1998.

O'Brien, Tim. *Going After Cacciato.* New York: Dell Publishing, 1978.

———. *If I Die in a Combat Zone: Box Me Up and Ship Me Home.* New York: Dell Publishing, 1973.

———. *The Things They Carried.* New York: Broadway Books, 1990.

O'Brien, Timothy D. "Oppositions in *In Country.*" *Critique* 41.2 (2000): 175–190.

O'Neill, John E., and Jerome R. Corsi. *Unfit for Command: Swift Boat Veterans Speak Out against John Kerry.* Washington, D.C.: Regnery Publishing, 2004.

Overboe, James. "'Difference in Itself': Disabled People's Lived Experience." *Body and Society* 5.4 (1999): 17–29.

———. Personal communication. January 30, 2003.

Parks, David. *G.I. Diary.* 1968. Washington, D.C.: Howard University Press, 1984.

"Patrick S. Duncan." Penguin UK Authors. http://www.penguin.co.uk/Author October 14, 2002.

Pfiffner, James P., and Roger H. Davidson, eds. *Understanding the Presidency.* New York: Longman, 1997.

Phillips, Kathy J. *Manipulating Masculinity: War and Gender in Modern British and American Literature.* New York: Palgrave Macmillan, 2006.

Platoon. Dir. Oliver Stone. Perf. Charlie Sheen, Tom Berenger, Willem Dafoe, Forest Whitaker, Kevin Dillon, Francesco Quinn, John G. McKinley, Keith David, Johnny Depp. Orion Pictures, 1986.

Pleck, Joseph H., and Jack Sawyer, eds. *Men and Masculinity.* Englewood Cliffs, NJ: Prentice-Hall, 1974.

Powell, Colin. *My American Journey.* New York: Random House, 1995.

Puller, Lewis B., Jr. *Fortunate Son: The Autobiography of Lewis B. Puller, Jr.* New York: Bantam Books, 1991.

"Pulling Strings to Avoid the Draft." Realchange website. http://www.realchange.org/quayle.htm July 8, 2002.

Quiñones, Juan Gómez. *Chicano Politics: Reality and Promise, 1940–1990*. The Calvin P. Horn Lectures in Western History and Culture. Albuquerque: University of New Mexico Press, 1990.

Rabe, David. *The Vietnam Plays: Volume One*. New York: Grove Press, 1993.

Rambo: First Blood. Dir. Ted Kotheff. Perf. Sylvester Stallone, Richard Crenna, Brian Dennehy, et al. Anabasis N. V., 1982.

Rambo: First Blood Part II. Dir. George B. Cosmatos. Perf. Sylvester Stallone, Richard Crenna, Charles Napier, Steven Berkoff, et al. Anabasis N. V., 1985.

Rambo III. Dir. Peter MacDonald. Perf. Sylvester Stallone, Richard Crenna, Mark de Jonge, Kurtwood Smith, et al. Carolco Pictures, 1988.

Reiter, Rayna, ed. *Toward an Anthropology of Women*. New York: Monthly Review Press, 1975.

Rescue Dawn. Dir. Werner Herzog. Perf. Christian Bale, Marshall Bell, François Chau, Jeremy Davies, et al. MGM, 2006.

Return with Honor. Dir. Freida Lee Mock and Terry Sanders. Perf. Everett Alvarez, Ron Bliss, Fred Cherry, George Day, Jeremiah Denton, et al. Sanders and Mock Productions, 1998.

Robinson, Sally. "Men's Liberation, Men's Wounds." Milette Shamir and Jennifer Travis, eds. *Boys Don't Cry? Rethinking Narratives of Masculinity and Emotion in the U.S.* 205–229.

Roediger, David R. *Towards the Abolition of Whiteness: Essays on Race, Politics, and Working Class History*. Haymarket Series. New York: Verso, 1994.

____, ed. *Black on White: Black Writers on What It Means to Be White*. New York: Shocken Books, 1998.

Roman, Leslie G. "White Is a Color! White Defensiveness, Postmodernism, and Anti-racist Pedagogy." Cameron McCarthy and Warren Crichlow, eds. *Race, Identity and Representation in Education*. 71–88.

Rosales, F. Arturo. *Testimonio: A Documentary History of the Mexican American Struggle for Civil Rights*. The Hispanic Civil Rights Series. Houston: Arte Público Press, 2000.

Rosen, David. *The Changing Fictions of Masculinity*. Urbana: University of Illinois Press, 1993.

Rosen, Jay. "Memo to Clinton: The Media and 'Character.'" *Tikkun* 8.1 (1993): 24–27.

Rotter, Andrew J. "Vietnam." *Foreign Policy in Focus*. http://foreignpolicy-infocus.org/commentary/vietnam_body.html July 10, 2002.

Rubin, Gayle. "The Traffic in Women: Notes toward a Political Economy of Sex." Rayna Reiter, ed. *Toward an Anthropology of Women*. 157–210.

Sabo, Donald, and David Frederick Gordon, eds. *Men's Health and Illness: Gender, Power, and the Body*. Research on Men and Masculinities 8. Thousand Oaks, CA: Sage, 1995.

Sackett, Paul R., and Anne S. Mavor. *Attitudes, Aptitudes, and Aspirations of American Youth: Implications for Military Recruiting*. National Research Council Committee on the Youth Population and Military Recruitment. Washington, D.C.: National Academies Press, 2003.

Sadker, David. *Being a Man: A Unit of Instructional Activities on Male Role Stereotyping*. U.S. Department of Health, Education, and Welfare, Office of Education, 1976.

Saving Private Ryan. Dir. Steven Spielberg. Perf. Tom Hanks, Tom Sizemore, Edward Burns, Barry Pepper, Adam Goldberg, Vin Diesel, Giovanni Ribisi, Jeremy Davies, Matt Damon, Ted Danson, Paul Giamatti, et al. Paramount Pictures, 1998.

Sayre, Alan. "High Court to Decide If Veterans May Sue." *The Columbus Dispatch*. February 23, 2003: A7.

Scarry, Elaine. *The Body in Pain: The Making and Unmaking of the World*. New York: Oxford University Press, 1985.

Schatz, Thomas. "World War II and the Hollywood 'War Film.'" Nick Browne, ed. *Refiguring American Film Genres: Theory and History*. 89–128.

Schroeder, Eric James. *Vietnam, We've All Been There: Interviews with American Writers*. Westport, CT: Praeger, 1992.

Scotch, Richard K. "American Disability Policy in the Twentieth Century." Paul K. Longmore and Lauri Umansky, eds. *The New Disability History: American Perspectives*. 375–392.

Scott, Wilbur J., and Sandra Carson Stanley, eds. *Gays and Lesbians in the Military: Issues, Concerns, and Contrasts*. Social Problems and Social Issues. New York: Aldine de Gruyter, 1994.

Scruggs, Jan C., and Joel L. Swerdlow. *To Heal a Nation: The Vietnam Veterans Memorial*. New York: Harper and Row, 1985.

Searle, William, ed. *Search and Clear: Critical Responses to Selected Literature and

Films of the Vietnam War. Bowling Green, OH: Bowling Green State University Popular Press, 1988.

Sedgwick, Eve Kosofsky. *Between Men: English Literature and Male Homosocial Desire.* New York: Columbia University Press, 1985.

———. *Epistemology of the Closet.* Berkeley: University of California Press, 1990.

Severo, Richard, and Lewis Milford. *The Wages of War: When America's Soldiers Came Home — From Valley Forge to Vietnam.* New York: Simon and Schuster, 1989.

Shakespeare, Tom, Kathy Gillespie-Sells, and Dominic Davies. *The Sexual Politics of Disability: Untold Desires.* New York: Cassell, 1996.

Shamir, Milette, and Jennifer Travis, eds. *Boys Don't Cry? Rethinking Narratives of Masculinity and Emotion in the U.S.* New York: Columbia University Press, 2002.

Shay, Jonathan. *Achilles in Vietnam: Combat Trauma and the Undoing of Character.* New York: Simon and Schuster, 1994.

Shenkman, Richard. "Is Presidential Character Everything?" *National Forum: The Phi Kappa Phi Journal.* 80.1 (2000): 17–25.

Shepard, Scott. "Gore's Vietnam Days Loom Large in Foreign Policy Views." *Cox News/Campaign 2000.* http://www.cox news.com/2000/news/cox/052900_gor e-vietnam.html July 10, 2002.

Shilts, Randy. *Conduct Unbecoming: Lesbians and Gays in the U.S. Military, Vietnam to the Persian Gulf.* New York: St. Martin's Press, 1993.

———. "Homosexuality in the United States Armed Forces." Robert M. Baird and M. Katherine Baird, eds. *Homosexuality: Debating the Issues.* 151–154.

———. "What's Fair in Love and War?" *Newsweek.* February 1, 1993. Qtd. at http://www.davidclemens.com/gaymilita ry/canfodder.htm.

Simons, Geoff. *Vietnam Syndrome: Impact on US Foreign Policy.* New York: St. Martin's Press, 1998.

Skaine, Rosemarie. *Women at War: Gender Issues of Americans in Combat.* Jefferson, NC: McFarland, 1999.

Small, Melvin. *Antiwarriors: The Vietnam War and the Battle for America's Hearts and Minds.* Vietnam: America in the War Years. Volume 1. Wilmington, DE: Scholarly Resources Books, 2002.

Smith, Lorrie N. "Disarming the War Story." Owen W. Gilman, Jr., and Lorrie Smith, eds. *America Rediscovered: Critical Essays on Literature and Film of the Vietnam War.* 87–99.

———. "'The Things Men Do': The Gendered Subtext in Tim O'Brien's *Esquire* Stories." *Critique* 36.1 (1994): 16–40.

Smith, Paul Chaat, and Robert Allen Warrior. *Like a Hurricane: The Indian Movement from Alcatraz to Wounded Knee.* New York: The New Press, 1996.

Smith, Sharon. "Ghost of Vietnam." *Socialist Review* 231 (1999). Qtd. at http:// pubs.socialistreviewindex.org.uk/sr231/s mith.htm July 10, 2002.

Smith, Stephen A., ed. *Bill Clinton on Stump, State, and Stage: The Rhetorical Road to the White House.* Fayetteville: University of Arkansas Press, 1994.

Snead, James. *White Screens/Black Images.* Edited by Colin McCabe and Cornel West. New York: Routledge, 1994.

Snyder, R. Claire. *Citizen-Soldiers and Manly Warriors: Military Service and Gender in the Civic Republic Tradition.* New York: Rowman and Littlefield Publishers, 1999.

Sollors, Werner. "Ethnicity." Frank Lentricchia and Thomas McLaughlin, eds. *Critical Terms for Literary Study.* 288–305.

Somerville, Siobhan B. *Queering the Color Line: Race and the Invention of Homosexuality in American Culture.* Durham: Duke University Press, 2000.

Starr, Paul. *The Discarded Army: Veterans after Vietnam.* The Nader Report on Vietnam Veterans and the Veterans Administration. New York: Charterhouse, 1973.

"Statement on Vietnam." Clyde Taylor, ed. *Vietnam and Black America: An Anthology of Protest and Resistance.* 258–260.

Stecopoulos, Harry, and Michael Uebel, eds. *Race and the Subject of Masculinities.* Durham: Duke University Press, 1997.

Stiehm, Judith, ed. *It's Our Military, Too! Women and the U.S. Military.* Philadelphia: Temple University Press, 1996.

Sturken, Marita. *Tangled Memories: The Vietnam War, the AIDS Epidemic, and the Politics of Remembering.* Berkeley: University of California Press, 1997.

Suid, Lawrence. *Guts and Glory: The Making of the American Military Image in Film.* 2nd ed. Louisville: University of Kentucky Press, 2002.

"Summary Report of the Military Working Group on Recommended Department of Defense Homosexual Policy." Robert M. Baird and M. Katherine Baird, eds. *Homosexuality: Debating the Issues,* 158–170.

Summers, Harry G., Jr. "The Vietnam Syndrome and the American People." *Parameters* 17.1 (1994): 53–58.

Suran, Justin David. "Coming Out against the War: Antimilitarism and the Politicization of Homosexuality in the Era of Vietnam." *American Quarterly* 53.3 (2001): 452–488.

Suro, Roberto, and Sharon Waxman. "Pentagon Wants Hollywood to Aid Recruiting." *The Washington Post.* January 29, 2000: A11.

Swain, John, Vic Finkelstein, Sally French, and Mike Oliver, eds. *Disabling Barriers — Enabling Environments.* London: Sage Publications, 1993.

Tang, Truong Nhu, David Chanoff, and Doan Van Toai. *A Viet Cong Memoir: An Inside Account of the Vietnam War and Its Aftermath.* New York: Random Books, 1985.

Taxi Driver. Dir. Martin Scorsese. Perf. Robert DeNiro, Cybill Shepherd, Peter Boyle, Jodi Foster, Harvey Keitel, Leonard Harris, Albert Brooks, et al. Columbia Pictures, 1976.

Taylor, Clyde, ed. *Vietnam and Black America: An Anthology of Protest and Resistance.* Garden City, NY: Anchor Press, 1973.

Team Xbox. "Call of Duty 4's Hank Keirsey Interview." http://interviews.teamxbox.com/xbox/2075/Call-of-Duty-4s-Hank-Keirsey-Interview/p1/ January 14, 2009.

Terry, Wallace. *Bloods: An Oral History of the Vietnam War by Black Veterans.* New York: Ballantine Books, 1984.

The Thin Red Line. Dir. Terrence Malick. Perf. John Travolta, Sean Penn, Elias Kosteas, Nick Nolte, John Cusack, Woody Harrelson, Adrien Brody, John Savage, Jim Caviezel. Twentieth Century Fox, 1998.

Thomas, Evan. "The Last of His Kind." Rev. of *Faith of My Fathers*, by John McCain. *Newsweek.* September 13, 1999: 31–32.

The Three Kings. Dir. David O. Russell. Perf. George Clooney, Mark Wahlberg, Ice Cube, Spike Jonze, et al. Warner Brothers, 1999.

Thurer, Shari. "Disability and Monstrosity: A Look at Literary Distortions of Handicapping Conditions." *Rehabilitation Literature* 41.1–2 (1980): 12–15.

Timberg, Robert. *John McCain: An American Odyssey.* New York: Simon and Schuster, 1999.

Toth, Elizabeth L., and Linda Aldoory, eds. *The Gender Challenge to Media: Diverse Voices from the Field.* Cresskill, NJ: Hampton Press, 2001.

Tour of Duty. With Stephen Caffrey, Terence Knox, Ramón Franco, Tony Becker, Miguel A. Núñez, Jr., Stan Foster, Dan Gauthier. 1987–1990.

The Trial of Billy Jack. Dir. Tom Laughlin. Perf. Tom Laughlin, Delores Taylor, Victor Izay. Taylor-Laughlin Productions, 1974.

Tripp, Nathaniel. *FatherSoldierSon: Memoir of a Platoon Leader in Vietnam.* South Royalton, VT: Steerforth Press, 1996.

Turner, Fred. *Echoes of Combat: Trauma, Memory, and the Vietnam War.* Minneapolis: University of Minnesota Press, 2001.

Uchmanowicz, Pauline. "Vanishing Vietnam: Whiteness and the Technology of Memory." *Literature and Psychology* 41.4 (1995): 30–50.

United States. Department of Defense. "Southeast Asia, Combat Area Casualties File." http://www.archives.gov/research_room/research_topics/vietman_war_casualty_lists/descriptive_handout/page_01.html March 12, 2003.

_____. _____. Equal Opportunity. "Negro Participation in the Armed Forces and in Southeast Asia, 31 March 1971." Bernard C. Nalty and Morris J. MacGregor, eds. *Blacks in the Military: Essential Documents.* 344–345.

_____. _____. Office of the Under Secretary of Defense (Personnel and Readiness). "Report to the Secretary of Defense: Review of the Effectiveness of the Application and Enforcement of the Department's Policy on Homosexual Conduct in the Military, April 1998." http://www.defenselink/mil/pubs/rpt040798.html February 6, 2009.

_____. Department of Justice. "A Guide to Disability Rights Laws." http://www.usdoj.gov/crt/ada/cguide.htm January 30, 2003.

_____. Department of Labor, Manpower Administration. "Jobs for Veterans with Disabilities." Manpower R&D Monograph 41, 1975.

Van Devanter, Lynda. *Home before Morning: The True Story of an Army Nurse in Vietnam.* New York: Warner Books, 1983.

Veterans Benefits and Services. "The Agent Orange Settlement Fund." http://www.vba.va.gov/bln/21/Benefits/Herbicide/AOno2.htm February 6, 2003.

Vicinus, Martha, ed. *Lesbian Subjects: A Feminist Studies Reader.* Bloomington: Indiana University Press, 1996.

Vietnam Veterans of America. "About the

War: Electronic Library." http://www.vva.org/about_the_war.htm February 1, 2003.

Vistica, Gregory L. *The Education of Lieutenant Kerrey*. New York: St. Martin's Press, 2003.

Walker, Barbara G. *The Woman's Encyclopedia of Myths and Secrets*. Philadelphia: Harper and Row Publishers, 1983.

Warner, Michael, ed. *Fear of a Queer Planet: Queer Politics and Social Theory*. Cultural Politics, vol. 6. Minneapolis: University of Minnesota Press, 1993.

We Were Soldiers. Dir. Randall Wallace. Perf. Mel Gibson, Madeleine Stowe, et al. Paramount and Icon, 2002.

Webb, James. *Fields of Fire*. New York: Bantam Books, 1978.

Weed, Elizabeth, and Naomi Schor, eds. *Feminism Meets Queer Theory*. Bloomington: Indiana University Press, 1997.

Weisbrot, Mark. "'Vietnam Syndrome' Is Alive and Thriving." Common Dreams News Center. http://www.commondreams.org/views02/0125-04.htm July 10, 2002.

Weisman, James J. "The Good Fight." *WE Magazine* 3.3 (1999): 106–107.

Welch, James. *The Death of Jim Loney*. New York: Penguin Books, 1979.

Wells, Tom. *The War Within: America's Battle over Vietnam*. Berkeley: University of California Press, 1994.

Westheider, James E. *Fighting on Two Fronts: African Americans and the Vietnam War*. New York: New York University Press, 1997.

Westwell, Guy. *War Cinema: Hollywood on the Front Line*. Short Cuts: Introductions to Film Studies. New York: Wallflower Press, 2006.

Weyler, Rex. *Blood of the Land: The Government and Corporate War against the American Indian Movement*. New York: Everest House Publishers, 1982.

Whitehead, Stephen M., and Frank J. Barrett, eds. *The Masculinities Reader*. Malden, MA: Blackwell Publishers, 2001.

Whitmore, Terry. *Memphis-Nam-Sweden: The Story of a Black Deserter*. 1971. Jackson: University Press of Mississippi, 1997.

Williams, Colin J., and Martin S. Weinberg. *Homosexuals and the Military: A Study of Less Than Honorable Discharge*. New York: Harper & Row, 1971.

Williams, John A. *Captain Blackman*. 1972. Minneapolis: Coffee House Press, 2000.

Williams, Tony. "Rites of Incorporation in *In Country* and *Indian Country*." Michael Bibby, ed. *The Vietnam War and Postmodernity*. 109–129.

Williams-Searle, John. "Cold Charity: Manhood, Brotherhood, and the Transformation of Disability, 1870–1900." Paul K. Longmore and Lauri Umansky, eds. *The New Disability History: American Perspectives*. 157–186.

Witteman, Paul, and Daniel S. Levy. "The Wound That Would Not Heal." *Time*. May 23, 1994. 75.

Wolff, Tobias. *In Pharaoh's Army: Memories of a Lost War*. New York: Random House, 1994.

Woodward, Bob, and David S. Broder. "Quayle's Reputation vs. the Record: Damaging Campaign Coverage Was Sometimes Inaccurate." *The Washington Post*. January 7, 1992. A1.

"The Worldview of Science Fiction." http://falcon.cc.ukans.edu/~sfcenter/sfview.htm July 17, 2002.

Wright, Evan. *Generation Kill: Devil Dogs, Iceman, Captain America, and the New Face of American War*. New York: G.P. Putnam's Sons, 2004.

Wyant, Dennis R. "Rehabilitation in the Veterans Administration." *Journal of Rehabilitation* 52.1 (1986): 56–57.

Young, Marilyn B. *The Vietnam Wars: 1945–1990*. New York: HarperCollins, 1991.

Index

Adair, R.D. 59–60, 170*n*.1
Adler, Jerry 177*n*.22, 177*n*.23
Afghanistan 5, 19
African-Americans: buffalo soldiers 167*n*.7; enlistment 30; integration into military 30, 178*n*.32; mortality rates 30, 166*n*.2
Agent Orange 111–112, 175*n*.10
Allen, Chadwick 166*n*.5
American Indians 166*n*.5
American War Library 167*n*.1, 168*n*.14
Americans with Disabilities Act 104
anti-war demonstrations 169*n*.19
Anzaldúa, Gloria 170*n*.3
Apocalypse Now 151, 160, 173*n*.17
Appiah, Kwame Anthony 30
Appy, Christian G. 115, 167*n*.10, 173*n*.14
Architectural Barriers Act of 1968 175*n*.5
Arnold, David 165*n*.1
Attaway, William 168*n*.11

The Bamboo Bed 168*n*.15
Barrett, Frank J. 165*n*.2
Bataan 168*n*.17
Bates, Milton J. 14, 15–16, 29, 49, 134–135, 166*n*.6, 171*n*.7, 172*n*.11, 174*n*.21
Baynton, Douglas C. 105
Beattie, Keith 166*n*.5
Beidler, Philip D. 23, 172*n*.11
Berger, Maurice 165*n*.2
Berlant, Lauren 7, 173*n*.16
Bernstein, Richard 48
Berubé, Alan 63, 170*n*.4, 172*n*.12
Bianco, William T. 150
Billy Jack films 174*n*.4
Blais, Ellen A. 173*n*.16
Bloods 168*n*.15
Bloom, Alexander 64, 173*n*.14
Body Shop 19, 109, 114–120, 176*n*.11
Booker, Christopher B. 165*n*.2, 166*n*.3
Born on the Fourth of July 107, 177*n*.25
Boyle, Brenda M. 176*n*.15
The Boys in Company C 150

Brigham, Robert K. 159, 181*n*.19
Brod, Harry 165*n*.2
Broder, David 178*n*.2
Browne, Corinne 19, 109, 114–120
Buckley, Gail 155, 166*n*.7
Bush, George H.W. 180*n*.9, 180*n*.10
Bush, George W. 179*n*.5
Butler, John Sibley 167*n*.8, 167*n*.9
Butler, Judith 9, 12–13, 131, 168*n*.16, 170*n*.3

Canellos, Peter S. 147
Captain Blackman 178*n*.32
Caputo, Philip 181*n*.16
Carbado, Devon W. 165*n*.2
Carn, John 166*n*.6
Carter, Jimmy 180*n*.9
Carton, Evan 173*n*.16
character 144–148, 179*n*.6
China Beach 151
Chomsky, Noam 149
Chosen Books 122, 177*n*.20
Cleland, Max 19, 109, 121–124, 176*n*.10, 177*n*.17, 177*n*.19, 177*n*.21
Clift, Eleanor 177*n*.22, 177*n*.23
Clinton, Bill 61, 63–64, 145, 146, 171*n*.5, 179*n*.3, 179*n*.9
Clinton, Hillary Rodham 178*n*.1
Cloud, Stanley W. 149
Clute, John 79
Colburn, David R. 43, 44, 166*n*.3, 169*n*.23
Coming Home 107, 151, 177*n*.25
Connell, R.W. 10, 24, 26, 27, 61, 172*n*.10
Conway, Jill Ker 181*n*.16
Cooke, Miriam 165*n*.2
Corber, Robert J. 172*n*.12
Corsi, Jerome R. 147
Crowley, Candy 179*n*.5
Cruise, Tom 177*n*.25

D'Agostino, Joseph A. 177*n*.19, 177*n*.24
Davis, George 166*n*.6

197

Davis, Lennard 19, 120
Dean, Robert Dale 147
The Deer Hunter 151, 173*n*.17, 177*n*.25
Deloria, Philip J. 166*n*.5
Del Vecchio, John 14, 31, 67–70, 166*n*.6, 168*n*.13, 168*n*.14
D'Emilio, John 125, 170*n*.4, 172*n*.13
Denton, Robert E., Jr. 179*n*.6
Devine, Jeremy 150, 173*n*.17, 173*n*.18, 174*n*.4, 180*n*.10
disability: accommodation versus compensation 104–106; hierarchy 106–108, 175*n*.7; images in literature 18; prostheses 177*n*.17; types 174*n*.1
Dispatches 168*n*.15
Duiker, William J. 42
Duncan, Patrick 18, 32, 46–57, 166*n*.6, 168*n*.13
Dyer, Richard 27, 31, 48, 51, 53, 54

Eastlake, William 168*n*.15
Eastman, Charles Alexander 167*n*.7
Edwards, John 178*n*.1
84 Charlie MoPic 18, 28, 32, 46–57
Eisenhower, Dwight David 179*n*.9
Ellmann, Mary 65
Eng, David L. 165*n*.2
Executive Order 9381 (racially integrating military) 167*n*.8, 178*n*.32

Faith of My Fathers 19, 157–158, 179*n*.4, 179*n*.7
Falk, Richard 180*n*.10
Faludi, Susan 62, 91
Farber, David 64, 144, 165*n*.4, 170*n*.2
A Farewell to Arms 176*n*.16
Farrell, Warren 169*n*.22
Feldman, Linda 147
Fick, Nathaniel 19, 158–164
Fiedler, Leslie A. 101, 174*n*.2
Fields of Fire 168*n*.15
film suturing 170*n*.25
Firestone, Shulamith 65
Flowers, A.R. 166*n*.6
Fontana, Alan 174*n*.1
Ford, Gerald 179*n*.9
The Forever War 18, 62, 78–83, 173*n*.14
Forrest Gump 177*n*.25
Fortunate Son 19, 109, 124–130
Foucault, Michel 8, 170*n*.3
Franklin, H. Bruce 78, 170*n*.24
Freedman, Estelle B. 125
Full Metal Jacket 151, 168*n*.15

Galloway, Joe 19, 153–157, 181*n*.16
Garber, Marjorie 170*n*.3

Garcia, Ignacio M. 166*n*.4
Garland-Thomson, Rosemarie 18, 100, 104, 107, 108, 113, 123, 124, 128–129, 138
Generation Kill (book) 19, 159–161
Generation Kill (miniseries) 182*n*.20
Gerber, David A. 101, 102
Gerschick, Thomas J. 100, 105, 106, 113, 131, 132, 175*n*.6
Gersten, David 180*n*.13
Gerstle, Gary 25
Gibson, Mel 153–157
Gilmore, Leigh 115, 181*n*.16
Gitlin, Todd 149, 164
Glass, Ira 4–5
Glenday, Michael K. 172*n*.11
Glover, David 165*n*.2
Go Tell the Spartans 150–151
Going After Cacciato 168*n*.15
Goldberg, Herb 169*n*.22
Goldstein, Joshua S. 6
Graham, Herman 167*n*.7
Graham-Silverman, Adam 177*n*.19
Graybill, Mark S. 173*n*.16
Guiliani, Rudy 178*n*.1
Gunn, James 79
Gutmann, Stephanie 65–66

Halberstam, Judith 12, 73
Haldeman, Joe 18, 62, 78–83, 173*n*.13, 173*n*.14
Hallett, Joe 147
Halperin, David M. 170*n*.3
Hanks, Tom 179*n*.7
Harbour, Wendy 175*n*.7
Harper, Philip Brian 165*n*.2
Harris, David 181*n*.16
Harris, Ian M. 165*n*.2
Hearn, Jeff 165*n*.2, 165*n*.4
Heinemann, Larry 19, 109, 131–143, 177*n*.29
Hellmann, John 70, 74–75, 171*n*.7, 172*n*.11
Hemingway, Ernest 176*n*.16
Herr, Michael 168*n*.15
Hess, Stephen 150
Hickel, K. Walter 175*n*.8
Hohenberg, John 146, 179*n*.3
Holloway, Rachel L. 179*n*.6
Holm, Tom 166*n*.5
homosexuality in the military 63, 170*n*.2, 170*n*.4, 171*n*.5, 172*n*.12, 172*n*.13
honor 179*n*.7
Hooper, Charlotte 165*n*.2
Hurley, Michael 83

If I Die in a Combat Zone 168*n*.15

In Country (book): 14, 18, 62, 83–89, 110–114, 174*n*.4
In Country (film): 18, 87–92
Iraq 4–5, 19, 149, 158–164, 181*n*.19

Jaehne, Karen 47, 48–49
Jagose, Annamarie 83
Jarraway, David R. 96
Jason, Philip K. 74, 78, 171*n*.7
Jeffords, Susan 5, 14–15, 59, 62, 70, 84, 134–135, 171*n*.7, 173*n*.17
Jewison, Norman 18, 62, 173*n*.16
Johnson, Loch 102
Johnson, Lyndon Baines 179*n*.9, 180*n*.10
Johnston, Craig 83
Jones, James 172*n*.12
Jordan, Harold 151

Kaplan, Cora 165*n*.2
Karnow, Stanley 179*n*.7
Kauffman, Stanley 48
Kaufman, Michael 165*n*.2
Keirsey, Hank 165*n*.1
Kennedy, John F. 179*n*.9
Kerrey, Robert 177*n*.22, 179*n*.4, 179*n*.8, 180*n*.10
Kimmel, Michael 7, 61, 165*n*.2, 165*n*.4, 170*n*.2
King, Debra Walker 39, 169*n*.21
Kinney, Katherine 14, 16, 29, 74–75, 95, 134–135, 166*n*.6, 171*n*.7
Kissinger, Henry 181*n*.16
Kleinhans, Chuck 48
Kolker, Robert 49, 170*n*.25, 170*n*.26
Krauthammer, Charles 179*n*.4, 181*n*.17
Kripke, Saul 168*n*.16
Kulka, Richard A. 102

Ladd, Everett Carll 146
Lanning, Michael Lee 48, 167*n*.7
Latino-Americans 166*n*.4, 180*n*.13
Lehman, Peter 165*n*.2
Leonard, Mary 147
Levy, Daniel 177*n*.22
Linton, Simi 105, 134
Lipsky, David 165*n*.1
Lloyd, Emily 87–92, 173*n*.18
Loeb, Jeff 24, 166*n*.6
Longmore, Paul K. 104
Lupack, Barbara Tepa 84–85, 173*n*.16

MacPherson, Myra 102, 107
Magnum P.I. 151
Mailer, Norman 18, 33, 62, 74–78, 172*n*.11, 172*n*.12, 173*n*.13

"Man Dance" masculinity 4–5, 19, 20–21, 153, 157, 158, 160
Maraniss, David 179*n*.3
Markham, Jamie 150
Mason, Bobbie Ann 14, 18, 62, 110–116, 173*n*.15
Mason, Robert 181*n*.16
Matthiessen, Peter 166*n*.5
Mavor, Anne S. 180*n*.14
McCain, John 19, 145, 157–158, 178*n*.1, 179*n*.4, 179*n*.7, 181*n*.17
McCarthy, Michael 180*n*.13
McMahon, Anthony 165*n*.2, 181*n*.18
McNamara, Robert S. 121, 181*n*.16
McNerney, Brian C. 94
memoirs 181*n*.16, 181*n*.17
Miami Vice 151
Michel, Sonya 100, 174*n*.3
Milford, Lewis 100, 102, 111
Miller, Adam Stephen 106, 113
Millett, Kate 65, 75
Mitchell, Billie 171*n*.8
Moddelmog, Debra A. 106
Moore, Harold G. 19, 153–157, 181*n*.16
Morris, Jenny 131
Moskos, Charles 6, 115, 167*n*.7, 167*n*.8, 167*n*.9
Moynihan, Daniel Patrick 40
Mulvey, Laura 178*n*.33
Myers, Joseph C. 59–60, 170*n*.1
Myers, Thomas 78, 171*n*.7

The Naked and the Dead 172*n*.12
narrative strategies: lighting 25, 26, 46–57; naming 25, 26, 29, 31–46, 56–57, 168*n*.15, 168*n*.16, 169*n*.20, 169*n*.21
National Symbolic 7–8, 9, 21, 60, 101, 149–150, 159
Nelson, Robert T. 181*n*.17
Nicosia, Gerald 177*n*.18, 177*n*.21, 177*n*.24
Nixon, Richard M. 179*n*.7, 179*n*.9
No Shining Armor 168*n*.15
Norden, Martin F. 103, 174*n*.2
"Notebook" 177*n*.24

Obama, Barack 178*n*.1
O'Brien, Tim 18, 62, 92–96, 168*n*.15, 174*n*.21, 179*n*.7
O'Brien, Timothy D. 173*n*.16
One Bullet Away 19, 159, 161–164
O'Neill, John E. 147
Overboe, James 108

Paco's Story 19, 109, 131–143, 168*n*.13, 169*n*.20, 178*n*.30, 31

Parks, David 166n.3
Phillips, Kathy J. 165n.3
Platoon 107, 151
Pleck, Joseph H. 169n.22
political correctness 17, 66
Post-traumatic Stress Disorder (PTSD) 88, 102, 112
Powell, Colin 166n.3
Pozzetta, George E. 43, 44, 166n.3, 169n.23
presidential elections 144–148
Puller, Lewis B., Jr. 19, 107, 109, 124–130, 177n.22, 177n.23

Quayle, Dan 178n.2
Queer theory 170n.3
Quiñones, Juan Gómez 43, 166n.4

Rabe, David 177n.26
Race: and ethnicity 167n.11; integration of military 167n.8; makeup of forces 166n.1, 167n.10, 168n.14; multiplication 24; oblique reference 24; prejudice 181n.15; racializing 155–156; tension 36
Rambo films 174n.4
Reagan, Ronald 180n.9
recognition 137–143
recruiting 151–153, 180n.13, 180n.14
The Rehabilitation Act of 1973 175n.5
rescue 156
Rescue Dawn 151
Return with Honor 179n.7
Robinson, Sally 173n.20
Roediger, David 168n.12
Romney, Mitt 178n.1
Rosales, F. Arturo 166n.4
Rosen, David 165n.2
Rosen, Jay 146
Rosenheck, Robert 174n.1
Rotter, Andrew J. 149
Rubin, Gayle 83, 170n.3

Sackett, Paul R. 180n.14
Salisbury, Neal 166n.5
Savage, John 177n.25
Saving Private Ryan 180n.11
Sawyer, Jack 169n.22
Sayre, Alan 176n.10
Scarry, Elaine 100, 115
Schatz, Thomas 169n.17, 180n.11
Schor, Naomi 11
Schroeder, Eric James 173n.15
science fiction 79
Scott, Wilbur J. 63, 165n.4, 170n.2, 170n.4

Sedgwick, Eve Kosofsky 83, 170n.2
Severo, Richard 100, 102, 111
Shakespeare, Tom 126
Shamir, Milette 152, 165n.2
Shay, Jonathan 175n.9
Shenkman, Richard 179n.6
Shepard, Scott 149
Shilts, Randy 61, 63, 64, 72, 74, 77, 83, 85, 165n.4, 170n.2, 170n.4, 174n.22
Simons, Geoff 180n.10
Sinise, Gary 177n.25
Skaine, Rosemarie 71, 171n.6
Small, Melvin 169n.19
Smith, Lorrie 35, 95–96, 174n.21
Smith, Paul Chaat 166n.5
Smith, Sharon 149
Smith, Stephen A. 179n.3, 179n.6
Snyder, R. Claire 165n.2
Sollors, Werner 167n.11
Somerville, Siobhan B. 167n.11
Stanley, Sandra Carlson 63, 165n.4, 170n.2, 170n.4
Starr, Paul 52, 101, 107–108, 136, 174n.1
"Statement on Vietnam." 166n.3
Stecopoulos, Harry 165n.2
Sticks and Bones 177n.26
Stiehm, Judith 171n.8
Stockdale, James 59–60
Stonewall Inn riots 15, 172n.13
Strong at the Broken Places 19, 109, 121–124
Sturken, Marita 45
Summers, Harry G., Jr. 180n.10
Suran, Justin David 172n.13
Suro, Roberto 180n.13
"The Sweetheart of the Song Tra Bong" 18, 62, 92–96, 174n.21

Tailhook 1991 170n.1, 171n.8
Taxi Driver 174n.4
Taylor, Clyde 36, 166n.3, 167n.9
The Thin Red Line 172n.12, 180n.11
The Things They Carried 92–96, 168n.15, 179n.7
The 13th Valley 14, 28, 31, 33–46, 67–70, 168n.12, 171n.7
Thomas, Evan 181n.17
The Three Kings 180n.11
Timberg, Robert 181n.17
Tour of Duty 151
Travis, Jennifer 152, 165n.2
Tripp, Nathaniel 181n.16
Turner, Fred 127–128, 171n.7, 176n.12

Uchmanowicz, Pauline 171n.7
Uebel, Michael 165n.2

Umansky, Lauri 104

Van Devanter, Lynda 181*n*.16
Viet Cong 177*n*.28
Vietnam Syndrome 121, 149, 170*n*.24, 180*n*.10
Vietnam veterans' images 173*n*.17
Vietnam Veterans Memorial 90, 127–128, 155
Vistica, Gregory L. 179*n*.8
visual rhetoric 124, 128–130; *see also* Garland-Thomson
Voight, Jon 177*n*.25

Wallace, Kathleen 180*n*.11
Wallis, Brian 165*n*.2
Warner, Michael 170*n*.3
Warrior, Robert Allen 166*n*.5
Watson, Simon 165*n*.2
Waxman, Sharon 180*n*.13
We Were Soldiers 19, 153, 154–157
We Were Soldiers Once ... and Young 19, 153–157, 168*n*.15

Webb, James 168*n*.15
Weed, Elizabeth 11
Weinberg, Martin S. 170*n*.4
Weisbrot, Mark 149
Weisman, James J. 104
Wells, Tom 169*n*.19
Westheider, James E. 30, 36, 166*n*.2, 166*n*.3, 169*n*.19, 178*n*.32
Westwell, Guy 180*n*.11
Weyler, Rex 166*n*.5
white race 27, 30, 31, 57, 168*n*.12
Whitehead, Stephen M. 165*n*.2
Whitmore, Terry 166*n*.6
Why Are We in Vietnam? 18, 62, 74–78
Williams, Colin J. 170*n*.4
Williams, John A. 166*n*.6, 178*n*.32
Willis, Bruce 89–92, 173*n*.18, n.20
Witteman, Paul 177*n*.22
Wolff, Tobias 181*n*.16
Woodward, Bob 178*n*.2
Woollacott, Angela 165*n*.2
Wright, Evan 19, 158–164, 182*n*.20

www.ingramcontent.com/pod-product-compliance
Ingram Content Group UK Ltd.
Pitfield, Milton Keynes, MK11 3LW, UK
UKHW042005140426
5217IPUK00015B/1001

9 780786 445387